ABOUT THE COVER
Brazilian Coffee Worker (1939)

This oil painting by Brazilian artist Candido Portinari (1903–1962) hangs in Sao Paulo's art museum. Grasping a crude hoe, a young worker gazes proudly across the newly cut forest, which had been transformed into coffee fields. He overlooks a vast landscape filled to the horizon with Brazil's burgeoning coffee plantations as a train puffs by in the distance—a clear-cut symbol of modernity. Portinari's employment of a nostalgic social realism, likely influenced by Mexican painter Diego Rivera (1885–1957), conveys the worker's dignity amid a somewhat ambivalent representation of economic development.

VOICES OF *A PEOPLE'S HISTORY OF THE WORLD*

VOICES OF A PEOPLE'S HISTORY OF THE WORLD

SINCE 1400

EDITED BY

Jeff Horn

OXFORD

UNIVERSITY PRESS

OXFORD
UNIVERSITY PRESS

Oxford University Press is a department of the University of Oxford.
It furthers the University's objective of excellence in research, scholarship,
and education by publishing worldwide. Oxford is a registered trade mark
of Oxford University Press in the UK and in certain other countries.

Published in the United States of America by Oxford University Press
198 Madison Avenue, New York, NY 10016, United States of America.

Library of Congress Cataloging-in-Publication Data
Names: Horn, Jeff (Historian), editor.
Title: Voices of "A people's history of the world, since 1400" / edited by
Jeff Horn.
Description: New York : Oxford University Press, [2023] | Includes
bibliographical references. | Summary: "A higher education history
sourcebook on World History"—Provided by publisher.
Identifiers: LCCN 2022010807 (print) | LCCN 2022010808 (ebook) | ISBN
9780190640637 (paperback) | ISBN 9780197630587 | ISBN 9780197630594
(epub) | ISBN 9780197630600 (pdf)
Subjects: LCSH: History, Modern—Sources. | Biographical sources. |
History, Modern—Textbooks.
Classification: LCC D209 .H57 2023 Suppl. (print) | LCC D209 (ebook) |
DDC 909—dc23/eng/20220601
LC record available at https://lccn.loc.gov/2022010807
LC ebook record available at https://lccn.loc.gov/2022010808

9 8 7 6 5 4 3 2 1
Printed by Lakeside Book Company, United States of America

CONTENTS

INTRODUCING *VOICES OF A PEOPLE'S HISTORY OF THE WORLD*

This companion volume to *A People's History of the World* presents primary documents that are completely integrated into the narrative. Each chapter of *A People's History* contains numerous maps and various types of images and graphical representations of data that complement the textual sources found in this volume. If you have read the introduction to that book, you probably do not need to spend much time on this section.

Primary sources are generated by people, groups, or institutions directly involved in an event as participants, witnesses, or commentators. They include a wide variety of types of texts, ranging from transcribed oral accounts like speeches, to autobiographies, to treaties between sovereign powers, to journalistic stories, to tweets, among many others. Explicating, evaluating, and contextualizing primary sources, especially when they contradict each other, are essential skills for the student of history to develop. The documents included in this volume extend and explain the chapter narratives either by providing individual and group perspectives or by illustrating the effects of a process or development, such as a United Nations resolution or the text of a law. The primary sources in this volume are also integral to addressing the "Be An Historian" and "Debate" features.

Primary sources require active reading; readers need to be curious about the language and point of view while appreciating the differences among fact, opinion, and interpretation. Examine what you are reading and consider how it fits into the chapter and the themes articulated by your instructor: the detailed index in both *People's* and *Voices* are vital tools in understanding how these sources link to other documents, other issues, and other places and times. Take notes, think of questions, mark up the text, consider contradictions or missing pieces of the puzzle. Careful attention to analyzing primary sources is required to appreciate *A People's History of the World*.

Embedded across *A People's History* and these primary sources are a series of arguments about who should be featured in the stories we tell about the global past, the nature and pace of historical change, and causality. I borrow heavily from the concerns articulated by Howard Zinn in *A People's History of the United States* (1980) where he sought to integrate the excluded, the marginalized, and resistance to the domination of elites into historical understandings. His book builds on the idea of "history from below" to restructure the analytical landscape and to inspire new ways of thinking about historical narratives. The need to consider a much longer timeframe and the diversity of world cultures in a much shorter book led me to adapt the approach of Fernand Braudel in *The Mediterranean and the Mediterranean World in the Age of Philip II* (1949, 1972–73). He split historical time into three divisions: 1) geographical or environmental time featuring slow, subtle changes marked by repetition and cycles; 2) social and economic changes within and between empires and civilizations considered over the course of a century or two; and 3) the history of events and individuals. These divisions should be kept in mind when considering how to contextualize the primary documents in this book. At the same time, *A People's History* prioritizes the concept of "political economy," which examines the economic foundations, motivations, and outcomes of political action as well as the interaction of individuals, groups, and societies with institutions. Political economy emphasizes how economic competitiveness shaped and shapes local, national, and international political action. Understanding my goals can help you develop your own analysis.

The texts in this volume were selected to highlight these concerns and to encourage readers to make connections and develop interpretations focused on the interests, challenges, and relationships of the common person as well as "the people" as a collectivity. Such connections and this type of analysis are by nature comparative and can stretch across time periods and within states and regions as well as globally. If you are trying to construct or find evidence to support an argument or answer a question, remember that the texts are meant to be compared and contrasted; they are not intended to be considered solely in isolation. The indexes are good places to look for texts that are in dialogue.

Whenever possible, the primary sources in this companion volume were chosen to provide the literal authorial "voices" of individuals who experienced or witnessed the event or issue. The selection process also intentionally sought to allow those who had been excluded or marginalized—which varied according to time, place, and subject—to express themselves directly. But such sources do not always exist, or I did not have access to them, or they were written in languages that I do not read and have not yet been translated. When you encounter a source by a person of European descent concerning other parts of the world—unless their experience is relevant, such as in examining imperialism—assume that I could not find a more appropriate source, but not for lack of trying!

Most of the texts excerpted in this book are quite short, and deliberately so. They are intended to explicate critical issues and to be used in comparison to or in contrast with other texts, including the visual sources in the narrative of *People's*. The short length was also a choice based on the realization that instructors frequently supplement such a book of sources with longer passages of key texts that are readily available on the World Wide Web. The relatively brief texts in *Voices* seek to encourage such customization and provide maximum flexibility for instructors and students to delve both broadly and deeply into the study of the global past.

Historians seek to understand the forces shaping how people lived, not to collect "facts." *Voices of a People's History* displays the amazing diversity of human experience. It calls attention to the peculiarities and distinctive elements of past societies while illustrating the roots of contemporary institutions, problems, and opportunities. *Voices* provides an introduction to the complexities of the past, but readers should remember that neither causes nor effects can usually be traced to a single factor. Weigh these factors and motivations in constructing your interpretations.

The multiplicity of influences that shaped the dynamics of personal, economic, social, and political interaction are why the narrative of *People's* is broken down into three temporal approaches. Chapters on religious practice, community, slavery, agriculture, trade, and taxation span the entire six-hundred-year period. Paired chapters on imperialism, industrialization, and decolonization divide the era in two to highlight continuities and changes, while five chapters focusing on politics examine shorter blocks of time. These seventeen chapters follow an introduction to the world in the fifteenth century, while a final chapter considers contemporary issues and possible lessons for the future. Attentive readers will see that each source can be used in multiple ways to support or construct myriad types of arguments. In conjunction with *A People's History of the World*, this volume is an opportunity for readers to take a carefully curated, yet exciting journey into the study of the global past. Enjoy!

ACKNOWLEDGMENTS

Writing *A People's History of the World* required a lot of help and encouragement along the way from some very special people. Teaching world history in various iterations at Stetson University and Manhattan College has been a fascinating and sometimes frustrating task. My departmental colleagues, especially Margaret Venzke and Paul Droubie, as well as far too many students to name individually, have been my instructors in the ways and means of world history. I hope that those who have helped me and pick up this book will recognize their contributions in its pages. Besides my own relative lack of expertise in many of the topics I sought to discuss, my biggest hindrance has always been how to engage students, especially those taking world history for some sort of distribution requirement. The exceptionally high prices of textbooks that were too focused on politics, culture, and ideas for my teaching style was also exasperating. The projected selling price of this book was important to me: watching textbook prices go beyond the willingness or ability of my students to afford them, especially in a general education class, was what sealed the deal in my decision to write a global history textbook.

Charles Geisst, Kelli Christiansen, and Lynn Hunt gave me wonderful advice about constructing the original proposal and negotiating the contract with Oxford University Press. Cliff Rosenberg provided insight from his own experience writing a world history textbook.

Many other colleagues have encouraged me during the writing process. Jeff Ravel, Heather Salter-Streets, and John Savage generously provided venues where I could try out ideas and gave me vital feedback at critical times. Len Rosenband, David Troyansky, Jen Popiel, Isser Woloch, and Cory Blad were stimulating discussion partners as I thought my way through how to write a textbook.

The lockdowns imposed by COVID-19 shaped this book and *Voices of a People's History* because more than half of the text was written and revised while I was on sabbatical in the spring and summer of 2020 without recourse to either a library or interlibrary loans. Manhattan College's librarians went above and beyond to help me get what I needed, in particular Susanne Markgren, whose responsiveness and assistance was very much appreciated.

My biggest acknowledgment must go to Charles Cavaliere, my editor. We met in a panel discussion about a prospective textbook, thanks to Sarah Shurts, in 2015. Not too long afterwards, we began an amazing adventure together when he asked me to propose a world history textbook to OUP. As he laid out why he thought I might be good at it and what kind of book he hoped to get, I realized that this was an opportunity that I could not ignore. Charles' optimism, experience, and good sense were always linked to the strictest professionalism and standards. He played a major role in helping me to conceptualize a different approach and then to put it into practice. Along the way, he has become my friend, and I know he will see a lot of himself in *Peoples*. Thanks, Charles—I could not have done it without you, and I would never have wanted to try!

Andrew Kotick wrote great questions for the book's website and instructor's manual and was a superb, tenacious fact-checker. The entire Oxford University Press team, spearheaded by Danica Donovan, was helpful and supportive throughout the process. They turned my ideas about map design and graphical tips for readers into reality. The distinctive look of this book comes from their talent and vision. I also got an enormous amount of useful feedback from OUP's readers: of the proposal in 2016; of five chapters in 2018; and of the entire manuscript in 2021. To all my readers: I could not implement all your suggestions or incorporate all your critiques, but I thought long and hard about what you had to say and took to heart the way you read my work.

My family has put up with the grind of this project. Since I began work on it, they have had to navigate mounds of books and many a distracted look from me as well as mild franticness over meeting repeated tight deadlines. This book is dedicated, with love, to them. Thanks Julie, David, and Cate: you make it all worthwhile.

ABOUT THE EDITOR

Jeff Horn has taught European and World History at Manhattan College since 2000 and has previously held positions at George Mason University and Stetson University. He served as president of the Western Society for French History in 2013–14 and as president of the Society for French Historical Studies in 2020–21. Horn will serve again in 2023–24. He is co-moderator of the New York French History Group.

Professor Horn writes about political economy, economic development, and political culture in the Age of Revolution. He is the author or editor of seven books, including, most recently, *The Making of a Terrorist: Alexandre Rousselin and the French Revolution* (Oxford University Press, 2021, paperback, 2022), *The Industrial Revolution: History, Documents, and Key Questions* (ABC-CLIO, 2016), and *Economic Development in Early Modern France: The Privilege of Liberty, 1650–1820* (Cambridge University Press, 2015, paperback 2017). His next project is *The Terror: Revolutionary Government in the French Revolution* for Polity Press, due in 2024.

ISOLATION, REGIONALISM, AND EXPLORATION

The World in 1400

1.1 FEI XIN, *DESCRIPTION OF THE STARRY RAFT* (1436)

Fei Xin (c.1385–after 1436) was a Chinese soldier who accompanied Zheng He on his third, fifth, and seventh expeditions, visiting many places in Southeast Asia and around the Indian Ocean. In this excerpt, he comments on the different customs found in Siam (the forerunner of today's Thailand) and the economic and political results of the voyages on behalf of two Chinese emperors. His observations also suggest the extent of Chinese technological superiority.

The customs are violent and fierce: they particularly respect bravery. They invade and despoil neighboring regions. They sharpen areca-palm wood for spears and [use] the skin of water-buffalos for shields. They [have] poisoned barbs and other such implements and are practiced and skillful at fighting on water. . . .

The principal chief and the lower classes, when considering their plans, whether the matter be great or small all decide in accordance with [the wishes of] the women. The men readily comply with [these wishes] and [both sexes] have illicit relations as it pleases them. . . .

Many of the women become Buddhist nuns. The Taoist priests all are adept at intoning the sutras and keeping the fasts. The color of [their] robes is roughly like that prescribed in the Middle Kingdom. They also make places for monasteries and Taoist temples. They pay [adroit] attention to [all] matters connected with funeral ceremonies. When a person has drawn his last breath, they inevitably pour quicksilver in the corpse to preserve it. Afterwards they select a spot on a high mound, and carrying out the service of Buddha, they bury him.

They ferment sugar cane to make wine and boil sea-water to obtain salt. It is customary, instead of money, to use cowries [the shells of a certain type of sea snail] which are current in the markets; every ten-thousand cowries are the equivalent of twenty strings in Chung-t'ung paper money.

The land produces lo-hu incense, which burns very clearly for a long time [but] is inferior to ordinary gharu-wood. In the second place they have sapan-wood, rhinoceros' horns, elephants' teeth, kingfisher feathers, yellow wax, and chaulmoogra oil.

The commodities used [in trade with them] are such things as porcelain articles, decorated in blue and white, cotton cloth with printed designs, colored thin silk, rolls of silk, gold, silver, brass, iron, melted beads, quicksilver, and umbrellas.

Their chief, greatly esteeming the far-reaching benevolence of the Heavenly Court, sent envoys who offered memorials written on leaves of gold and brought local products as tribute.

QUESTIONS

- How did Xin depict the customs of those he found? What did he think about them?
- What can this source teach you about "Chinese technological superiority"?

Source: Hsin Fei, *Hsing-Ch'a Sheng-Lan [The Overall Survey of the Star Raft]*, ed. Roderich Ptak, trans. J. V. Mills with contributions by Roderich Ptak (Wiesbaden: Harrassowitz Verlag, 1996), 42–44.

1.2 NICOLAS V, *ROMANUS PONTIFEX* (1455)

This papal bull granted Portugal a monopoly over the exploitation of Africa and justified the enslavement of all non-Christians. It was issued in response to Portugal's explorations and their stated goal of finding Christian kingdoms like that of the fabled Prester John to come to their aid in the aftermath of the fall of the eastern Roman Empire to the Ottoman Turks in 1453. This measure extended an earlier bull issued three years before granting the Portuguese the right to conquer and enslave pagans; it set the stage for the Roman Catholic division of the rest of the world between Spain and Portugal in the 1494 Treaty of Tordesillas.

[The King of Portugal and Prince Henry] have ordained that none, unless with their sailors and ships and on payment of a certain tribute and with an express license previously obtained from the said king or infante [second son of the ruling monarch], should presume to sail to the said provinces [of Africa] or to trade in their ports or to fish in the sea. In time it might happen that persons of other kingdoms or nations, led by envy, malice, or covetousness, might presume, contrary to the prohibition aforesaid, with-out license and payment of such tribute, to go to the said provinces, and in the provinces, harbors, islands, and sea, so acquired, to sail, trade, and fish . . . very many hatreds, rancors [bitterness or resentfulness], dissensions, wars, and scandals, to the highest offense of God and danger of souls, probably might and would ensue. We weighing all and singular the premises with due meditation, and noting that since we had formerly by other letters of ours granted among other things free and ample faculty to the aforesaid King Alfonso—to invade, search out, capture, vanquish, and subdue all Saracens [Muslims] and pagans whatsoever, and other enemies of Christ wheresoever placed, and the kingdoms, dukedoms, principalities, dominions, possessions, and all movable and unmovable goods whatsoever held and possessed by them and to reduce their persons to perpetual slavery, and to apply and appropriate to himself and his successors the kingdoms, dukedoms, counties, principalities, dominions, possessions, and goods, and to convert them to his and their use and profit. . . . We do by the tenor of these presents decree . . . to the aforesaid king and to his successors and to the infante . . . that the right of conquest which in the course of these letters we declare to be extended from the capes of Bojador and of Não, as far as through all Guinea, and beyond toward that southern shore, has belonged and pertained, and forever of right belongs and pertains to the said King Alfonso, his successors, and the infante, and not to any others.

QUESTIONS

- How did Nicolas V justify this proclamation?
- What can this source teach us about European views of Africa and Africans at the time?

Source: Nicolas V, *Romanus Pontifex* in *Africa and the West: A Documentary History*, ed. William H. Worger, Nancy L. Clark, and Edward A. Alpers, vol. 1, *From the Slave Trade to Conquest, 1441–1905* (New York: Oxford University Press, 2010), 16–17.

1.3 RUY DE GONZALEZ DE CLAVIJO, "JOURNEY THROUGH KHORASSAN" (1403)

Ruy de Gonzalez de Clavijo (d. 1412) was an ambassador from Henry III of Castille to the court of Timur from 1403–1406. He took extensive notes and wrote up a diary of his travels that was published in 1582. This excerpt details his observations about the nomadic life and governing style of the rulers of the inhabitants of the steppes of northeastern Persia.

When they arrived at a village, the people brought out all the things that the ambassadors required. You must know that, from the time that they took leave of the son-in-law of the lord, the ambassadors and the ambassador of the Sultan of Babylon travelled in company; and these things were not only done for the ambassadors, but for everyone who travelled with orders from the lord. They were to kill anyone who impeded the execution of his orders, and thus it was that the people were in marvelous terror of the lord, and of his servants. . . .

The people of these tents have no other dwelling place, and they wander over the plains, during both winter and summer. In summer they go to the banks of the rivers, and sow their corn, cotton, and melons, which I believe to be the best that can be found in the world. They also sow much millet, which they boil with their milk. In the winter they go to the warm districts. The lord, with all his host, wanders in the same way over the plains, winter and summer. His people do not march all together, but the lord, with his knights and friends, servants and women, go by one road, and the rest of the army by another, and so they pass their lives.

These people have many sheep, camels, and horses, and but few cows; and when the lord orders them to march with his army, they go with all that belongs to them, flocks and herds, women and children; and so they supply the host with flocks, especially with sheep, camels, and horses.

With these people the lord has performed many deeds, and conquered in many battles; for they are a people of great valor, excellent horsemen, expert with the bow, and enured [accustomed] to hardships. If they have food, they eat; and if not, they suffer cold and heat, hunger and thirst, better than any people in the world. When they have no meat, they feed on milk and water boiled together, and they make their food in this manner: --they fill a great cauldron with water, and, when it is hot, they pour in sour milk, and make a sort of cheese, which is as sour as vinegar. They then take thin cakes of flour, cut them very small, and put them in the cauldron. When this mess is cooked, they take it out, and they go without other food very well, and this is the food upon which they live.

They have no wood to cook their food, but they use the dung of the horses and camels; and this food, which has been described to you, is called *haz*.

QUESTIONS

- Based on this reading, what are some adjectives you would use to describe steppe cultures at the time?
- What did Gonzalez think of the peoples and customs he encountered?

Source: Clements Markham, ed. and trans., *Narrative of the Embassy of Ruy Gonzalez de Clavijo to the Court of Timour at Samacand, A.D. 1403–06* (London: Hakluyt Society, 1859), 181–82.

1.4 FRANCESCO BALDUCCI PEGOLOTTI, *MERCHANT HANDBOOK* (c. 1340)

Francesco Balducci Pegolotti (1290–1347), a banker from the republic of Florence, wrote the *Book of Descriptions of Lands* in 1339–1340, based on documents held by the commercial firm he represented and on his own observations, to serve as a reference for international trade. It was printed in the eighteenth century with the title used here. His endorsement of the safety and profitability of the steppe route because of Mongol power was notable.

The road you travel from Tana [trading city in Crimea in the Black Sea] to Cathay [China, about 3,700 miles] is perfectly safe, whether by day or by night, according to what the merchants say who have used it. Only if the merchant, in going or coming, should die upon the road, everything belonging to him will become the perquisite of the lord of the country in which he dies, and the officers of the lord will take possession of all. . . .

You may calculate that a merchant with a dragoman [translator], and with two men servants, and with goods to the value of twenty-five thousand golden florins, should spend on his way to Cathay from sixty to eighty *sommi* [a weight of silver] of silver, and not more if he manage well; and for all the road back again from Cathay to Tana, including the expenses of living and the pay of servants, and all other charges, the cost will be about five *sommi* per head of pack animals, or something less. And you may reckon the *sommo* to be worth five golden florins. You may reckon also that each ox-waggon will require one ox, and will carry ten cantars Genoese weight; and the camel-waggon will require three camels, and will carry thirty cantars Genoese weight; and the horse-waggon will require one horse,

and will commonly carry six and half cantars of silk, at 250 Genoese pounds to the cantar [a Genoese pound was apparently about 12 ounces]. And a bale of silk may be reckoned at between 110 and 115 Genoese pounds.

You may reckon also that from Tana to Sara [Selitryanoe north of the Caspian Sea] the road is less safe than on any other part of the journey; and yet even when this part of the road is at its worst, if you are some sixty men in the company you will go as safely as if you were in your own house. . . .

Whatever silver the merchants may carry with them as far as Cathay the lord of Cathay will take from them and put into his treasury. And to merchants who thus bring silver they give that paper money of theirs in exchange. This is of yellow paper, stamped with the seal of the lord aforesaid. And this money is called *balishi*; and with this money you can readily buy silk and all other merchandize that you have a desire to buy. And all the people of the country are bound to receive it. And yet you shall not pay a higher price for your goods because your money is of paper. And of the said paper money there are three kinds, one being worth more than another,

Source: Adapted from Henry Yule and Henri Cordier, ed. and trans., *Cathay and the Way Thither, Being a Collection of Medieval Notices of China*, vol. 3 (London: Hakluyt Society, 1916), 143–71. Reproduced on Silk Road Seattle—University of Washington: http://depts.washington.edu/silkroad/texts/pegol.html (consulted December 26, 2020).

according to the value which has been established for each by that lord.

And you may reckon that you can buy for one *sommo* of silver nineteen or twenty pounds of Cathay silk, when reduced to Genoese weight, and that the *sommo* should weigh eight and a half ounces of Genoa, and should be of the alloy of eleven ounces and seventeen deniers to the pound.

You may reckon also that in Cathay you should get three or three and a half pieces of damasked silk for a *sommo*; and from three and a half to five pieces of *nacchetti* of silk and gold, likewise for a *sommo* of silver.

QUESTIONS

- Why do you think Pegolotti spent so much time discussing exact prices for the journey? What does this tell you about contemporary trade?
- Does this sound like a fair system to you? Why or why not?

1.5 *THE FOUNDING OF TENOCHTITLAN*

This account of the establishment of the Mexicas' chief settlement is a long story written down in 1558 and based on materials described far earlier in pictographs. In this version, Huitzilopochtli is a priest rather than the god of war. The god-priest Quauhcoatl (Quetzalcoatl) is a complicated culture-bearer for the peoples of the region. The eagle was sacred to the Mexica, and its presence in this spot convinced them to build their settlement after generations of wandering. Huitzilopochtli had consecrated the site long before by tearing out the heart of the wizard Copil and burying it on this reedy island in Lake Texcoco. This founding story or myth exists in different versions based on oral and pictographic tradition.

Then Quauhcoatl gathered the Mexicans together,
he had them hear the words of Huitzilopochtli
The Mexicans listened.
And then, once more, they went in among the rushes, I among the reeds, to the edge of the spring.
And when they came out into the reeds,
There, at the edge of the spring, was the tenochtli [prickly pear cactus],
And they saw an eagle on the tenochtli, perched on it, standing on it.
It was eating something, it was feeding,
It was pecking at what it was eating.
And when the eagle saw the Mexicans, he bowed his head low.
(They had only seen the eagle from afar.)

Its nest, its pallet, was of every kind of precious feather—
Lovely cotinga feathers, roseate
Spoonbill feathers, quetzal feathers.
And they also saw strewn around the heads of sundry birds,
The heads of previous birds strung together,
And some bird's feet and bones.
And the god called out to them, he said to them,
"O Mexicans, it shall be there!"
(But the Mexicans did not see who spoke.)
It is for this reason they call it Tenochtitlan.
And then the Mexicans wept, they said,
"O happy, O blessed are we!
We have beheld the city that shall be ours!
Let us go, now, let us rest. . . ."
This was the year 2-House, 1325.

QUESTIONS

- What is the main message of the storm?
- What can you learn about Mexica civilization from the story?

Source: From Fernando Alvarado Tezozomoc, *Crónica Mexicayotl*, trans. Thelma Sullivan, *Tlalocan VI* (1971), 313–35, in *In the Language of Kings: An Anthology of Mesoamerican Literature—Pre-Columbian to the Present*, ed. Miguel León-Portilla and Earl Shorris (New York: W. W. Norton & Company, 2001), 192–205, 204–05.

1.6 IBN BATTUTA, "ON *HAJJ*" (1326)

Ibn Battuta (1304–c.1369) was from a Berber family of legal scholars that lived in Tangier, Morocco. He went on *hajj* in 1325 expecting to be gone for sixteen months, but kept going and did not return for twenty-four years. He became known as the greatest traveler of the eastern hemisphere, more than doubling the voyages of Zheng Ze and surpassing Marco Polo by a factor of five. In this excerpt, Battuta arrived at Mecca and Medina on a desert caravan that originated in Damascus, Syria.

The great caravan halts at Tabuk for four days to rest and to water the camels and lay in water for the terrible desert between Tabuk and al-Ula. The custom of the watercarriers is to camp beside the spring, and they have tanks made of buffalo hides, like great cisterns, from which they water the camels and fill the waterskins. Each amir [an Arab ruler] or person of rank has a special tank for the needs of his own camels and personnel; the other people make private agreements with the watercarriers to water their camels and fill their waterskins for a fixed sum of money.

From Tabuk the caravan travels with great speed night and day, for fear of this desert. Halfway through is the valley of al-Ukhaydir, which might well be the valley of Hell (may God preserve us from it). One year the pilgrims suffered terribly here from the samoom-wind [hot, dry, desert wind]; the water-supplies dried up and the price of a single drink rose to a thousand dinars, but both seller and buyer perished. Their story is written on a rock in the valley. . . .

Al-Ula, a large and pleasant village with palm-gardens and water-springs, lies half a day's journey or less from al-Hijr. The pilgrims halt there four days to provision themselves and wash their clothes. They leave behind them here any surplus of provisions they may have, taking with them nothing but what is strictly necessary. The people of the village are very trustworthy. The Christian merchants of Syria may come as far as this and no further, and they trade in provisions and other goods with the pilgrims here. On the third day after leaving al-Ula the caravan halts in the outskirts of the holy city of Medina.

That same evening [the third day after leaving al-Ula, on the route from Syria and Damascus] we entered the holy sanctuary and reached the illustrious mosque, halting in salutation at the Gate of Peace; then we prayed in the illustrious "garden" between the tomb of the Prophet and the noble pulpit, and reverently touched the fragment that remains of the palm-trunk against which the Prophet stood when he preached. . . .

On this journey, our stay at Medina lasted four days. We used to spend every night in the illustrious mosque, where the people, after forming circles in the courtyard and, lighting large numbers of candles, would pass the time either in reciting the Koran from volumes set on rests in front of them, or in intoning litanies, or in visiting the sanctuaries of the holy tomb.

Source: Adapted from Ibn Battuta, *Travels in Asia and Africa 1325–1354*, ed. and trans. H. A. R. Gibb (London: Broadway House, 1929), 72–77. https://sourcebooks.fordham.edu/source/1354-ibnbattuta.asp (consulted December 29, 2020).

We then set out from Medina towards Mecca, and halted near the mosque of Dhu'l-Hulayfa, five miles away. It was at this point that the Prophet assumed the pilgrim garb and obligations, and here too I divested myself of my tailored clothes, bathed, and putting on the pilgrim's garment I prayed and dedicated myself to the pilgrimage. . . .

Thence we travelled through 'Usfan to the Bottom of Marr, a fertile valley with numerous palms and a spring supplying a stream from which the district is irrigated. From this valley fruit and vegetables are transported to Mecca.

We set out at night from this blessed valley, with hearts full of joy at reaching the goal of our hopes, and in the morning arrived at the City of Surety, Mecca (may God ennoble her!), where we immediately entered the holy sanctuary and began the rites of pilgrimage.

QUESTIONS

- What did Battuta think of the system set up to support the Hajj?
- Does this document change how you think about fourteenth-century trade and transit? Why or why not?

RELIGIOUS PRACTICE IN THE MODERN WORLD

2.1 DELIBERATIONS OF THE COUNCIL OF CONSTANCE: SENTENCE AGAINST JOHN HUS (1415)

John Hus (1369–1415) was a Roman Catholic clergy from Bohemia who was much influenced by the reformist ideas of Englishman John Wyclif (d. 1384). He preached against the corruption of the clergy and Roman Catholic fundraising practices. Hus challenged certain theological orthodoxies. Many people in Bohemia and surrounding areas adopted his views. Tasked with ending the simultaneous reign of three different popes, the Church Council of Constance summoned Hus, denounced his ideas, ejected him from the priesthood, and burned him at the stake. His ideas continued to spread leading to a series of Hussite wars lasting from 1419 to 1434. Although various popes called five crusades to annihilate the Hussites, Roman Catholics were obliged to allow the different rite developed by Hus to be practiced in Bohemia.

The most holy general council of Constance, divinely assembled and representing the catholic church, for an everlasting record. Since a bad tree is wont to bear bad fruit, as truth itself testifies, so it is that John Wyclif, of cursed memory, by his deadly teaching, like a poisonous root, has brought forth many noxious sons, not in Christ Jesus through the gospel, as once the holy fathers brought forth faithful sons, but rather contrary to the saving faith of Christ, and he has left these sons as successors to his perverse teaching. This holy synod of Constance is compelled to act against these men as against spurious and illegitimate sons, and to cut away their errors from the Lord's field as if they were harmful briars, by means of vigilant care and the knife of ecclesiastical authority, lest they spread as a cancer to destroy others. . . .

[Regarding John Hus] This most holy synod of Constance therefore declares and defines that the articles listed below, which have been found on examination, by many masters in sacred scripture, to be contained in his books and pamphlets written in his own hand, and which the same John Hus at a public hearing, before the fathers and prelates of this sacred council, has confessed to be contained in his books and pamphlets, are not catholic and should not be taught to be such but rather many of them are erroneous, others scandalous, others offensive to the ears of the devout, many of them are rash and seditious, and some of them are notoriously heretical and have long ago been rejected and condemned by holy fathers and by general councils, and it strictly forbids them to be preached, taught or in any way approved. Moreover, since the articles listed below are explicitly contained in his books or treatises, namely in the book entitled *De ecclesia* and in his other pamphlets, this most holy synod therefore reproves and condemns the aforesaid books and his teaching . . . [to] be publicly and solemnly burnt in the presence of the clergy and

Source: Found in Norman P. Tanner, ed., *Decrees of the Ecumenical Councils* (London: Sheed & Ward, 1990,), 426–31. https://web.archive.org/web/20080101090223/http://www.piar.hu/councils/ecum16.htm (consulted July 11, 2020).

people in the city of Constance and elsewhere. . . . This same holy synod decrees that local ordinaries and inquisitors of heresy are to proceed against any who violate or defy this sentence and decree as if they were persons suspected of heresy. . . .

John Hus was and is a true and manifest heretic and has taught and publicly preached, to the great offence of the divine Majesty, to the scandal of the universal church and to the detriment of the catholic faith, errors and heresies. . . . [The council] declares that the said John Hus seduced the Christian people, especially in the kingdom of Bohemia, in his public sermons and in his writings . . . and as such does not desire to return to the bosom of holy mother the church, and is unwilling to abjure the heresies and errors which he has publicly defended and preached, this holy synod of Constance therefore declares and decrees that the same John Hus is to be deposed and degraded from the order of the priesthood. . . .

This holy synod of Constance, seeing that God's church has nothing more that it can do, relinquishes John Hus to the judgment of the secular authority and decrees that he is to be relinquished to the secular court. [to be burnt at the stake].

QUESTIONS

- How did the Council justify its sentence?
- Why do you think Hus' ideas were viewed as so dangerous?

2.2 MOTOORI NORINAGA, "KAMI" (1798)

Shintoism is an ancient set of beliefs and practices that has gone through many phases of adaptation and renewal. It was strongly affected by Buddhism and Neo-Confucianism. In the late eighteenth century, Japanese scholar Motoori Norinaga (1730–1801) sought to understand the idea of kami as gods, ancestors, and spirits of place through contemplating the Shinto shrine at Ise. This shrine was primarily dedicated to the Sun Goddess, who was perceived as the ancestor of the ruling dynasty, as a fertility goddess, and as the embodiment of nature. In this brief excerpt from *The Two Shrines of Ise: An Essay of Split Bamboo* (1798), Motoori Norinaga grapples with the ancient views of the relationship between humanity and the divine.

I do not yet understand the meaning of the term *kami*. Speaking in general, however, it may be said that *kami* signifies, in the first place, the deities of heaven and earth that appear in the ancient records and also the spirits of the shrines where they are worshipped.

It is hardly necessary to say that it includes human beings. It also includes such objects as birds, beasts, trees, plants, sees, mountains, and so forth. In ancient usage, anything whatsoever which was outside the ordinary, which possessed superior power, or which was awe-inspiring was called *kami*. Eminence here does not refer merely to the superiority of nobility, goodness, or meritorious deeds. Evil and mysterious things, if they are extraordinary and dreadful are called *kami*. It is needless to say that among human beings who are called *kami* the successive generations of sacred emperors are all included. The fact that emperors are also called "distant kami" is because, from the standpoint of common people, they are far-separated, majestic, and worthy of reverence. In a lesser degree we find, in the present as well as in ancient times, the human beings who are *kami*. Although they may not be accepted throughout the whole country, yet in each province, each village, and each family there are human beings who are *kami*, each one according to his proper position. The *kami* of the divine age were for the most part human beings of that time and, because the people of that time were all *kami*, it is called the Age of the Gods (*kami*).

QUESTIONS

- What can you glean about Shintoism from the text?
- Why do you think Norinaga struggled with some Shinto values?

Source: Ryusaku Tsunoda, Wm. Theodore de Bary, and Donald Keene, eds., *Sources of Japanese Tradition* (New York: Columbia University Press, 1958), 23–24.

2.3 SRI RĀMAKRISHNA PARAMAHANSA, "THE WORLD AS SEEN BY A MYSTIC" (1880s)

Sri Rāmakrishna Paramahansa (1836–1886) was born Gadadhar Chattopadhyaya to a relatively poor but pious Brahmin family in Bengal. He served as a priest in several temples including one devoted to the goddess Kali. He was well known as an ascetic, mystic, and teacher. His message of focusing on god and the domination of the body by the mind through discipline melded the ideas of several Hindu schools with elements more common to Buddhism. These teachings had wide impact during the nineteenth-century renaissance of Hindu thought and practice. Paramahansa generally taught through the use of parables such as the one included in the last paragraph.

I practiced austerities for a long time. I cared very little for the body. My longing for the Divine Mother [Kali] was so great that I would not eat or sleep. . . . I used to have ecstasy all the time. . . .

When I reached the state of continuous ecstasy, I gave up all external forms of worship; I could no longer perform them. . . .

Brāhmo: Revered Sir, is it true that God cannot be realized without giving up the world?

The Bhagavān [blessed one], smiling: Oh no! you do not have to give up everything. You are better off where you are. By living in the world you are enjoying the taste of both the pure crystalized sugar and of the molasses with all its impurities . . . but you will have to fix your mind on God, otherwise you cannot realize Him. . . .

Everything is in the mind. Bondage and freedom are in the mind. . . . If you keep your mind in evil company, your thoughts, ideas, and words will be colored with evil; but keep in the company of Bhaktas [devotees or worshippers], then your thoughts ideas and words will be of God. The mind is everything. On one side is the wife, on the other side is the child; it loves the wife in one way and the child in another way, yet the mind is the same.

By the mind one is bound; by the mind one is freed. If I think I am absolutely free, whether I live in the world or in the forest, where is my bondage? I am the child of God, the son of the King of kings; who can bind me? When bitten by a snake, if you assert with firmness: "There is no venom in me," you will be cured. In the same way, he who asserts with strong conviction: "I am no bound, I am free," becomes free. . . .

A man woke up at midnight and desired to smoke. He wanted a light, so he went to a neighbor's house and knocked at the door. Someone opened the door and asked him what he wanted. The man said: "I wish

Source: Wm. Theodore de Bary, Stephen N. Hay, Royal Weiler, and Andrew Yarrow, eds., *Sources of Indian Tradition* (New York: Columbia University Press, 1958), 638, 641–2, 644.

to smoke. Can you give me a light?" The neighbor replied: "Bah! What is the matter with you? You have taken so much trouble to come and [awaken] us at this hour, when in your hand you have a lighted lantern!" What a man wants is already within him; but he still wanders here and there in search of it.

QUESTIONS

- How, according to the document, can a "state of continuous ecstasy" be achieved?
- Why do you think the document had such an impact? What about the ideology would have been appealing?

2.4 SAYYID QUTB, "JIHAD IN THE CAUSE OF GOD" (1964)

Egyptian writer, teacher, and literary critic Sayyid Qutb (1906–1966) became increasingly radical after a visit to the United States from 1948 to 1951, rejecting many aspects of modern economy and society as false "progress" in favor of what he believed to be a more moral, just, and faithful society, espoused as an ideal by the Islamic community. He joined the Muslim Brotherhood and advocated the overthrow of existing governments as betraying the faith in *Milestones* (1964), the source of this excerpt. Qutb's radical, universalistic views rejected traditional Muslim tolerance of others. Jailed, tortured, and executed by the Egyptian government, Qutb helped to inspire an Islamic religious revival and influenced many radical political figures across the Muslim world.

If we insist on calling Islamic Jihad a defensive movement, then we must change the meaning of the word "defense" and mean by it "the defense of man" against all those elements which limit his freedom. These elements take the form of beliefs and concepts, as well as political systems, based on economic, racial and class distinctions. . . .

When we take this broad meaning of the word "defense," we understand the true character of Islam, and that it is a universal proclamation of the freedom of man from servitude to other men, the establishment of the sovereignty of God and His Lordship throughout the world, the end of man's arrogance and selfishness, and the implementation of the rule of the Divine Shari'ah [Islamic religious law] in human affairs. . . .

It would be naïve to assume that a call is raised to free the whole of humankind throughout the earth, and it is confined to preaching and exposition. . . .

Since the objective of the message of Islam is a decisive declaration, not merely on the philosophical plane but also in the actual conditions of life, it must employ jihad. It is immaterial whether the homeland of Islam—in the true Islamic sense, Dar ul-Islam—is in a condition of peace or whether it is threatened by its neighbors. When Islam strives for peace, its objective is not that superficial peace which requires that only that part of the earth where the followers of Islam are residing remain secure. The peace which Islam desires is that the religion [i.e., the law of the society] be purified for God, that the obedience of all people be for God alone, and that some people should be lords over others. . . .

What kind of a man is it who, after listening to the commandment of God and the Traditions of the Prophet—peace be on him—and after reading about the events which occurred during the Islamic jihad, still thinks that it is concerned only with the defense of the borders? . . .

In the verse giving permission to fight, God has informed the believers that the life of this world is such that checking one group of people by another is the law of God, so that the earth may be cleansed of

Source: Walter Laqueur, ed., *Voices of Terror: Manifestos, Writings and Manuals of Al Qaeda, Hamas, and other Terrorists from around the World and throughout the Ages* (New York: Reed Press, 2004), 394–96.

corruption. . . . Thus, this struggle is not a temporary phase, but an eternal state—an eternal state, as truth and falsehood cannot co-exist on this earth. Whenever Islam stood up with the universal declaration that God's lordship should be established over the entire earth and that men should become free from servitude to other men, the usurpers of God's authority on earth have struck out against it fiercely and have never tolerated it. It became incumbent upon Islam to strike back and release man throughout the earth from the grip of these usurpers. The eternal struggle for the freedom of man will continue until the religion is purified for God.

QUESTIONS

- What are the core tenets of Qutb's philosophy?
- Why do you think the document had such an impact? What about the ideology would have been appealing?

2.5 ANIMAL SACRIFICE IN THE *BOOK OF BEREISHIT*

This excerpt is the first eighteen verses of Chapter 15 of the *Book of Bereishit* (Genesis) in the Hebrew Bible. This ancient text describes a covenant between Abram (Abraham) and his deity concerning the eventual occupation of the land of Canaan by his descendants. That covenant was to be sealed by animal sacrifice. The Jewish practice of animal sacrifice ended in the first century of the Common Era with the destruction of the Second Temple.

After these things the word of the LORD came unto Abram in a vision, saying, Fear not, Abram: I am thy shield, and thy exceeding great reward.

And Abram said, LORD God, what wilt thou give me, seeing I go childless, and the steward of my house is this Eliezer of Damascus?

And Abram said, Behold, to me thou hast given no seed: and, lo, one born in my house is mine heir.

And, behold, the word of the LORD came unto him, saying, This shall not be thine heir; but he that shall come forth out of thine own bowels shall be thine heir.

And he brought him forth abroad, and said, Look now toward heaven, and tell the stars, if thou be able to number them: and he said unto him, So shall thy seed be.

And he believed in the LORD; and he counted it to him for righteousness.

And he said unto him, I am the LORD that brought thee out of Ur of the Chaldees [Assyria], to give thee this land to inherit it.

And he said, LORD God, whereby shall I know that I shall inherit it?

And he said unto him, Take me an heifer of three years old, and a she goat of three years old, and a ram of three years old, and a turtledove, and a young pigeon.

And he took unto him all these, and divided them in the midst, and laid each piece one against another: but the birds divided he not.

And when the fowls came down upon the carcases [sic], Abram drove them away.

And when the sun was going down, a deep sleep fell upon Abram; and, lo, an horror of great darkness fell upon him.

And he said unto Abram, Know of a surety that thy seed shall be a stranger in a land that is not their's, and shall serve them; and they shall afflict them four hundred years;

And also that nation, whom they shall serve, will I judge: and afterward shall they come out with great substance.

And thou shalt go to thy fathers in peace; thou shalt be buried in a good old age.

But in the fourth generation they shall come hither again: for the iniquity of the Amorites is not yet full.

Source: Jewish Virtual Library, *Book of Genesis*, based on the Jewish Publication Society translation, ed. Benyamin Pilant (1997), https://www.jewishvirtuallibrary.org/bereishit-genesis-full-text (consulted August 16, 2020).

And it came to pass, that, when the sun went down, and it was dark, behold a smoking furnace, and a burning lamp that passed between those pieces.

In the same day the LORD made a covenant with Abram, saying, Unto thy seed have I given this land, from the river of Egypt unto the great river, the river Euphrates. . . .

QUESTIONS

- What was the "covenant" agreed to? Why was it significant?
- Why was animal sacrifice such a crucial part of the story?

2.6 SPAIN'S EFFORTS TO ELIMINATE IDOLATRY IN NEW GRANADA (1595)

This document relates the actions of Egas de Guzmán, a judge in New Granada [modern Columbia] in 1595. He was tasked with eradicating all physical remnants of the Indigenous Muisca religion, which was believed to include the worship of idols and the veneration of ancestors, particularly those who had resisted Spanish Roman Catholicism. This investigation was undertaken not by the Inquisition but by the civil authorities, illustrating their close collaboration and joint interest in conversion. Varied forms of torture were employed on many occasions throughout the process to force Indigenous people to talk. Particularly close attention was paid to Indigenous possession of gold or any other valuables.

Speaking through the interpreter Cristóbal de Sanabria, his honor told the Indians that he came on a visit of inspection, to precure that they be good Christians, and to see that they did not keep old shrines and idols. To this effect and to extirpate all idolatrous practices, eh commanded that anyone among them who maintained such shrines or temples dedicated to the devil declare it openly. In the name of His Majesty the King he promised to forgive those who told the truth, but vowed that all who concealed such practices would be dealt with and brought to justice in accord with the will of God and His Majesty.

There immediately appeared before the judge an Indian *principal* [prominent inhabitant] named Pedro Conba, who stated that he possessed a shrine known as a *cuca* or holy house. . . .

Accompanied by me [the notary], as well as the interpreter and others, the judge and *visitador-general* went directly to inspect the houses and huts referred to by the Indians and searched each one thoroughly in order to see if they contained idols or shrines. He discovered none and given that there were no shrines in any of these huts, he ordered that one of the Indians be threatened. . . .

Thereupon the judge ordered that the Indian Pedro Conba be stripped of his clothing and asked him to state and to declare if he or other Indians have any such shrines. Conba said that he knew nothing, and in light of the Indian's reticence and previous declaration, the judge, to intimidate and frighten him ordered Alonso de Molina to tie the man's arms with a rope, telling the Indian through the interpreter that he should speak the truth, because if he did not he would have to be tortured. . . . He said that an Indian woman named Clara kept a cotton idol [but] that he did not know what was inside it. . . .

We were led by the Indian woman to a field some five hundred strides from the village, where she pointed to some stones under which there was a small clay pot containing two hollow figurines made of unrefined gold wrapped in a bit of cotton and colored cloth and filled with earth. Beneath other stones

Quoted in Richard Boyer and Geoffrey Spurling, eds., *Colonial Lives: Documents on Latin American History, 1550–1850* (New York: Oxford University Press, 2000), 40–42, 44–45, 50.

shown us by the Indian woman was found a piece of white cloth the width of the palm of the hand and a bit of cotton, within which was wrapped a figurine of unrefined gold filled with earth and six tiny emerald-like gems of no value. [Six other sites with similar types of figurines were turned over to the Roman Catholic authorities. Several Indigenous were tortured to gain information]. . . .

There . . . in some stone caves facing a hill and impossible to reach on horseback, Diego [Raga] indicated a cave inside which there was found a large *tunjo* [offering] of cotton cloth. Wrapped within it were bones a skull that Diego Raga said were those of the old *cacique* named Unbaguya, who was not a Christian and whose remains were kept for veneration. When it was untied no gold was found, and there were only a few small, worthless emeralds and five or six moldy and torn cotton blankets. . . .

The judge ordered that all of this be burned along with the bones and blankets in the small square in front of the church. . . .

Although it is recorded in these proceedings that his grace the juge [judge] inspected these houses and found no idols there is reason to believe that since these Indians kept them that they retain some memory of the old rites and ceremonies and that it is right in the service of the Lord our God to extirpate all idolatrous abuses and to see that no trace or memory remain among the Indians. To make an example the judge intended and did so order that the seven houses and temples of idolatry in which the Indians used to perform their ceremonies and idolatrous rites, be immediately burned and demolished, reserving as his grace does the right to impose upon these Indians whatever punishment he sees fit.

QUESTIONS

- Why were the authorities so insistent on destroying the items mentioned in this excerpt?
- Does this change how you think about Spain during the era of the Inquisition? Why or why not?

2.7 GONZALO DE LA MASA ON SANTA ROSA OF LIMA (1617)

Santa Rosa de Lima (1586–1617) was born Isabel Flores de Oliva to a noble Spanish family in Lima, Peru. Denied their permission to enter a convent as a nun, she joined the Third Order of St. Dominic, a lay group devoted to pious action and Dominican spirituality, to live an ascetic, humble life. In her home, she cared for sick people, homeless children, and the elderly. This account by Gonzalo de la Maza, a Spanish accountant whose family had close contact with her, was recorded in 1617 as part of the information-gathering process that culminated in the papal declaration of Rosa as a saint in 1671. She was the first person born in the western hemisphere to be canonized and is the patron of the city of Lima, the Americas, and the Philippines.

[F]rom that moment on she did not do a thing, not one thing, which she understood to be a sin and an offense to God Our Father. From this fear [five-year-old] Rosa gained some knowledge of the divine goodness, which helped her [understand things about her] grandmother [who had died] and a sister, a little older than her, who died at the age of fourteen. [Rosa was now able to see them] as souls that, in her opinion, had been very pleasing to Our Lord, [and] whose deaths had been a great consolation to her because the things she had seen in them and been given to understand by His Divine Majesty convinced her that they had certainly gone to Heaven. . . .

Thus, the said Rosa de Sancta María said to this witness that at that tender age she had dedicated to God Our Lord the gift of her virginity, with a vow [of chastity], and that, to this witness's understanding, the great outward modesty and purity of life attained by the said Rosa suggested that she honored the said promise not only in her deeds, but also in her thoughts, as one of her spiritual fathers expressed it to this witness that in her life she had neither seen nor longed for a feast day or worldly celebration, not even a common procession, and that during the time that he knew her he clearly perceived this [to be a true account of] her way of withdrawal [from the world] and devotion. She withdrew not only from direct communication but also from seeing people and [worldly] things in order that they might neither impede nor delay the serenity of her soul, the power of which this witness saw at that time to be so focused that he beheld it with great admiration. . . .

To the seventh question this witness answered that he knew for a fact that since the beginning of her life the said Rosa de Sancta María performed continuous and rigorous mortifications of the flesh, usually with iron chains. . . .

With the same certainty, this witness learned that for a long time she [Rosa] had worn an iron chain wrapped two or three times around her waist and fastened with a padlock for which she had no key. [At one point when] she was in her mother's house, she

Source: Kenneth Mills and William B. Taylor, eds., *Colonial Spanish America: A Documentary History* (Wilmington, DE: SR Books, 1998), 198–202.

developed a very severe pain in her abdomen, and the chain had to be removed in order for her to be helped. She suffered much as the lock was broken because her skin and, at some parts, her flesh had become stuck to the said chain, as this witness saw after Rosa's death. . . .

[H]e has heard said that there have been many, and very exceptional, miracles performed by Our Lord God for the greater glory of His name and in demonstration of the virtue and sanctity of the blessed Rosa. [By these miracles] many people with different maladies, [who] entrust themselves to her intercession [by]

touching some traces of her clothing and the earth from around her tomb, have been restored to health. This witness defers to the testimonies and proof of the said miracles. . . .

What this witness had most noticed were the tears shed by many people [while] talking about the life and things of the blessed Rosa. Some friar-confessors told him of the exceptional conversions of souls and arduous transformations of [people's] lives that had occurred among those who commended themselves to the blessed Rosa after her death.

QUESTIONS

- What kind of actions were deemed most important in determining Santa Rosa's sainthood?
- What insights can you glean into sixteenth-century Spanish Catholicism through this account?

2.8 TRI HAI, "WHY WE MUST REVIVE BUDDHISM" (1938)

In Indochina, Mahayana Buddhism dominated. This movement is known for focusing on ritualism, metaphysical speculation, and universal ethics. Beginning in the 1920s, reformist Buddhists sought more traditional training and stricter education for monks and nuns as a first step in reforming society. In this address published in 1938, Tri Hai (1906–1979) took advantage of greater literacy among some segments of the population to advocate educating the rest of the population both in the tenets of Buddhism and more generally. He believed that by ending ignorance, he could eliminate dependence.

Many people have not read the Buddhist sutras and do not understand the teachings of Buddhism. . . .

Buddhism also teaches that the human body is ephemeral and all will disintegrate in a few decades, and therefore when human beings are still healthy, they should perform good and useful deeds for people, society and sentient beings. All the buddhas, bodhisattvas, sages, and worthies also relied on their human bodies to accomplish their mission. Therefore, human beings must cultivate themselves and not allow their bodies to be wasted. To this end, they must do away with excessive desires for position, fame, and wealth. . . . The Lord Buddha warned people against excessive greed and advised them to focus on fidelity, filial piety, righteousness, and ethical behavior to attain everlasting spiritual pleasure. . . .

It is wrong to regard ritual as a troublesome thing and as superstition. Because we live in the world, polite and courteous behavior shows that someone is honest and good. Courtesy entails certain rites that should not be constrained as superstitious. When we perform rituals in honor of Confucius or at the Hung kings' temple, or offer wreaths on the death anniversaries of meritorious mandarins and heroes and righteous persons, this is not superstition. The same applies to the Lord Buddha, whose teachings guide people to understand self-cultivation, mutual affection and respect, sinfulness and blessedness, the law of cause and effect, samsara, and the karmic rewards of good and evil. If the world correctly abides by the Lord Buddha's teachings, everyone will attain peace. . . .

[W]e need to revive Buddhism and impart the teachings of the Buddha to enlighten the population. To this end, our association has set up a research committee on the Buddha's teachings, to translate them into Vietnamese and publish them as books and in the *Duoc Tue* [*Torch of Wisdom*] journal so that Buddhist followers can understand the Buddha's teachings and the Way and follow it.

The lecture committee has decided that on every first and fifteenth of each lunar month, the pagodas will teach the Buddhist sutras to the public so that

Source: George E. Dutton, Jayne S. Werner, and John K. Whitmore, eds., *Sources of Vietnamese Tradition* (New York: Columbia University Press, 2012), 435–38.

Buddhist followers may properly understand their own religion. . . .

At present, the objective of our association is to make as many people as possible understand and abide by the principles of Buddhism. To this end, the branches of our association and its members should strengthen their religious devotion, encourage more people to join the association and to read our books and journals, and should provide financial assistance to Buddhist schools, making further study possible so that many people can propagate Buddhism to benefit all sentient beings. In this way, everyone will return to the right path and enjoy peace and happiness together. We thus will earn immeasurable merit.

QUESTIONS

- What steps did Hai advocate for "reviving" Buddhism?
- Why did he defend "ritual"? Is his defense effective? Why or why not?

3

IMPERIALISM AND THE EVOLUTION OF EMPIRE, 1500–1800

3.1 CAPITULATIONS OF THE REPUBLIC OF FLORENCE WITH THE SULTAN OF EGYPT (1488)

Although Muslims and Christians engaged in religious war in Europe, Africa, and Asia, trade continued to flourish. Despite ongoing conflict, various European states were Muslim Egypt's largest trading partners. This excerpt of the "capitulations," or agreements, made between the Republic of Florence and the ruler of Egypt illustrates that religious conflict was not permitted to stifle commerce. The sultan sought to eliminate corrupt restrictions on Florentine merchants, even allowing them to dress as Muslims to avoid additional taxes or harassment. Nor were religious prohibitions on alcohol enforced, in order to maximize customs revenue. This agreement became the model for other states, and, after Egypt was conquered by the Ottomans in 1517, these capitulations were ratified and remained in force until the end of the eighteenth century. Ruling a diverse and extensive empire required trade to furnish goods and provide tax revenue.

2. That the Florentine merchants or their comrades on presenting themselves at the place of Alexandria or at another port of our Moslem dominion with cloth, silk, soap, oil, nuts, ointments, coral, sulfur, and every other sort of ware, be safe in their persons and goods, and be able to sell freely their merchandise for cash or for exchange, and that no one can or dare to hinder them, damage them, not even so much as a farthing. . . .

3. Furthermore, that formerly the officials of the custom-house of Alexandria, upon the arrival of the merchandise of the Florentines, proceeded to open the bales with violence and confusion, in such a way that some of them appropriated to themselves in the meantime a part of said merchandise by falsely asserting to have bought the same, whereby the trade of the Florentines was hurt; that in the future no one of the vicars, presidents, and officials of the custom-house, and also no one of the said Florentine nation, dare to take the merchandise of the Florentines without their full consent; and also that in order to obviate the recurrence of the disorders above referred to, the Florentine merchants be permitted to quickly transfer the goods into their own magazines, and that they be then visited by the ministers of the custom-house, so as not to defraud the rights of the custom-house. . . .

5. That the Florentine having paid according to custom one *surifo* for each barrel of liquid extract [as wine or spirits] in the ports of our Moslem dominion, no one shall dare to burden or vex them not even for a farthing. Whereof we do ordain the execution. . . .

Art. 14. Should any controversy or disagreement arise between the said Florentines, none of the governors or Moslem judges may interfere in their affairs, but jurisdiction therein belongs to the consul of the Florentines; which is to be brought in such cases in accordance with the legal custom of the Florentines.

Art. 15. That should any Florentine make a voyage from one country to another in our Moslem

Source: Reprinted in Edward A. Van Dyck, *Report upon the Capitulations of the Ottoman Empire since the Year 1150,* part 1 (Washington, DC: Government Printing Office, 1881), 91–92.

dominion, he can, for greater security of his person and effects while traveling on the way, dress himself like a Moslem so as to free himself from bad encounters and vexations, and no one may dare disturb him as to eating and drinking, nor burden him with any costs and charges. . . .

QUESTIONS

• Why would the sultan make such "capitulations"?
• What do you think the effect of this document would have been on Florentine behavior?

TABLE 3.1 POPULATION COMPOSITION OF EUROPEAN EMPIRES IN THE WESTERN HEMISPHERE

	Year	European/white	African/Black	Indigenous	Share of Population in Western Hemisphere
Spanish America	1570	1.3	2.5	96.3	83.5
	1650	6.3	9.3	84.4	84.5
	1825	18.0	22.5	59.5	55.2
U.S./Canada	1570	0.2	0.2	99.6	8.9
	1650	12.0	2.2	85.8	9.1
	1825	79.6	16.7	3.7	33.2
Brazil	1570	2.4	3.5	94.1	7.6
	1650	7.4	13.7	78.9	7.7
	1825	23.4	55.6	21.0	11.6

Note: All numbers except dates are percentages.

Source: Stanley L. Engerman and Kenneth L. Sokoloff, "Once Upon a Time in the Americas: Land and Immigration Policies in the New World," in *Understanding Long-Run Economic Growth: Geography, Institutions, and the Knowledge Economy*, ed. Dora L. Costa and Naomi R. Lamoreaux (Chicago: University of Chicago Press, 2011), 13–48, 24.

3.2 DE CHAMPLAIN FIGHTS FOR THE HURON AGAINST THE IROQUOIS

Samuel de Champlain (1567–1635) was a major French explorer of the Saint Lawrence River Valley. After the establishment of a permanent settlement at Québec in 1608, the French allied with diverse Indigenous groups to get beaver pelts (to make hats) that paid for the colony. Champlain participated actively in military campaigns by the Hurons against their mortal enemies, the Iroquois, who were supported by the Dutch. This power struggle continued for two generations, until several groups of Iroquois united successfully to push the Huron across the Saint Lawrence. But France's alliance with the Huron, who provided interpreters, porters, hunters, and access to Indigenous groups and furs farther west and south, made New France a paying proposition.

I directed our interpreter to say to our savages . . . that Sieur de Monts [the founder of New France] had sent me to them to see them . . . to preserve friendship with them and to reconcile them with their enemies, the Souriquois [Iroquois] and Canadians, and moreover that he desired to inhabit their country and show them how to cultivate it, in order that they might not continue to lead so miserable a life as they were doing, and some other words on the same subject. This our savages interpreted to them, at which they signified their great satisfaction, saying that no greater good could come to them than to have our friendship, and that they desired to live in peace with their enemies, and that we should dwell in their land, in order that they might in future more than ever before engage in hunting beavers, and give us a part of them in return for our providing them with things which they wanted. After he had finished his discourse, I presented them with hatchets, paternosters, caps, knives, and other little knickknacks, when we separated from each other. All the rest of this day and the following night, until break of day, they did nothing but dance, sing, and make merry, after which we traded for a certain number of beavers. . . .

The next day, the two chiefs came to see me [complaining] . . . that nearly ten moons ago, according to their mode of reckoning, the son of Yroquet had seen me, and that I had given him a good reception, and declared that Pont Grave and I desired to assist them against their enemies, with whom they had for a long time been at warfare, on account of many cruel acts committed by them against their tribe, under color of friendship; that, having ever since longed for vengeance, they had solicited all the savages, whom I saw on the bank of the river, to come and make an alliance with us, and that their never having seen Christians also impelled them to come and visit us; that I should do with them and their companions as I wished; that they had no children with them, but men versed in war and full of courage, acquainted with the country and rivers in the land of the Iroquois; that now they entreated me

Source: *Voyages of Samuel de Champlain, 1604–1618*, ed. W. L. Grant (New York: Charles Scribner's Sons, 1907), 49–50, 151–52.

to return to our settlement, that they might see our houses, and that, after three days, we should all together come back to engage in the war. . . .

After hearing them, I replied that, if they desired, I should be very glad to return to our settlement . . . they might conclude that I had no other purpose than to engage in the war, since we carried with us nothing but arms, and not merchandise for barter, as they had been given to understand; and that my only desire was to fulfil what I had promised them. . . .

QUESTIONS

- How does Champlain view the Native Americans he fought with and against?
- What stands out about French colonization at the time?

3.3 LETTER FROM THE COUNCIL OF HUEJOTZINGO TO THE KING OF SPAIN (1560)

The municipal government of this city wrote to King Philip II for assistance when their taxes were raised sevenfold with no warning and for no apparent reason. They described the assistance they had given to Spain's conquests and reminded the King that they had adopted Roman Catholicism voluntarily and peaceably. This group of Indigenous noblemen also made it clear how the Spanish forced their subjects to figure out ways to earn gold even if it was not native to the region.

. . . Before the faith reached us, and before we were Christians, when your servants the Spaniards reached us and your captain general don Hernando Cortés arrived . . . not a single town surpassed us here in New Spain in that first and earliest we threw ourselves toward you, we gave ourselves to you, and furthermore no one intimidates us, no one forced us into it. . . . Nowhere did we attack them. Truly we fed them and served them; some arrived sick, so that we carried them in our arms and on our backs, and we served them in many other ways. . . .

And when they began their conquest and war-making, then also we well prepared ourselves to aid them, for out came all of our war gear, our arms and provisions and all our equipment, and we not merely named someone, we went in person, we who rule, and we brought all our nobles and all of our vassals to aid the Spaniards. We helped not only in warfare, but also we gave them everything they needed; we fed and clothed them, and we would carry in our arms and on our backs those whom they wounded in war or who were very ill. . . . And when they went to conquer Michoacan, Jalisco, and Colhuancan, and there at Pánnuco and there at Oaxaca and Tehuantepec and Guatemala, [we were] the only ones who went along while they conquered and made war here in New Spain until they finished the conquest. . . .

Also when they gave us the holy gospel, the holy Catholic faith, with very good will and desire we received and grasped it; no one frightened us into it, no one forced us, but very willingly we seized it, and they gave us all the sacraments. Quietly and peacefully we arranged and order it among ourselves; no one, neither nobleman nor commoner, was ever tortured or burned for this, as was done on every hand here in New Spain. [The people of] many towns were forced and tortured, were hanged or burned because they did not want to leave idolatry, and unwillingly they received the gospel and faith. . . .

We are afflicted and sore pressed, and your town and city of Huejotzingo is as if it was about to disappear and be destroyed. . . . And we your poor vassals, we of Huejotzingo who dwell in your city, when Licentiate Salmerón came to us and entered the city of Huejotzingo, then he saw how troubled the town was with our tribute in gold, sixty pieces that we gave each

Source: Quoted in *Beyond the Codices: The Nahua View of View of Colonial Mexico*, trans. and ed. Arthur J. O. Anderson, Frances Berdan, and James Lockhart (Berkeley: University of California Press, 1976), 181, 183, 185, 187, 189.

year, and that it troubled us because gold does not appear here, and is not to be found in our province, though we searched for it everywhere; then at once Licentiate Salmerón pardoned it on your behalf, so that he made a replacement and substitution of the money. He set our tribute in money at 2,050 pesos. . . . [N]ow this very great tribute has fallen up upon us, seven times exceeding all we had paid before. . . .

QUESTIONS

- What strategies did the council use to try to persuade the King of their argument?
- Do you find the argument persuasive? Why or why not?

3.4 SPANISH *REQUERIMIENTO* (1510)

This statement of the Council of Castile, the institution established to rule the Spanish overseas empire, is usually attributed to jurist Juan López de Palacios Rubios (1450–1524). It was intended to be read as an ultimatum to Indigenous people to accept the religious authority of the papacy, upon whose grant the Spanish monarchy claimed to rule the western hemisphere (other than Brazil). Spain stated that if Christianity and their own power was not accepted immediately, then the Indigenous people could be justly enslaved or killed. Often the text was read in Latin with no translation provided or without any Indigenous people present.

On the part of the King, Don Fernando, and of Doña Juana, his daughter, Queen of Castile and León, subduers of the barbarous nations, we their servants notify and make known to you, as best we can, that the Lord our God, Living and Eternal, created the Heaven and the Earth, and one man and one woman, of whom you and we, all the men of the world, were and are descendants, and all those who came after us. But, on account of the multitude which has sprung from this man and woman in the five thousand years since the world was created, it was necessary that some men should go one way and some another, and that they should be divided into many kingdoms and provinces, for in one alone they could not be sustained.

Of all these nations God our Lord gave charge to one man, called St. Peter, that he should be Lord and Superior of all the men in the world, that all should obey him, and that he should be the head of the whole human race, wherever men should live, and under whatever law, sect, or belief they should be; and he gave him the world for his kingdom and jurisdiction.

And he commanded him to place his seat in Rome as the spot most fitting to rule the world from; but also he permitted him to have his seat in any other part of the world, and to judge and govern all Christians, Moors [Muslims], Jews, Gentiles, and all other sects. This man was called Pope, as if to say, Admirable Great Father and Governor of men. . . .

One of these Pontiffs [popes] who succeeded that St. Peter as Lord of the world, in the dignity and seat which I have before mentioned, made donation of these isles and Tierra-firma [mainland] to the aforesaid King and Queen and to their successors, our lords, with all that there are in these territories, as is contained in certain writings which passed upon the subject as aforesaid, which you can see if you wish.

So their Highnesses are kings and lords of these islands and land of Tierra-firma by virtue of this donation: and some islands, and indeed almost all those to whom this has been notified, have received and served their Highnesses, as lords and kings, in the way that subjects ought to do, with good will, without any resistance, immediately, without delay, when they were informed of the aforesaid facts. And also they received and obeyed the priests whom their Highnesses sent to preach to them and to teach them our Holy Faith; and

Source: Requiremiento: Pronouncement to be Read by Spanish Conquerors to defeated Indians (1510), http://nationalhumanitiescenter.org/pds/amerbegin/contact/text7/requirement.pdf (consulted December 29, 2019).

all these, of their own free will, without any reward or condition, have become Christians, and are so, and their Highnesses have joyfully and benignantly received them, and also have commanded them to be treated as their subjects and vassals; and you too are held and obliged to do the same. Wherefore, as best we can, we ask and require you that you consider what we have said to you, and that you take the time that shall be necessary to understand and deliberate upon it, and that you acknowledge the Church as the Ruler and Superior of the whole world, and the high priest called Pope, and in his name the King and Queen Doña Juana our lords, in his place, as superiors and lords and kings of these islands and this Tierra-firme by virtue of the said donation, and that you consent and give place that these religious fathers should declare and preach to you the aforesaid. If you do so, you will do well, and that which you are obliged to do for their Highnesses, and we in their name shall receive you in all love and charity, and shall leave you, your wives, and your children, and your lands, free without servitude, that you may do with them and with yourselves freely that which you like and think best, and they shall not compel you to turn Christians, unless you yourselves, when informed of the truth, should wish to be converted to our Holy Catholic Faith, as almost all the inhabitants of the rest of the islands have done. And, besides this, their Highnesses award you many privileges and exemptions and will grant you many benefits. But, if you do not do this, and maliciously make delay in it, I certify to you that, with the help of God, we shall powerfully enter into your country, and shall make war against you in all ways and manners that we can, and shall subject you to the yoke and obedience of the Church and of their Highnesses; we shall take you and your wives and your children, and shall make slaves of them, and as such shall sell and dispose of them as their Highnesses may command; and we shall take away your goods, and shall do you all the mischief and damage that we can, as to vassals who do not obey, and refuse to receive their lord, and resist and contradict him; and we protest that the deaths and losses which shall accrue from this are your fault, and not that of their Highnesses, or ours, nor of these cavaliers who come with us. And that we have said this to you and made this Requisition, we request the notary here present to give us his testimony in writing, and we ask the rest who are present that they should be witnesses of this Requisition.

QUESTIONS

- How did the Spanish throne defend its prerogative for conquest?
- What does the fact that this document was often read in Latin tell you about Spanish views of Native Americans?

3.5 ALONZO ORTIZ WRITES TO HIS WIFE, LEONOR GONZÁLEZ (1574?)

This letter from a recent immigrant in Mexico City to his wife in Zafra, Spain, reveals the piety but also the desire for financial benefit behind his decision to immigrate to the Americas. He started a business that employed a significant number of Indigenous people and found a partner. Remarkably, he remained healthy, even though tanning was dangerous and difficult. That such work was the best available shows both his lack of other choices and how hard it was to get people to fill vital economic tasks. We do not know whether Ortiz's plan to bring his family to across the Atlantic was successful.

My lady,

Juan López Sayago gave me some of your letters, and I have others from a sailor who told me he got them from a certain de la Parra, who died at sea. From both sets of letters, I was most pleased to learn that you and all my children are well. . . . Up to now I have simply not been able to write. But be assured that in all I have done, I have asked God and His Blessed Mother to grant me health and, even more, the ability to take advantage of this time and my good health. . . . Because, over here, even though it seems that one suffers much work and tribulation, one knows that God does not harm and that even a leaf on a tree does not move without his will.

I endured difficulties before God guided me here, to the place where I am and will remain. And all that I have suffered since coming is nothing to be because the troubles that you and my children have endured are what give me great sadness and torment. . . . And now I feel it more than ever because God has led me to become a tanner, and there is no better position than

this over here. Moreover, the great expectations which I brought, I still have. In order that I will make good use of the health with which God has blessed me, and that this time not be lost, I have worked, and I continue to work, with great care; I try not to spend money wastefully, and I earn much more than I need to make ends meet. There is, in all this, only one thing wrong, and this is that I do not have you and the children with me. . . .

I have between six and eight Indians who work with me, and each one that I have brings in thirty pesos, twenty, fifteen, or some only ten. About them I will not say more than that I pay them each week for what they do. I tell you all this so that you might consider that here, where I do suffer, I also earn very abundantly.

God has also brought me a partner . . . and when I formed the partnership with him, I made no other condition than that if I wanted to depart for Castile within the three years of our contract, I could do so. He, who will not be leaving because

Source: Quoted in Kenneth Mills and William B. Taylor, eds., *Colonial Spanish America: A Documentary History* (Wilmington, DE: SR Books, 1998), 106–07.

he sees that much profit can be made in the long term, agreed to send 150 pesos to Seville with a merchant friend of his, a sum which is meant entirely for you, that you and the children may come. . . . So, if you decide to come, send your letter by the advance ship preceding the fleet on which you will sail. And to those men to whom I am indebted, you may say that on another fleet I will send one hundred hides that will be worth enough for everyone to be paid.

QUESTIONS

- How did Ortiz try to defend his decision to move?
- Do you think his wife found the letter persuasive? Would you have made the journey, if you were her?

3.6 INDIGENOUS REBELLION IN THE ANDES MOUNTAINS (1781)

These two documents were from the Charcas region of modern Bolivia. Mariano Ramon del Valle was the parish priest for the community. Most members of the clergy could not imagine Indigenous people wanting to make decisions for themselves or withholding their labor; the Indigenous people, for their part, recognized that Spanish-born settlers would find native allies and use violence to overwhelm their minor resistance.

LETTER FROM JOSEPH BALZEDA, CHAPLAIN OF CULTA, TO MARIANO RAMON DEL VALLE (FEBRUARY 18, 1781)

It is not possible to evaluate the frightening things that I live with in this parish. Every day we have more surprises with these Indians who want to live without either GOD or King, making themselves judges over their own legal cases without any respect for GOD and his ministers, and it can all be attributed to the enormous rapacity with which, until the present, they have acted, taking lives and robbing from them when they can. . . .

We have received news that the parish of Macha is without either priest, assistant, sacristan, or cantor because all of them are fugitives for what they have seen. Also they have told us that they will not supply *mitanis* [laborers], *pongos* [house servants]), nor any other things according to the *cartas de favor* written by [Nicolás] Catari [that spread the rebellion]. In fact, I went to the annex of Cahuayo to oversee the election of the *alférez* and *mayordomo* [officers in Roman Catholic confraternities], and they would not supply a *pongo* or *mitani*, leaving me in the dark and dying of cold. . . .

CIRCULAR LETTER TO THE COMMUNITIES (MARCH 8, 1781)

I am informing you that I have just arrived from the province of Cochabamba and the Cochabambinos and the *chapetones* [peninsular Spaniards] have united. They are coming, destroying towns; they have destroyed two towns, and thus Your

Source: *Colonial Lives: Documents on Latin American History, 1550–1850,* ed. Richard Boyer and Geoffrey Spurling (New York: Oxford University Press, 2000), 206–08.

Mercies, when you see this, prepare yourselves for our defense. Everyone should come immediately. Pass this letter to every town in this province of Paria. . . .

For these reasons, whoever would resist this order, should suffer a vile death. As soon as you see this letter, hit the road, even if it's in the middle of the night, for God's sake.

QUESTIONS

- How did the priests wish to run the Charcas region?
- How did they view its Indigenous inhabitants?

3.7 TLAXCALAN CONSPIRATORS

This version of the Spanish intervention in the Valley of Mexico illustrates the significance of the support of Tlaxcala, the twin city to Tenochtitlan, the capital of the Mexica Empire. This version, found in Bernadino De Sahagún's *Florentine Codex*, compiled in the late sixteenth century, was based on the testimony of Nahuatl-speaking elders who witnessed events. Clearly, the Tlaxcalans sought to use the Spanish to further their rivalry with the Mexica. The ability of the Spanish, and indeed of most Europeans, to take advantage of local political divisions was a major reason for their success.

Here it is said how the Spaniards reached Tlaxcala, [also] called Texcallan.

[The Tlaxcalans] guided, accompanied, and led them until they brought them to their palace<s> and placed them there. They showed them great honors, they gave them what they needed and attended to them, and then they gave them their daughters.

Then [the Spaniards] asked them, "Where is Mexico? What kind of a place is it? Is it still far?"

They answered them, "It's not far now. Perhaps one can get there in three days. It is a very favored place, and [the Mexica] are very strong, great warriors, conquerors, who go about conquering everywhere."

Now before this there had been friction between the Tlaxcalans and the Cholulans. They viewed each other with anger, fury, hate, and disgust; they could come together on nothing. Because of this they put [the Spaniards] up to killing them treacherously.

They said to them, "The Cholulans are very evil; they are our enemies. They are as strong as the Mexica, and they are the Mexica's friends."

When the Spaniards heard this, they went to Cholula. The Tlaxcalans and Cempoalans went with them, outfitted for war. When they arrived, there was a general summons and cry that all the noblemen, rulers, subordinate leaders, warriors, and commoners should come., and everyone assembled in the temple courtyard. When they had all come together, [the Spaniards] and their [friends] blocked the entrances, all of the places where one entered. Thereupon people were stabbed, struck, and killed. No such thing was in the minds of the Cholulans; they did not meet the Spaniards with weapons of war. It just seemed that they were stealthily and treacherously killed, because the Tlaxcalans persuaded [the Spaniards] to do it. . . .

And after the dying in Cholula, [the Spaniards] set off on their way to Mexico, coming gathered and bunched, raising dust. Their iron lances and halberds seemed to sparkle, and their iron swords were curved like a stream of water. Their cuirasses and iron helmets seemed to make a clattering sound. Some of them came wearing iron all over, turned into iron beings, gleaming, so that they aroused great fear and were generally seen with fear and dread. . . .

Source: James Lockhart, *We People Here*, cited in *In the Language of Kings*, 292–93. Originally from the *Florentine Codex*.

QUESTIONS

- What do you think the Spanish were thinking during these events?
- What can you learn about Spanish colonization from this source?

4

THE EMERGENCE AND SPREAD OF GUNPOWDER EMPIRES

Political Change, 1500–1650

4.1 TOYATOMI HIDEYOSHI, THE SWORD COLLECTION EDICT

Toyatomi Hideyoshi (1537–1598) issued this edict in 1588 near the end of his campaigns to conquer Japan and end a long era of civil war and disorder. Part of his plan was to impose strict hierarchy on Japanese society. Only the hereditary warrior caste, the samurai, was to be allowed weapons, but they were to be made dependent on the state by taking away their right to own land. The common people lost the ability to defend themselves as Japanese society was demilitarized in the name of economic development and social peace.

[1] The people of the various provinces are strictly forbidden to have in their possession any swords, short swords, bows, spears, firearms, or other types of arms. The possession of unnecessary implements [of war] makes difficult the collection of taxes and dues and tends to foment uprisings. Needless to say, the perpetrators of improper acts against official agents shall be summarily punished, but in that event the paddy fields and farms of the violators will remain unattended and there will be no yield of crops. Therefore the heads of provinces, official agents, and deputies are ordered to collect all the weapons mentioned above and turn them over to the government.

[2] Swords and short swords thus collected will not be wasted. They shall be used as nails and bolts in the construction of the Great Image of Buddha. This will benefit the people not only in this life but also in the life hereafter.

[3] If the people are in possession of agricultural implements only and devote themselves exclusively to agriculture, they and their descendants will prosper. Sincere concern for the well-being of the people is the motive for the issuance of this order, which is fundamental for the peace and security of the country and the happiness of the people. In other lands, such as China, the ruler Yao converted rare swords and short weapons into agricultural implements after he had established peace. In our country such an experiment has never been made. Thus, all the people should abide by and understand the aims of this act and give their undivided attention to agriculture and sericulture.

All implements mentioned above shall be collected and submitted forthwith.

Hideyoshi [*Seal*]
Tenshō 16 [1588]: Seventh
Month, 8th Day

QUESTIONS

- What specific parts of the edict seem likely to achieve "economic development and social peace"?
- What negative effects do you imagine the edict would have sparked?

Source: Ryusaku Tsunoda, Wm. Theodore de Bary, and Donald Keene, eds., *Sources of Japanese Tradition* (New York: Columbia University, 1958), 328–29.

4.2 ẒAHĪR AL-DĪN MUḤAMMAD, BABUR'S AUTOBIOGRAPHY

Ẓahīr al-Dīn Muḥammad (1483–1530), the founder of the Mughal Empire, became known as Babur "the Tiger." After decades of fighting in Central Asia, Babur invaded the subcontinent of India with only 10,000 cavalry in search of greater financial and material resources. Although the motives for his incursion were partly religious, his first conquests were almost all of other Muslims. This autobiography was written in diary form during his campaigns, providing an invaluable account of his motives and reactions.

The one nice aspect of Hindustan is that it is a large country with lots of gold and money. . . . Another nice thing is the unlimited numbers of craftsmen and practitioners of every trade. For every labor and every product there is an established group who have been practicing that craft or professing that trade for generations. . . . during Temür Beg's building of the stone mosque [in Samarkand] two hundred stonemasons from Azerbaijan, Fars, Hindustan, and other places were employed on it daily. In Agra alone there were 680 stonemasons at work on my building every day. Aside from that, in Agra, Sikri, Bayana, Dholpur, Gwalior, and Koil, 1,491 stonemasons were laboring on my buildings. There are similar vast numbers of every type of craftsman and laborers of every description in Hindustan.

The regions from Bhera to Bihar that are currently under my control are worth 52 crores [52 million rupees], as can be seen in the following table. Of these, eight to nine crores' worth are districts of rays and rajahs who are in obedience and have been awarded these districts for their maintenance as of old.

Estimate of the total revenue of as much of Hindustan as has presently come under conquest: [A table listing revenue of more than 431,094,000 tanka follows. In the most important calculation of the era, every 1,000 tanka could support one fully armed horse soldier. Thus Babur believed that his income could support a massive army of 431,000. He had invaded with fewer than 10,000.]

With the glint of the swords of our army, the refuge of Islam, lighted the land of India with flashes of the luminescence of conquest and victory, and, as had been reported in former notices of victory, the hands of success raised our victory-inscribed banners in the realms of Delhi, Agra, Jaunpur, Kharid, Bihar, and other places, most of the infidel tribes and Muslims elected obedience to our felicitous lord and trod the path of servitude with the feet of truth and sincerity. However, Sanga the Infidel . . . caused an amassing of tribes, some of whom bore the accursed band of the *zunnar* [the cloth that non-Muslims had to wear] around their necks, and the skirts of others of whom were sullied with the brambles of apostasy. . . . In around two hundred cities within the realm of Islam he raised the banner of infidelity and undertook the destruction of mosques and places of worship, taking captive the wives and children of believers in those cities and towns. . . . During these days many renowned

Source: Wheeler M. Thackston, ed. and trans., *The Baburnama: Memoirs of Babur, Prince and Emperor* (New York: The Modern Library, 2002 [1996]), 353–55, 386–87, 394–95.

infidels, not one of whom had ever helped him in any battle, joined his wretched forces out of enmity toward the Army of Islam. . . .

Muhammad-Ali Jang-Jang, Shaykh Guran, and Abdul-Malik Qorchï were dispatched with a large force to attack Ilyas Khan, who had rebelled in the Doab . . . they captured him and brought him in. I had him skinned alive. When the army was camped at Koh Bachcha, they were ordered to erect a tower of infidel skulls on the top of the mountain. . . . When I came to the camp, I summoned the Turk and India officers and consulted them on the advisability of proceeding against the infidels' territories: the expedition was postponed due to the paucity of water along the way and the intense heat. . . . However, the province of Mewat was near Delhi. . . . Hasan Khan of Mewat and his forefathers had been ruling Mewat independently for a century of two, giving only halfhearted allegiance to the sultans of Delhi. . . . After the conquest of India we too maintained this favor to Hasan Khan as had past rulers, but this heretical, heathen ingrate, in blatant disregard of our kindness and favor and expressing no gratitude for our patronage, was the instigator of all sedition and the cause of all evil, as has been mentioned.

QUESTIONS

- How did Babur present his actions in the excerpt?
- Reading between the lines, what negative effects do you imagine Babur's actions would have sparked?

4.3 EMPEROR JAHANGIR, POLICIES TOWARD THE HINDUS

The vast extent of Babur's conquests did not long survive him. His grandson Akbar (r. 1556–1605) restored and extended the fortunes of the Mughal dynasty. A major reason for his success and for the longevity of the Empire was a significant degree of religious tolerance. Many Hindu practices were allowed, and captives were not forced to convert to Islam. In this account, Akbar's son, Emperor Nur-ud-din Muhammad Jahangir (r. 1605–1627) recalled his father's actions. Originally written in Persian, most probably in the decade of the 1610s, this text is both homage and an explanation of why the policy of tolerance was so important.

In the city of Banaras, a temple had been erected . . . [whose] principal idol had on its head a tiara or cap, enriched with jewels. . . . it was the belief of these non-believers that a dead Hindu, if he had been a worshipper when alive, was laid before this idol, he would be restored to life. As I could not possibly give credit to such a pretense, I employed a confidential person to ascertain the truth; it was, as I justly supposed, an impudent fraud. . . .

On this subject I must however acknowledge that having on one occasion asked my father [Akbar] the reason why he had forbidden anyone to prevent or interfere with the building of these haunts of idolatry, his reply was in the following terms: "My dear child," said he, "I find myself a powerful monarch, the shadow of God on earth. I have seen that he bestows the blessings of his gracious providence upon all his creatures without distinction. I would not be discharging the duties of my exalted station if I withheld my compassion and indulgence from any of those entrusted to my charge. With all of the human race, I am at peace: why then should I permit myself, under any consideration, to be the cause of molestation or aggression to anyone? Besides, are not five parts in six of mankind either Hindus or aliens to the faith; and were I to be governed by motives of the kind suggested in your inquiry, what alternative can I have but to put them all to death! I have thought it therefore my wisest plan to let these men alone. Neither is it to be forgotten, that the class of whom we are speaking, in common with the other inhabitants of [the city of] Agra, are usefully engaged, either in the pursuits of science or the arts, or of improvements for the benefit of mankind, and have in numerous instances arrived at the highest distinctions in the state, there being, indeed, to be found in this city men of every description, and of every religion on the face of the earth."

QUESTIONS

- How did Jahangir's policies seek to achieve "tolerance"?
- Does this strike you as an effective set of policies? Why or why not?

Source: Adapted from David Price, ed. and trans., *Memoirs of the Emperor Jahangueir* (London: Oriental Translation Committee, 1829), 14–15.

4.4 LETTER OF QUEEN ANA NZINGA OF NDONGO TO THE GOVERNOR GENERAL OF ANGOLA

On December 13, 1655, Queen Nzinga (r. 1623–1663) of Ndongo wrote to the Governor General of Angola asking for the release of her sister Barbara, held as a hostage for the good behavior of the Queen. Nzinga discusses the slave trade's practical politics as part of Ndongo's relationship with the Portuguese, but she and the Ndongo nobles (grandees) feared that the governors were not acting in good faith despite their shared Roman Catholic faith.

My Lord,

. . . I have many complaints about past governors, who always promised to return my sister to me. [To secure her return,] I have given an infinite number of slaves and created thousands of *banzos* [sad people], but they never returned her to me. Rather they waged war against my person and harried me, and constantly forced me to live like a *Jaga* [roaming warrior band] and resort to tyrannical edicts, such as prohibiting the raising of children and other ceremonies because this is what life in a *quilombo* [community of escaped slaves] entails. I give Your Lordship my royal word that I will give up these warlike [practices], as long as I have clergymen among us who will provide me and my grandees with good examples and teach them to live in the Holy Catholic Faith. . . .

As soon as I get news that my sister has arrived in Ambaca, I will dispatch Captain Manuel Frois Peixoto from my court to get her. This task falls to him, since he made the effort of appeasing my grandees, who are quite suspicious of past treacheries. Your Lordship ought not to suppose that Captain Manuel Frois Peixoto is undeserving of high praise, for he succeeded in convincing them and me that this delegation was in good faith and not like the previous ones I mentioned. . . . Because of this and other treacheries, I roam the forests, far from my own lands, with no one to inform His Majesty, may God protect him, of my unease, when to be at peace with the said commander and His Majesty's governors is what I most desire. Yet all of His Majesty's past [agents and governors] acted out of personal gain and not in the king's service, as I have been informed His Majesty bids them do, for this kingdom is of the utmost importance to his royal privilege. It would be worth even more if I were allowed to live in peace and quiet, bringing my markets closer [to the coast] so the *pombeiros* [slave merchants] need not go through so much trouble to bring their wares so far, and I could enjoy them at a cheaper price. Finally, I trust with God that your Lordship will be in His Majesty's good graces only if you leave me in peace and tranquility and conquer Quissama [a region of small independent states], a thing that no governor has earned the glory of accomplishing.

I offer Your Lordship my assistance in the conquest of Quissama. If it refuses to pay obeisance to

Source: Adapted from Kathryn Joy McKnight and Leo J. Garofalo, eds., *Afro-Latino Voices: Narratives from the Early Modern Ibero-Atlantic World, 1550–1812* (Indianapolis: Hackett Publishing Company, 2009), 45–51.

you, and if it pleases Your Lordship, I will dispatch one of my grandees with as large a force as can be mustered. This I will do as a sign of obeisance to His Majesty, may God protect him. I also give my word that as soon as the reverend fathers arrive with my sister, I will immediately endeavor to allow women to give birth to and raise their children, which I have not permitted until now because we have been living in the countryside, in *quilombos*. This would not happen if we had a firm and lasting peace. It would only take a few years for my lands to be repopulated as they once were, for up to now I have taken as servants only people from other provinces and *nations* that I have conquered, and they have obeyed me as if I were their native queen, some out of love and others out of fear. . . .

Caotaub Nabyek Frois Peixoto requested on His Majesty's behalf that I [hand over to him], the *Jaga* Cabuco. [He asked me] with such fine manners that I could not refuse him, even though I have had many grievances against Cabuco for having devastated my lands. The satisfaction of so many losses as he caused me should be good enough reason for him to remain in my service a few years longer. Nevertheless, so great is my desire to see my sister again [to make her the heir to the throne] that as soon as Captain Manuel Frois Peixoto arrives in my court, I will give the said *Jaga* permission to leave with him and place himself at his orders. Of this Your Lordship can be certain, as well as of the aid I promised to give you in [subduing] Quissama, should Your Honor need it. This I will do and everything you may instruct me to do. My friends' friends are my friends, and my enemies' enemies my own enemies.

With respect to the two hundred slaves Your Lordship requests as ransom for my sister Dona Barbara, that is a very exacting price, particularly since I have already given the slaves Your Honor must know of to past governors and envoys, to say nothing of my gifts to secretaries and servants from your noble house and to many settlers whose treachery I still endure to this day. What I am so bold as to offer Your Honor is one hundred and thirty slaves, a hundred of whom I will send as soon as my sister reaches Ambaca. I will keep your envoy hostage until I can see with my own eyes my sister arriving in my court to make sure that I will not be wrongly used again as I have been by past governors. Your Lordship should not regard it as strange that I want these precautions. Even though I understand that this delegation is a very honest one, I will avoid further grief, because they remember the deceits of the past, my grandees remain suspicious.

May Your Lordship forgive so long a letter as this, but it needed to be thus. The offering Your Lordship sent me, and for which I render you my thanks, was delivered to me by your envoy. I appreciated the mother-of-pearl goblet very much. Do not be weary of me, Your Lordship, but I want for nothing in my court. What I miss the most is my sister. Once she returns to me, Your Lordship will see that I will serve your Lordship much to your liking. The bearer of this letter will relay to you by post what I have agreed upon with your envoy. Because he leaves in haste, he takes no more than twelve slaves. [Accept them as] my offering to mollify Your Lordship.

My Court at Matamba, on the thirteenth of December of the year 1655.

Queen Dona Ana de Sousa

QUESTIONS

- What did the Queen offer in exchange for the release of her sister?
- Do you find the request persuasive? Why or why not?

4.5 DISSENSION AT THE DIET OF WORMS (1521)

The Diet of the Holy Roman Empire was the formal deliberative assembly of the numerous sovereign rulers. A Diet held in the city of Worms from February 28 to May 26, 1521, was presided over by Emperor Charles V of the Habsburg dynasty. It was focused on the protests of religious reformer and Augustinian monk Martin Luther and Pope Leo X's demand that this independent-minded university professor renounce all his published work. In the first selection, Luther defends his work and his critique of Roman Catholic practice and doctrine in a printed broadsheet while asserting the right to resist the authority of the papacy. The second selection is Charles V's assertion of the power of the institution to discipline an individual and contains his own determination to silence Luther. The Edict issued at Worms is the final selection. It proclaimed that Luther was a heretic and that his writings were to be destroyed and the property of his supporters seized. Soon afterward, Leo X excommunicated Luther, who remained under the protection of German princes who found his critique justified and politically useful.

LUTHER AT THE DIET OF WORMS, BROADSHEET

"Most serene Emperor, gracious electors, nobles and lords. Yesterday I was asked two questions: whether I would confess those pamphlets which were published under my name to be mine and whether I would persist in them or revoke them. . . .

Now I am called upon to answer the second question. I humbly pray your Imperial Majesty and Lords, to consider carefully that my books are not all of the same kind. There are some in which I dealt with faith and life in such an evangelical and simple manner that even my opponents must admit that they are useful, innocent and worthy to be read by Christian people. . . .

The second group of my books is written against the papacy and papal scheming and action, that is against those who through evil teaching and example have ruined Christendom laying it waste with the evils of the spirit and the soul. No one can deny or obscure this fact, since experience and complaint of all men testify that the conscience of Christian believers is sneered at, harassed and tormented by the laws of the Pope and the doctrines of men. Likewise the goods and wealth of this most famous German nation were and are devoured through unbelievable tyranny in unreasonable manner, through decretals and laws, regulations and orders. Yet Canon Law states (Distinctions 9 and 25, Questions 1 and 2) that the law and teaching of the Pope, whenever contrary to the Gospel and the opinions of the holy Fathers, are to be considered in error and be rejected. Were I, therefore, to revoke these books I would only strengthen this tyranny and open not only windows, but also doors for such unchristian ways, which would then flourish and rage more freely than ever before. The testimony of my opposition will make the rule of their bold and ignominious malice most intolerable for the poor suffering people. . . .

Source: Hans J. Hillerbrand, ed., *The Reformation* (New York: Harper & Row, 1964), 89–91, 94, 99–100. Source of original German text: Detlef Ploese and Guenther Vogler, eds., *Buch der Reformation. Eine Auswahl zeitgenössischer Zeugnisse (1476–1555)* (Berlin: Union Verlag, 1989), 245–53. Reprinted on: http://germanhistorydocs.ghi-dc.org/pdf/eng/Doc.64-ENG-Luther_Charles.pdf (consulted January 2, 2018).

What more shall I say? Since I am a man and not God, I cannot support my pamphlets through any other means than that which the Lord Jesus employed when he was questioned before Ananias and asked concerning his teaching and smitten on his cheek by a servant. He said then: "If I have spoken evil bear witness of the evil." If the Lord, who knew that he could not err, did not refuse to hear testimony against his doctrine even from the most miserable servant, how much more should I, the scum of the earth and prone to error, hope and expect that someone should testify against my doctrine. Therefore I pray by the grace of God that your Imperial Majesty and Lordships, and everyone, high or low, should give such testimony, convict me of error and convince me with evangelical and prophetic writings. Should I thus be persuaded, I am most ready and willing to revoke all errors and be the first to throw my books into the fire.

From this it should be evident that I have carefully considered and weighed such discord, peril, uproar and rebellion which is rampant in the world today on account of my teaching, as I was gravely and urgently made aware yesterday. It is quite revealing as far as I am concerned that the divine Word causes factions, misunderstanding, and discord to arise. Such, of course, must be the fate and the consequence of the divine Word, even as the Lord himself said: "I am come not to send peace but a sword, to set a man against his father, etc." Therefore we must ponder how wonderful and terrible God is in his counsels, plans and intentions. Perhaps we condemn the Word of God if we do away with our factions and dissensions. It would be a deluge of inestimable evils, indeed a cause of concern lest the imperial rule of our most pious and youthful Emperor (in whom, next to God, great hope is to be placed) should have an unfortunate beginning. . . .

I cannot and will not recant, since it is difficult, unprofitable and dangerous indeed to do anything against one's conscience. God help me. Amen."

[. . .]

EMPEROR CHARLES'S RESPONSE

The morning after Luther's second appearance, Emperor Charles V assembled the rulers and stated his own position.

"You know that my ancestors were the most Christian Emperors of the illustrious German nation, the Catholic kings of Spain, the archdukes of Austria, and the dukes of Burgundy, who all were, until death, faithful sons of the Roman Church. Always they defended the Catholic faith, the sacred ceremonies, decretals, ordinances and holy rites to the honor of God, the propagation of the faith and the salvation of souls. After their deaths they left, by natural law and heritage, these holy Catholic rites, for us to live and to die following their example.

I am therefore resolved to maintain everything which these my forebears have established to the present, especially that which my predecessors ordered at the Council of Constance and at other councils. It is certain that a single monk errs in his opinion which is against what all of Christendom has held for over a thousand years to the present. According to his opinion all of Christendom has always been in error. To settle this matter I am therefore determined to use all my dominions and possessions, my friends, my body, my blood, my life and my soul. It would be a great disgrace for you and me, the illustrious and renowned German nation, appointed by privilege and singular pre-eminence to be the defenders and protectors of the Catholic faith, as well as a perpetual dishonor for both us and our posterity, if in our time not only heresy, but the suspicion of heresy and the degradation of the Christian religion were due to our negligence.

After the impertinent reply which Luther gave yesterday in our presence, I declare that I now regret having delayed so long the proceedings against him and his false doctrines. I am resolved that I will never again hear him talk. He is to be taken back immediately according to the arrangements of the mandate with due regard for the stipulations of his safe-conduct. He is not to preach or seduce the people with his evil doctrine and is not to incite rebellion. As said above, I am resolved to act and proceed against him as against a notorious heretic, asking you to state your opinion as good Christians and to keep the vow given me."

EDICT OF WORMS

In May 1521, Emperor Charles V issued, in the name of the Diet, the following edict against Luther and his followers:

. . . And now, particularly on account of these things, we have summoned here to Worms the electors, princes and estates of this our Holy Empire, and carefully examined the aforesaid matters with great diligence, as evident necessity demands, and with unanimous advice and consent of all, we decree what follows.

Although one so condemned and persisting in his obstinate perversity, separated from the rites of the Christian Church and a manifest heretic, is denied a hearing under all laws; nevertheless, to prevent all unprofitable dispute . . . we, through our herald, gave him a safe-conduct to come hither, in order that he might be questioned in our own presence and in that of the electors, princes, and estates of the empire; whether he had composed the books which were then laid before his eyes. . . .

Accordingly, in view of all these considerations and the fact that Martin Luther still persists obstinately and perversely in maintaining his heretical opinions, and consequently all pious and God-fearing persons abominate and abhor him as one mad or possessed by a demon . . . we have declared and made known that the said Martin Luther shall hereafter be held and esteemed by each and all of us as a limb cut off from the Church of God, an obstinate schismatic and manifest heretic. . . .

We strictly order that immediately after the expiration of the appointed twenty days, terminating on the fourteenth day of May, you shall refuse to give the aforesaid Martin Luther hospitality, lodging, food, or drink; neither shall anyone, by word or deed, secretly or openly, succor or assist him by counsel or help; but in whatever place you meet him, you shall proceed against him; if you have sufficient force, you shall take him prisoner and keep him in close custody; you shall deliver him, or cause him to be delivered, to us or at least let us know where he may be captured. In the meanwhile you shall keep him closely imprisoned until you receive notice from us what further to do, according to the direction of the laws. And for such holy and pious work we will indemnify you for your trouble and expense.

In like manner you shall proceed against his friends, adherents, patrons, maintainers, abettors, sympathizers, emulators and followers. And the property of these, whether personal or real, you shall, in virtue of the sacred ordinances and of our imperial ban and over-ban, treat in this way; namely, you shall attack and overthrow its possessors and wrest their property from them and transfer it to your own custody and uses; and no one shall hinder or impede these measures, unless the owner shall abandon his unrighteous way and secure papal absolution.

Consequently we command you, each and all, under the penalties already prescribed, that henceforth no one shall dare to buy, sell, read, preserve, copy, print, or cause to be copied or printed, any books of the aforesaid Martin Luther, condemned by our holy father the Pope as aforesaid, or any other writings in German or Latin hitherto composed by him, since they are foul, harmful, suspected, and published by a notorious and stiff-necked heretic. Neither shall any dare to approve his opinions, nor to proclaim, defend, or assert them, in any other way that human ingenuity can invent, notwithstanding he may have put some good in them to deceive the simple man."

QUESTIONS

- What were Luther's criticism of the Roman Catholic Church? Do you find them persuasive?
- Why do you think Charles V viewed Luther's works as so dangerous to his Catholic mission? What would have been the effect of the edict?

4.6 JOACHIM OPSER, MASSACRE OF PROTESTANTS: SAINT BARTHOLOMEW'S DAY (AUGUST 24, 1572)

Charles IX, of the Valois dynasty, decided to decapitate (literally) the Protestant opposition. His sister Marguerite's marriage to Henry, King of Navarre, brought many prominent Huguenot leaders to Paris, where they were attacked by royal troops, the city militia, and crowds of hardline Roman Catholics on Saint Bartholomew's Day (August 24, 1572). This letter from a Jesuit priest to an important Roman Catholic leader illustrates the exultant attitude of many observers who hoped that this violence would end civil strife over religion by imposing uniformity.

Letter from Joachim Opser, S.J. to the Abbot of Saint-Gall

I think I shall not bore you if I mention in detail an event as unexpected as it is useful to our cause, and which not only delights the Christian world with admiration, but brings it to a peak of rejoicing. Concerning this you will hear what the Captain has to say [the commander of the royal troops that broke into the home of the chief Protestant or Huguenot leader, Admiral Gaspard de Coligny and murdered him]. Rejoice in advance, but do not for that disdain or reject as superfluous the lines I write with more satisfaction perhaps than seems quite proper, for I affirm nothing I have not got from authoritative sources.

The Admiral has perished miserably on August 24, with all the heretical French nobility. (One can say it without exaggeration.) What immense carnage! I shuddered at the sight of this river [the Seine] full of naked and horribly mutilated corpses. Up to the present, the King has spared none but the King of Navarre [his brother-in-law]. In effect, today, August 26, towards one o'clock, the King of Navarre attended Mass with the King Charles, so that all conceive the greatest hopes of seeing him change his religion. . . . Everyone agrees in praising the prudence and magnanimity of the King who, after having his kindness and indulgence fattened, as it were, the heretics like cattle, has suddenly had them slaughtered by his soldiers. . . .

All heretical booksellers that one could find have been massacred and cast naked into the river. Ramus, who had jumped out of his bedroom, quite high up, still lies naked on the river bank, pierced by numerous dagger-blows. In a word, there is no one (even women not excepted) who has not been either killed or wounded.

QUESTIONS

- What specific word choices give you the sense that the letter writer was "exultant"?
- Do you imagine that the massacre would have "ended civil strife over religion by imposing uniformity"? Why or why not?

Source: Adapted from Eugen Weber, ed., *The Western Tradition*, vol. 2, *From the Renaissance to the Present*, 5th ed. (Lexington, MA: D. C. Heath and Co, 1995), 86–87.

4.7 FRANCISCO HERNÁNDEZ ARANA XAJILA, *THE ANNALS OF THE CAKCHIQUELS*

The Cakchiquel were part of the Mayan peoples who lived, and still live, in southern Mexico and parts of Central America. This chronicle was written by a Hispanicized leader later in the sixteenth century. It depicts the transition from Indigenous infighting to the intervention of the Spanish and their growing domination of the political scene through violence and the threat of violence.

HERE IS THE BEGINNING OF THE REVOLT AGAINST QIKAB

Then began the revolt of the Quichés against the king Qikab and also against the clan of the king. The revolt spread, and the king's clan was destroyed together with the principal chiefs. The Quichés did not wish the vassals to serve [the king]. They wanted the Quiché people to travel [freely] on the roads, but the king did not wish this. The principal chiefs became angry with the king and refused to pay him homage. For this reason the Quiché people rose against the king and so his glory diminished.

The two sons of the king had become arrogant. One was called *Tatayac* and the other *Ah Ytzá*. The king's two sons also held the titles of *Chituy* and *Quehnay*. The Quichés then gathered together to confer; the sons had turned them against the king so that they should not pay him tribute, now that they were angered by having to render him services. In this way the sons turned against the king. In addition, the two called Tatayac and Ah Ytzá had a grudge against their father because they coveted the royal power and also the precious stones, the metal, the slaves, and their father's people. Then the Quichés gathered in council to plot against the principal chiefs who served the king, and they killed those of the first rank in the sovereign's service. . . .

After the soldiers entered the house of the lords, they were slain by the soldiery and not by order of the king. The king at the time was in the city of *Panpetak*. The soldiers wished to kill the king also, but by order of his sons his house in Panpetak was well guarded. King Qikab humbled himself before the soldiers, and they returned then with the intention of killing the lords of the house of Xahil. After the king had humbled himself before the soldiers, he arranged to deliver to them the precious stones and the metal, as well as the government and the supreme command, and he delivered the power and majesty to the soldiers. The heart of King Qikab was full of bitterness because of the wrong his sons had done him, the two called Tatayac and Ah Ytzá. Thus the soldiers and the people seized the government and the power. Afterwards and by order of the tribes, they assigned their dwellings to the thirteen lords, the principal lords, the principal chiefs who initiated the revolt; and the greatness of the Quiché was ended after this act of King Qikab. Thus it was that the tribes seized command of old, oh, our

Source: Adapted from: Adrián Recinos and Delia Goetz, ed. and trans., *The Annals of the Cakchiquels: translated from the Cakchiquel Maya* (Norman, OK: University of Oklahoma Press, 1953), 94–97, 119–21, 123–4, 129–30.

sons! Since that time, because of this act of the soldiers, the people and the vassals have ceased to exalt the kings. . . .

ANOTHER REVOLT BEGINS

Immediately another revolt started against the kings *Huntoh, Vukubatz, Chuluc,* and *Xitamal Queh,* who were the four kings. A woman was the cause of this other revolt against the Zoltzils and the Tukuchés. The woman who caused the revolt was called *Nimapam Ixcacauh.* This woman had gone to the city of Gumarcaah to sell bread, and a soldier of the king's guard wished to snatch it from her. The woman refused to let him take the bread by force, and the soldier was driven away with a stick by the woman. They wished to hang the soldier then, they wished to hang him on account of the woman called Nimapam Ixcacauh. For this reason the revolt of the Quichés was resumed. These people wished to have the woman killed, but our grandfathers Huntoh, and Vukubatz refused to give her up to the Quichés or to the soldiers.

The Quichés then desired to humiliate the [Cakchiquel] kings and they wished King Qikab to be the one to do this. Furious, the Quichés gathered in council and they said: "Only the Ahpozotzil and the Ahpoxahil have received greatness and majesty; let us kill Huntoh and Vukubatz because are becoming great." Thus said the soldiers about our grandfathers. They wished to persuade King Qikab to consent to having the Zotzils and the Tukuchés slain, but the king did not listen to the words of the Quichés. In truth, in his heart the king favored Huntoh and Vukabatz. Because the wisdom of Qikab, a wonderful king, was truly great. Not only was he an illustrious king, but his judgment and wisdom, brought from Tulán, aroused admiration. But the soldiery were ignorant, they were only the common people; and because, in addition, they coveted power, they did not obey the king's orders and they continued to carry on the war.

ARRIVAL OF THE SPANIARDS AT XETULUL

On the day 1 Ganel [February 20, 1524] the Quichés were destroyed by the Spaniards. Their chief, he who was called *Tunatiuh Avilantaro* [Pedro de Alvarado], conquered all the people. Their faces were not known before that time. Until a short time ago the wood and the stone were worshiped.

Having arrived at *Xelahub,* they defeated the Quichés; all the Quiché who had gone out to meet the Spaniards were exterminated. Then the Quichés were destroyed before Xelahub.

Then [the Spaniards] went forth to the city of Gumarcaah, where they were received by the kings, the Ahpop and the Ahpop Qamahay, and the Quichés paid them tribute. Soon the kings were tortured by Tunatiuh.

On the day 4 Qat [March 7, 1524] the kings Ahpop and Ahpop Qamahay were burned by Tunatiuh. The heart of Tunatiuh was without compassion for the people during the war.

Soon a messenger from Tunatiuh came before the [Cakchiquel] kings to ask them to send soldiers: "Let the warriors of the Ahpozotzil and the Ahpoxahil come to kill the Quichés," the messenger said to the kings. The order of Tunatiuh was instantly obeyed, and two thousand soldiers marched to the slaughter of the Quichés.

Only the men of the city went; the other warriors did not go down to present themselves before the kings. The soldiers went three times only to collect tribute from the Quichés. We also went to collect it for Tunatiuh, oh, my sons!

THE DEMAND FOR MONEY

Then Tunatiuh asked the kings for money. He wished them to give him piles of metal, their vessels and crowns. And as they did not bring them to him immediately, Tunatiuh became angry with the kings and said to them: "Why have you not brought me the metal? If you do not bring with you all the money of the tribes, I will burn you and I will hang you," he said to the lords.

Next Tunatiuh ordered them to pay twelve hundred pesos of gold. The kings tried to have the amount reduced and they began to weep, but Tunatiuh did not consent, and he said to them, "Get the metal and bring it within five days. Woe to you if you do not bring it! I know my heart!" Thus he said to the lords.

THE BEGINNING OF THE TRIBUTE

During this year [1530] heavy tribute was imposed. Gold was contributed to Tunatiuh; four hundred men and four hundred women were delivered to him to be sent to wash gold. All the people extracted the gold. Four hundred men and four hundred women were contributed to work in *Pangán* [Guatemala city] on the construction of the city, by order of Tunatiuh. . . .

During the two months of the third year which had passed since the lords presented themselves, the king Belehé Qat died; he died on the day 7 Queh [September 24, 1532] while he was washing gold. Immediately after the death of the king, Tunatiuh came here to choose a successor to the king. Then the lord *Don Jorge* was installed in the government by order of Tunatiuh alone. There was no election by the people to name him. Afterwards Tunatiuh talked to the lords and his orders were obeyed by the chiefs, for in truth they feared Tunatiuh.

QUESTIONS

- What kind of political situation were the Spanish stepping into?
- Do you think the contemporary political situation made it easier for the Spanish to conquer? Why or why not?

CHAPTER

5

LIFE IN COMMON
Community in the Modern World

5.1 CHINUA ACHEBE, *THINGS FALL APART* (1958)

Nigerian author Chinua Achebe's (1930–2013) novel *Things Fall Apart* appeared in 1958 and has sold more than 10 million copies. Set among the Ibo people of southeastern Nigeria in the late nineteenth century during British colonial intervention, this excerpt looks at how a network of clan villages adjudicates cases and keeps the peace. Village elders masqueraded as ancestral spirits to preserve their autonomy and to ensure that their decisions have the weight of tradition.

Each of the nine *egwugwu* [masquerader impersonating village ancestral spirits] represented a village of the clan. Their leader was called Evil Forest. Smoke poured out of his head.

The nine villages of Umuofia had grown out of the nine sons of the first father of the clan. Evil Forest represented the village of Umueru, or the children of Eru, who was the eldest of the nine sons. . . .

Evil Forest then thrust the pointed end of his rattling staff into the earth. And it began to shake and rattle, like something agitating with a metallic life. He took the first of the empty stools and the eight other *egwugwu* began to sit in the order of seniority after him. . . .

Uzowulu stepped forward and presented his case.

"That woman there is my wife, Mgbafo. I married her with my money and with my yams. I do not owe my in-laws anything. I owe them no yams. I owe them no coco-yams. One morning three of them came to my house, beat me up and took my wife and children away. This happened in the rainy season. I have waited in vain for my wife to return. At last I went to my in-laws and said to them, 'You have taken back your sister. I did not send her away. You yourselves took her. The law of the clan is that you should return her bride-price.' But my wife's brothers said they had nothing to tell me. So I have brought the matter to the fathers of the clan. My case is finished. I salute you. . . ."

[Odokwe:] "My in-law, Uzowulu, is a beast. My sister lived with him for nine years. During those years no single day passed in the sky without his beating the woman. We have tried to settle their quarrels time without number. . . . Her two children belong to Uzowulu. We do not dispute it, but they are too young to leave their mother. If, in the other hand, Uzowulu should recover from his madness and come in the proper way to beg his wife to return she will do so on the understanding that if he ever beats her again we shall cut off his genitals for him." . . .

"We have heard both sides of the case," said Evil Forest. "Our duty is not to blame this man or to praise that, but to settle the dispute." He turned to Uzowulu's group and allowed a short pause.

"Go to your in-laws with a pot of wine and beg your wife to return to you. It is not bravery when a man fights with a woman." . . .

He pulled his staff from the hard earth and thrust it back.

Source: Chinua Achebe, *Things Fall Apart* (New York: Anchor Books, 1994 [1959]), 85–89.

"*Umuofia kwenu!*" he roared, and the crowd answered.

"I don't know why such a trifle should come before the *egwugwu*," said one elder to another.

"Don't you know what kind of man Uzowulu is? He will not listen to any other decision," replied the other.

QUESTIONS

- In the text, how did the elders try to "ensure that their decisions have the weight of tradition"?
- What does the last line of the excerpt indicate about acceptance of such decisions?

5.2 QING CHINA: SACRED EDICT

These instructions were issued by the Kangxi emperor (r. 1662–1722) and put into this form by the Yongzheng emperor (r. 1723–1735). Read aloud twice monthly across China until the twentieth century as part of a community ritual, these instructions were intended to inculcate morality and the principles of village harmony according to the Confucian tradition. Some of the Qing instructions seem aimed at officials rather than peasants; these were the ones added later. They build on traditions of "village lectures" going back to the twelfth century of the Common Era and were also used to teach Confucian ideals about proper behavior to conquered peoples. Although women were not referred to explicitly, their relations with each other, especially inside the family, were part of these injunctions.

1. Esteem most highly filial piety and brotherly submission, in order to give due importance to human moral relations.
2. Behave with generosity toward your kindred, in order to illustrate harmony and benignity.
3. Cultivate peace and concord in your neighborhoods, in order to prevent quarrels and litigations.
4. Give importance to agriculture and sericulture, in order to ensure a sufficiency of clothing and food.
5. Show that you prize moderation and economy, in order to prevent the lavish waste of your means.
6. Foster colleges and schools, in order to give the training of scholars a proper start.
7. Do away with errant teachings, in order to exalt the correct doctrine.
8. Expound on the laws, in order to warn the ignorant and obstinate.
9. Explain ritual decorum and deference, in order to enrich manners and customs.
10. Attend to proper callings, in order to stabilize the people's sense of dedication [to their work].
11. Instruct sons and younger brothers, in order to prevent them from doing what is wrong.
12. Put a stop to false accusations, in order to protect the honest and good.
13. Warn against sheltering deserters, in order to avoid being involved in their punishment.
14. Promptly remit your taxes, in order to avoid being pressed for payment.
15. Combine in collective security groups (*baojia*), in order to put an end to theft and robbery.
16. Eschew enmity and anger, in order to show respect for the person and life.

QUESTIONS

- What themes do you see that tie the various principles together?
- What gender roles did the edict seek to enforce?

Source: Wm. Theodore de Bary and Richard Lufrano, eds., *Sources of Chinese Tradition: From 1600 Through the Twentieth Century*, 2nd ed., vol. 2 (New York: Columbia University Press, 2000), 71–72.

5.3 DIGEST OF HINDU LAW (1797)

To govern its increasingly vast and diverse holdings, the British East India Company sought to base judicial decisions on the legal precedents generated by Hindu and Muslim cultures. In searching for the earliest cases, the British legalized the most traditional versions of the most educated parts of society and applied them to the whole. By establishing the arguments about process and action as law, the British limited the independence and legal rights of women and children in favor of men and families. This translation of opinions by Howard T. Colebrooke (1765–1829) from Sanskrit suggests some of those limitations.

Cátyáyana: A wife or a son, or the whole of a man's estate, shall not be given away or sold without the assent of the persons interested; he must keep them himself.

2. But, in extreme necessity, he may give or sell them *with their assent*: otherwise, he must attempt no such thing: this has been settled in codes of law. . . .

Smr̄iti: 3. All wives, sons, slaves, and unmarried girls are dependent: and a householder is not uncontrolled in regard to what has descended from an ancestor.

4. An infant, before his eighth year, must be considered as similar to a child in the womb; but a youth or adolescent is called a minor until he has entered his sixteenth year:

5. Afterwards *he is considered* as acquainted with affairs, *or adult in law*, and becomes independent on the death of both parents; *but*, however old, he is not deemed independent while they live. . . .

Vyása: What shall be given *to a bride* at the time of her nuptials, with a declaration *of its use, made by the giver* to the bridegroom, shall be her entire property, and shall not be shared by her kindred. . . .

Menu: Three persons, a wife, a son, and a slave, are declared by law to have *in general* no wealth exclusively their own; the wealth which they may earn is *regularly* acquired for the man to whom they belong.

QUESTIONS

- What gender roles did the Digest seek to enforce?
- Why do you think the British legalized the "most traditional versions" of societal norms? What did they hope to achieve?

Source: *Digest of Hindu Law on Contracts and Successions with a Commentary by Jagannát'ha Tercapanchánana*, trans. H. T. Colebrooke, 4th ed., 2 vols. (Madras: Higginbotham & Co., 1874), I: 406, 412, 436, and 459.

5.4 MARY HENRIETTA KINGSLEY, "ON POLYGAMY" (1894)

English scientific writer and explorer Mary Henrietta Kingsley (1862–1900) visited equatorial Africa in 1894, collecting fish and insect specimens for the British Museum and taking ethnographic notes on the cultures she encountered. After lecturing widely and writing two accounts of her travels, she died nursing sick prisoners during the Anglo–Boer War. She acerbically expressed her sympathy for Africans, who had been confronted with very different practices by their European conquerors, by focusing on the practical aspects of African polygamy and the hypocrisy of those seeking to change them.

[Reasons for polygamy:] One is that it is totally impossible for one woman to do the whole work of a house—look after the children, prepare and cook the food, prepare the rubber, carry the same to the markets, fetch the daily supply of water from the stream, cultivate the plantation, &c, &c. . . .

The African lady does not care a travelling whitesmith's execration if her husband does flirt, so long as he does not go and give to other women the cloth, &c, that she should have. The more wives the less work, says the African lady; and I have known men who would rather have had one wife and spent the rest of the money on themselves, in a civilized way, driven into polygamy by the women; and of course this state of affairs is most common in non-slave-holding tribes like the Fan[g of the Cameroons]. . . .

Polygamy is the institution which above all others governs the daily life of the native; and it is therefore the one which the missionaries who enter into this daily life, and not merely into the mercantile and legal, as do the trader and the government official, are constantly confronted with and hindered by. All the missionaries have set their faces against it and deny Church membership to those men who practice it; whereby it falls out that many men are excluded from the fold who would make quite as good Christians as those within it. They hesitate about turning off from their homes women who have lived and worked with them for years, and not only for them, but often for their fathers before them. One case in the Rivers I know of is almost tragic if you put yourself in his place. An old chief, who had three wives, profoundly and vividly believed that exclusion from the Holy Communion meant an eternal damnation . . . and the chief did not like the prospect at all; but on the other hand he did not like to turn off the three wives he had lived with for years. He found the matter was not even to be compromised by turning off two and going to church to be married with accompanying hymns and orange-blossoms with number three, for the ladies held together; not one of them would marry him and let the other two go. . . .

Many a keen old chief turns on his pastor and asks driving questions regarding the patriarchs, until I have

Source: Mary Henrietta Kingsley, *Travels in West Africa: Congo Française, Corisco and Cameroons* (London: Macmillan, 1897), 211–14.

heard a sorely tried pastor question the wisdom of introducing the Old Testament to the heathen. Many a young man hesitates about joining the Church that will require his entering into the married state with only one woman, whom he knows he may not whack, and who, he knows, will also know this and carry on in all directions, and go and report all his little failings up at the mission, and get him into hot water with the missionary whose good opinion he values highly. And he is artful enough to know he enjoys this good opinion more as an interesting possible convert, than he would as a Church member requiring "discipline."

QUESTIONS

- How did Kingsley defend polygamy?
- Do you find her argument persuasive? Why or why not?

5.5 AYUBA SULEIMAN DIALLO, "MARRIAGE IN BUNDU"

From a prominent family of Muslim clerics in Bundu (now Senegal), Ayuba Suleiman Diallo (1701–1773), also known as Job Ben Solomon, was captured and sold into slavery, made the trans-Atlantic passage, and worked as an enslaved person in Maryland's tobacco fields. After running away, he was recognized as an educated, devout Muslim and freed in hopes he would work for slave traders in Africa. This account, written down by Thomas Bluett, one of his benefactors, describes the marriage practices of Diallo's homeland, suggesting the cultural, economic, and sexual components of Muslim marriages in West Africa and the symbolic remnant of the practice of bride kidnapping.

The Manner of their Marriages and Baptisms is something remarkable. When a Man has a mind to marry his Son (which they generally do much sooner than in England) and has found out a suitable Match for him, he goes to the Girl's Father, proposes the Matter to him, and agrees for the Price that he is to pay for her; which the Father of the Woman always gives to her as a Dowry. All Things being concluded on, the two Fathers and the young Man go to the Priest, and declare their Agreement; which finishes the Marriage.

But now comes the great Difficulty, viz. how the Young Man shall get his Wife home; for the Women, Cousins, and Relations, take on mightily, and guard the Door of the House, to prevent her being carried away; but at last the young Man's Presents and Generosity to them, makes them abate their Grief. He then provides a Friend, well mounted, to carry her off; but as soon as she is up on Horseback, the Women renew their Lamentations, and rush in to dismount her. However, the Man is generally successful, and rides off with his Prize to the House provided for her.

After this they make a Treat for their Friends, but the Woman never appears at it; and tho' the Ladies here in England are generally more free after Marriage than before, with the Women in JOB's Country it is quite contrary; for they are so very bashful, that they will never permit their Husbands to see them without a Vail [veil] on for three Years after they are married; insomuch, that altho' JOB has a Daughter by his last Wife, yet he never saw her unveiled since Marriage, having been married to her but about two Years before he came from home. To prevent Quarrels, and keep Peace among their Wives, the Husbands divide their Time equally betwixt them; and are so exact in this Affair, that if one Wife lies in, the Husband lies alone in her Apartment those Nights, that are her Turn, and not with the other Wife. If a Wife proves very bad, they put her away, and she keeps her Dowry, and any one

Source: Thomas Bluett, *Some Memoirs of the Life of Job, the Son of Solomon, the High Priest of Boonda in Africa; Who was a Slave About Two Years in Maryland; and Afterwards Being Brought to England, was Set Free, and Sent to His Native Land in the Year 1734* (London: Richard Ford, 1734), 40–43, reproduced at: https://docsouth.unc.edu/neh/bluett/bluett.html (consulted June 17, 2020).

may marry her after her Divorce; but they don't use to put them away upon slight Occasions. If a Woman puts away her Husband, she must return him her Dowry; and she is look'd upon always after as a scandalous Person, no Man caring to have any thing to do with her.

QUESTIONS

- Why do you think the practice of "bride kidnapping" remained?
- Do you think the author approved of these marriage practices? What makes you think that?

5.6 A MARRIAGE ANNULMENT IN PERU (1618)

This extraordinary set of documents gathered by Nancy van Deusen concerns a woman's petition for the annulment of her marriage. Women were frequently beaten, confined, and starved if they did not agree to their father's plans for their marriage. This case went through the Roman Catholic Church in Huánuco Peru and was decided in her favor in 1618. The second excerpt is from a witness to the marriage, and the final excerpt is from the vicar general of the archbishopric of Lima.

Ysabel Allay Suyo: Diego Andrés: he alleges in his statement he presented on May 7th that I willingly married him, and my parents and sister supported the marriage. I deny this: I never willingly consented, but as I have claimed in other written documents, Father Alonso Sarmiento forced me to marry Diego against my will in the settlement of Guachagaro, [which is] outside of his parish, because he is his [Diego's] master. . . . At the same time, he makes other absurd assertions that are false, all with the intention of running roughshod over me; he does not declare the truth and is side-stepping the evidence. . . .

Domingo de Ariçola: Friar Alonso Sarmiento of the Mercedarian Order married Diego Andrés de Arenas and Ysabel Allay Suyo in the settlement of Guachagaro. They called this witness to the home of the parents . . . [and l]ater they called Ysabel Allay Suyo, who was in [another] room in the house and did not want to come out, and even though they called for her to come out various times, she did not want to, and her mother went in to get her and brought her out crying. In the main room the padre [priest] asked her two times if she would marry Diego Andrés, and both times she said "no." This witness stood by her side and reprimanded her by saying why didn't she want to marry to make her parents happy, and that it was better to be in the service of God, our Father. Then Firar Alonso Sarmiento asked her again if she wished to marry, and this witness never heard her say "yes," and then the padre took her hand and that of Diego Andrés and married them. Ysabel was crying throughout, and after the wedding she returned to the room where she had been. And this witness asked the padre why he hadn't asked [the couple] to embrace, and he said, "you are right, I didn't," and they called for Ysabel to come out again and told her she had to embrace her husband, Diego Andrés, which she refused to do. Diego Andrés then threw his arms around her. Diego Andrés served Friar Alonso Sarmiento. The marriage is not valid because this witness never heard Ysabel Allay Suyo say "yes." . . .

Diego Andrés [letter to Ysabel Allay Suyo]: . . . I repent and cry when I remember when I caused you to fall to the ground when you, Ysabel, were planting potatoes above in the area near the cliff. I break down weeping, my Ysabel, when I remember how I injured your mouth for so many days. . . . Married, we lived together, my Ysabel, for one year and five months; how

Source: Richard Boyer and Geoffrey Spurling, eds., *Colonial Lives: Documents on Latin American History, 1550–1850* (New York: Oxford University Press, 2000), 131–33, 136, 138.

hard, how rough, how cruel was I to a dove and lamb of God . . . forgive me wife, for the love of the death and the passion of Jesus Christ. And you see that God has such great mercy in this life, and in the next we will live in peace and joy. . . .

Recently, some Indians of Guánuco told me that you were walking around free and unconfined, and, evidently, it was understood that you were causing me to lose my honor and self-esteem. I don't believe this,

my señora Ysabel; I am confident in your virtue and honesty and purity and the watchfulness of your parents. . . .

Feliciano de Vega: I declare the marriage carried out by Friar Alonso Sarmiento of the Mercedarian Order to be nullified, because it was done against her will and by force, and because Friar Alonso Sarmiento married them outside the district of his parish. . . .

QUESTIONS

- On which grounds did Ysabel protest the marriage?
- From the excerpt, do you believe that this situation was common or rare? Why do you think that?

5.7 SHEN FU, *SIX RECORDS OF A FLOATING LIFE* (1809)

This autobiography was written in 1809 by Shen Fu (1763–1825), a magistrate's secretary, failed businessman, and painter. The first section is a love story of his marital relationship with Chen Yün (1763–1803). They had an arranged marriage at the age of 17 and lived happily together despite Shen Fu's lack of professional success. Yün's intense interest in the world is evident, as is her desire to get her beloved husband a concubine named Han-yüan. Yün died of a lingering illness after being separated from her "sister." The manuscript was first published in 1877 and became an instant bestseller.

I married Chen Yün, the daughter of my uncle, Mr Chen Hsin-yü. Her literary name was Shu-chen.

Even while small, she was very clever. While she was learning to talk she was taught the poem *The Mandolin Song* and could repeat it almost immediately.

Yün's father died when she was four years old. . . . At first they had virtually nothing, but as Yün grew older she became very adept at needlework, and the labor of her ten fingers came to provide for all three of them. Thanks to her work, they were always able to afford to pay the tuition for her brother's teachers.

One day Yün found a copy of *The Mandolin Song* in her brother's book-box and, remembering her lessons as a child, was able to pick out the characters one by one. That is how she began learning to read. . . .

Yün's habits and tastes were the same as mine. She understood what my eyes said, and the language of my brows. She did everything according to my expression, and everything she did was as I wished it. . . .

When Chien Shi-chu of Wuchiang County fell ill and died, my father wrote and ordered me to represent him at the funeral. Hearing this, Yün took me aside. "If you are going to Wuchiang, you have to cross Lake Tai. I would love to go with you and see something more of the world. . . ."

"Is this the Lake Tai that everyone speaks of?" asked Yün. "Now that I see how grand the world is, I have not lived in vain! There are women who have lived their entire lives without seeing a vista like this." . . .

"Today I have met someone who is both beautiful and charming," said Yün. "I have just invited Han-yüan to come and see me tomorrow, so I can try to arrange things for you."

"But we're not a rich family," I said, worried. "We cannot afford to keep someone like that. How could people as poor as ourselves dare think of such a thing? And we are so happily married, why should we look for someone else?"

Source: Shen Fu, *Six Records of a Floating Life*, trans. Leonard Pratt and Chiang Su-hui (London: Penguin Books, 1983), 25–26, 40, 45–46, 50–51.

"But I love her too," Yün said, laughing. "You just let me take care of everything. . . ."

"She has agreed," Yün told me happily. . . . From that time on there was a day that Yün did not talk about Han-yüan. But later Han-yüan was taken off by a powerful man, and all the plans came to nothing. In fact, it was because of this that Yün died.

QUESTIONS

- How did Fu present the marriage? Do you find the account believable?
- Why do you think his wife desired to get him a concubine?

5.8 RIGOBERTA MENCHÚ, "CHILDHOOD IN GUATEMALA" (1983)

Rigoberta Menchú Tum (b.1959) is a Quiché woman from Guatemala. She championed the rights of women and Indigenous people during Guatemala's long civil wars (1960–1996) and won the Nobel Peace Prize in 1992. These passages assert that "it takes a village" to raise a child and discuss her experience of childhood; the writing represents not only her people, but also, in its broad outlines, many preindustrial, colonized, and post-colonial societies.

In our community there is an elected representative, someone who is highly respected. . . . Well, then the whole community becomes the children of the woman who's elected. So a mother, on her first day of pregnancy goes with her husband to tell these elected leaders that she's going to have a child, because the child will not only belong to them but to the whole community. . . . The leaders then pledge the support of the community and say: "We will help you, we will be the child's second parents". They are known as *abuelos*, "grandparents" or "forefathers". . . .

As we grow up we have a series of obligations. Our parents teach us to be responsible; just as they have been responsible. The eldest son is responsible for the house. Whatever the father cannot correct is up to the eldest son to correct. He is like a second father to all of us and is responsible for our upbringing. The mother is the one who is responsible for keeping an account of what the family eats, and what she has to buy. . . . But the father has to solve a lot of problems too. And each one of us, as we grow up, has our own small area of responsibility. This comes from the promises made for the child when he is born, and from the continuity of our customs. The child can make the promise for himself when his parents have taught him to do it. The mother, who is closest to the children, does this, or sometimes the father. They talk to their children explaining what they have to do and what our ancestors used to do. They don't impose it as a law, but just give the example of what our ancestors have always done. This is how we all learn our own small responsibilities. for example, the little girl begins by carrying water, and the little boy begins by tying up the dogs. . . . Both girls and boys have their tasks and are told the reasons for doing them. They learn responsibility because if they don't do their little jobs well, their father has the right to scold them, or even beat them. . . .

I worked from when I was very small, but I didn't earn anything. I was really helping my mother because she always had to carry a baby, my little brother, on her back as she picked coffee. It made me very sad to see my mother's face covered in sweat as she tried to finish her work load, and I wanted to help her. But my work wasn't paid, it just contributed to my mother's work. . . . When I was eight, I started to earn money. . . .

Source: Elisabeth Burgos-Debray, ed., *I, Rigoberta Menchú: An Indian Woman in Guatemala*, trans. Ann Wright (London: Verso Books, 1984 [1983]), 7, 16–17, 34–35, 210–12, 219.

But when I was ten I was closer to my mother. That's the age she told me about the facts of life. She taught me by talking about the experiences of her grandmother: she told me about when her grandmother was pregnant. She didn't pass on her own experiences, not that she hadn't had them, but because she felt more comfortable teaching me through the experiences of others. . . .

Our tenth year actually marks the stage when we enter womanhood. It's when parents buy their daughters everything they need: two aprons; two *cortes* [multi-colored blouse]; two *perrajes* [shawls]; so that when one is being washed she can wear the other. . . .

Mamá used to get very angry. She taught us to do all our jobs well, and if we didn't do them right, she'd punish us. She said: "If it's not put right now, who'll teach you later on? This is for your own good, not mine." . . .

My mother had the same idea of women as our women had had in the past. They were very strict and believed a woman should learn her womanly occupation so that she could live and face many things. And she was right. . . . My father was very tender and always protected me, but it was my mother who coped with the big problems of our family. She was capable of seeing her son even when he was dying and doing everything she could to save him.

QUESTIONS

- After reading the excerpt, do you think the author enjoyed her childhood?
- How do the gender norms in the excerpt compare to those portrayed in any other document you have read in this chapter?

5.9 AMY CHUA, *BATTLE HYMN OF THE TIGER MOM* (2011)

Amy Chua (b. 1962), an American law professor of ethnic Chinese descent via the Philippines, wrote this account of raising two daughters according to what she describes as strict Confucian principles. In it, she describes how children become rebellious when confronted with educational approaches that do not match their interests or aptitudes. It also demonstrates dedication of time and money to parenting that, while not unknown in earlier eras, became much more widespread in the last two generations among the well-to-do. Chua did not seek to write a parenting manual, though some critics read it that way.

"Lulu, you know that Mommy loves you, and everything I do, I do for you, for your future."

My own voice sounded artificial to me, and Lulu must have thought so too, because her response was, "That's great," in a flat, apathetic tone.

Jed's fiftieth birthday was coming up. I organized a huge surprise party. . . . I asked Sophia and Lulu each to write her own toast. . . . Lulu said, "I don't want to give a toast."

"You *have* to give a toast," I replied.

"No one my age [13] gives toasts," Lulu said. . . .

"Lulu, you are so ungrateful. When I was your age, I worked nonstop. I built a treehouse for my sisters because my father asked me to. I obeyed everything he said, and that's why I know how to use a chainsaw. I also built a hummingbird house. I was a newspaper carrier for the *El Cerrito Journal* and had to wear a huge fifty-pound pouch over my head stuffed with papers and walk five miles. And look at you—you've been given every opportunity, every privilege. You've never had to wear imitation Adidas with four stripes instead of three. And you can't even do this one tiny thing for Daddy. It's disgusting."

"I don't want to give a toast," was Lulu's response.

I pulled out the big guns. I threatened everything I could think of. I bribed her. I tried to inspire her. I tried to shame her. I offered to help her write it. I jacked up the stakes and gave her an ultimatum, knowing it was a pivotal battle.

When the party came . . . [Lulu] had written nothing, and she refused to say a single word.

I had lost. It was the first time. Through all the turbulence and warfare in our household, I'd never lost before, at least not on something important.

This act of defiance and disrespect infuriated me. My anger simmered for a while, then I unleashed my full wrath. "You've dishonored the family—and yourself," I said to Lulu. "You're going to have to live with your mistake for the rest of your life."

Lulu snapped back, "You're a showoff. It's all about you. . . ."

There was now a wall between us. In the old days, we'd fight ferociously but always make up. We'd end

Source: Amy Chua, *Battle Hymn of the Tiger Mom* (New York: Penguin Press, 2011), 179–81, 218–21.

up snuggling in her bed or mine, hugging each other, giggling as we imitated ourselves arguing. I'd say things totally inappropriate for a parent, like "I'm going to be dead soon" or "I can't believe you love me so much it hurts." And Lulu would say, "Mommy! You are so weird!" but smile despite herself. Now Lulu stopped coming to my room at night. . . .

Ever since I'd given her the choice, we'd gotten along much better. My pain seemed to be her gain, and she was more patient and good humored. . . .

I started to gear up. . . . Lulu overheard me one day. "What are you doing?" she demanded. When I explained that I was just doing a little research, she suddenly got furious. "No, Mommy—*no!*" she said fiercely. "Don't wreck tennis for me like you wrecked violin."

That really hurt. I backed off. . . .

"No, Mommy—please stop," Lulu said. "I can do this on my own. I don't need you to be involved."

"Lulu, what we need to do is to channel your strength—"

"Mommy, I *get* it. I've watched you and listened to your lectures a million times. But I don't want you controlling my life."

"Okay Lulu, I can accept that," I said. . . . But I didn't really give up.

QUESTIONS

- Do you agree with Chua's parenting style? Why or why not?
- How does this parenting style compare with that of other families you know?

THE EXCHANGE OF GOODS AND SERVICES

Trade

6.1 ZHANG HAN, "ON MERCHANTS" (c. 1577)

In retirement, Ming official Zhang Han (1511–1593) wrote about the four traditional social classes of Confucian China: artisans, farmers, merchants, and scholars. "On Merchants" demonstrates how trade drove an increasingly complex Chinese economy. Zhang Han also illustrates both the possibility of great profit and how the government's heavy hand sometimes stifled trade.

Money and profit are of great importance to men. They seek profit, then suffer by it, yet they cannot forget it. They exhaust their bodies and spirits, run day and night, yet they still regard what they have gained as insufficient. . . . Merchants boast that their wisdom and ability are such as to give them a free hand in affairs. They believe that they know all the possible transformations in the universe and therefore can calculate all the changes in the human world, and that the rise and fall of prices are under their command. They are confident that they will not make one mistake in a hundred in their calculations. These merchants do not know how insignificant their wisdom and ability really are. . . .

The capital is located in an area with mountains at its back and a great plain stretching in front. The region is rich in millet, grain, donkeys, horses, fruit, and vegetables, and has become a center where goods from distant places are brought. Those who engage in commerce, including the foot peddler, the cart peddler, and the shopkeeper, display not only clothing and fresh foods from the fields but also numerous luxury items such as priceless jade from Kunlun, pearls from the island of Hainan, gold from Yunnan, and coral from Vietnam. These precious items, coming from the mountains or the sea, are not found in central China.

But people in remote areas and in other countries, unafraid of the dangers and difficulties of travel, transport these items step by step to the capital, making it the most prosperous place in the empire. . . .

The profits from the tea and salt trades are especially great, but only large-scale merchants can undertake these businesses. Furthermore, there are government regulations on their distribution, which prohibit the sale of tea in the northwest and salt in the southeast. Since tea is produced primarily in the southeast, prohibiting its sale to the non-Chinese on the northern border is wise and can be enforced. Selling privately produced salt where it is manufactured is also prohibited. This law is rigidly applied to all areas where salt is produced during the Ming dynasty. Yet there are so many private salt producers there now that the regulation seems too rigid and is hard to enforce.

Profits from selling tea and the officials' income from the tea tax are usually ten to twenty percent of the original investment. By contrast, merchants' profits from selling salt and official income from the salt tax can reach seventy to eighty percent of the original invested capital. In either case, the more the invested capital, the greater the profit; the less the invested capital, the less the profit. The profits from selling tea and salt enrich the nation as well as the merchants. Skillful

Source: Zhang Han, "Essay on Merchants," *Chinese Civilization: A Sourcebook,* ed. Patricia Buckley Ebrey, 2nd ed. (New York: The Free Press, 1993), 155–57.

merchants can make great profits for themselves while the inept ones suffer losses. This is the present state of the tea and salt business. . . .

As to the foreigners in the southeast, their goods are useful to us just as ours are to them. To use what one has to exchange for what one does not have is what trade is all about. Moreover, these foreigners trade with China under the name of tributary contributions. That means China's authority is established and the foreigners are submissive. Even if the gifts we grant them are great and the tribute they send us is small, our expense is still less than one ten-thousandth of the benefit we gain from trading with them. Moreover, the southeast sea foreigners are more concerned with trading with China than with gaining gifts from China. Even if they send a large tribute offering only to receive small gifts in return, they will still be content. In addition, trading with them can enrich our people. So why should we refrain from the trade? Some people may say that the southeast sea foreigners have invaded us several times so they are not the kind of people with whom we should trade. But they should realize that the southeast sea foreigners need Chinese goods and the Chinese need their goods. If we prohibit the natural flow of this merchandise, how can we prevent them from invading us? I believe that if the sea trade were opened, the trouble with foreign pirates would cease. . . .

Turning to the taxes levied on China merchants, though these taxes are needed to fill the national treasury, excessive exploitation should be prohibited. Merchants from all areas are ordered to stop their carts and boats and have their bags and cases examined whenever they pass through a road or river checkpoint. Often the cargoes are overestimated and thus a falsely high duty is demanded. Usually merchants are taxed when they enter the checkpoint and are taxed again at the marketplace. When a piece of goods is taxed once, the merchant can still make some profit while complying with the state's regulations. But today's merchants often are stopped on the road for additional payments and also suffer extortions from the clerks. Such exploitation is hard and bitter enough but, in addition, the merchants are taxed twice. How can they avoid becoming more and more impoverished?

QUESTIONS

- What did Han mean by "These merchants do not know how insignificant their wisdom and ability really are"?
- Does this economic system seem rational to you? Why or why not?

6.2 TOMÉ PIRES, AN ACCOUNT OF THE EAST (1515)

Portuguese royal apothecary Tomé Pires (1465?–1540) participated in an expedition to Malacca in 1512–1515 where he traveled extensively in the archipelagos of maritime Southeast Asia to scout out markets and new drugs or spices to trade. He died leading Portugal's first embassy to the court of China.

The men of these islands are warlike and great robbers; they plunder in many places; people going and of with merchandise take precautions. Those in the sea-ports are civilized; the other people are savages. These islands have an infinity of mats of three or four kinds; they have a few rattans; they have dried fish, pitch, foodstuffs, many vegetables; they have wines. . . . These islands trade with Malacca and with Java and with Borneo and with Siam and with all the places between Pahang and Siam. . . .

These men in these islands are greater thieves than any in the world, and they are powerful and have many paraos [double-outrigger sailboats]. They sail about plundering, from their country up to Pegu, to the Moluccas and Banda, and among all the islands around Java; and they take women to sea. They have fairs where they dispose of the merchandise they steal and sell the slaves they capture. They run all round the island of Sumatra. They are mainly corsairs. The Javanese call them Bugis (Bujuus), and the Malays call them this and Celates. They take their spoils to Jumaia which is near Pahang, where they sell and have a fair continually. . . .

Most of these islands have gold, and they also have corsairs and robbers who live by that alone. The corsairs only sail in paraos and therefore they do not attack junks [Chinese sailing ships]. And the corsairs who are nearest to Pahang make in Pahang their trading ports, and those near the Moluccas and Banda trade in Bima and Sumbawa and Sapeh, and those near us hold a fair and trade in Am and in Arcat, Rupat. They bring countless slaves, and therefore a large number of slaves are used in Malacca, because they all go there on account of the great trade it has, more than all the kingdoms and ports over here; and so it is called the fortunate river. There are certainly great sailings from here; no trading port as large as Malacca is known, nor any where they deal in such fine and highly-prized merchandise. Goods from all over the east are found here; goods from all over the west are sold here. There is no doubt that the affairs of Malacca are of great importance, and of much profit and great honor. It is a land [that] cannot depreciate, on account of its position, but must always grow. It is at the end of the monsoons, where you find what you want, and sometimes more than you are looking for.

QUESTIONS

- How did Pires present Malacca as a land of opportunity? Was he effective?
- What might have been the effect of Pires' account on contemporary trading expeditions?

Source: Tomé Pires, *The Suma Oriental of Tomé Pires*, ed. and trans. Armando Cortesao, 2 vols. (London: Hakluyt Society, 1944), I: 225–28, https://archive.org/stream/McGillLibrary–136385–182/136385_djvu.txt (consulted March 18, 2020).

6.3 JAMES STEUART, *AN INQUIRY INTO THE PRINCIPLES OF POLITICAL ECONOMY* (1767)

Scots nobleman James Steuart (1707–1780) spent more than two decades on the continent of Europe exploring different approaches to mercantilism and to political economy more generally. His arguments in favor of government action are often compared and contrasted to those of Adam Smith. His policy recommendations in this first full-fledged examination of political economy were often followed by British policymakers in succeeding decades.

A nation which remains passive in her commerce, is at the mercy of those who are active, and must be greatly favored, indeed, by natural advantages, or by a constant flux of gold and silver from her mines, to be able to support a correspondence, not entirely hurtful to the augmentation of her wealth. . . .

When I look upon the wide field which here opens to my view, I am perplexed with too great a variety of objects. In one part, I see a decent and comely beginning of industry; wealth flowing gently in, to recompence ingenuity; numbers both augmenting, and every one becoming daily more useful to another; agriculture proportionally extending itself; no violent revolutions; no exorbitant profits; no insolence among the rich; no excessive misery among the poor; multitudes employed in producing; great economy upon consumption; and all the instruments of luxury, daily produced by the hands of the diligent, going out of the country for the service of strangers; not remaining at home for the gratification of sensuality. . . .

Wealth will be found daily to augment, from the rising of prices, in many branches of industry. This will encourage the industrious classes, and the idle consumers at home will complain. I have already dwelt abundantly long upon the effects resulting from this to the lower classes of the people, in providing them with a certain means of subsistence. Let me now examine in what respect the higher classes will be likewise made to feel the good effects of this general change, although at first they may suffer a temporary inconvenience from it. . . .

In a trading nation every man must turn his talents to account, or he will undoubtedly be left behind in this universal emulation, in which the most industrious, the most ingenious, and the most frugal will constantly carry off the prize.

This consideration ought to be a spur to every body. The richest men in a trading nation have no security against poverty, I mean proportional poverty; for though they diminish nothing of their income, yet by not increasing it in proportion to others, they lose their rank in wealth, and from the first class in which they stood, they will slide insensibly down to a lower.

Source: James Steuart, *An Inquiry into the Principles of Political Economy: Being an Essay on the Science of Domestic Policy of Free Nations*, 2 vols. (London: A. Millar and T. Cadell, 1767), I: 207, 209–11.

This is one consequence of an additional beneficial trade, that it raises demand and increases wealth; but if we suppose no proportional augmentation of supply, it will prove at best but an airy dream which lasts for a moment, and when the gilded scene is passed away, numberless are the inconveniences which are seen to follow.

QUESTIONS

- To Steuart, what were the signs of a positive economy? What were negative signs?
- Do his ideas seem rational? Why or why not?

6.4 GUILLAUME-ANTOINE OLIVIER, THE PEOPLES OF THE OTTOMAN EMPIRE

Entomologist Guillaume-Antoine Olivier (1756–1814) left France in 1792 on an official scientific journey that took six years. He visited much of the Middle East, including Turkey, Persia, and Egypt, and brought back an impressive collection that is still displayed in Paris' National Museum of Natural History. This excerpt from his visit to Constantinople (now Istanbul) shows his perspective on the commercial behavior of the religious minority groups that conducted most of the trade in the region.

The Greeks are gay, witty, and cunning: they exercise various trades, carry on some commerce, apply themselves to maritime affairs, visit the different towns of the coast, and never travel far inland, except into European Turkey. . . . The rich are well informed, supple, and very intriguing; they study languages and spare nothing to be employed as physicians, as droguemans [interpreters], or as men of business by the Turks. . . .

The Armenians are all traders; in the Ottoman Empire, it is they who are engaged in the greatest traffic, and who carry it on with the most intelligence. They are patient, economical, and indefatigable; they travel into the interior of Asia and into India; they have storehouses and correspondents everywhere. The greater part of them exercise mechanic arts; they are bankers, contractors, and men of business of the pashas or other great personages. They are reproached with sparing no means of enriching themselves, and of cheating, when they have an opportunity, in the quality of merchandise. Nevertheless, in endeavoring to gain the most they possibly can, they seldom fail in their engagements, and are punctual in the performance of their promises. . . .

The Jews present themselves here under colors far more unfavorable than in Europe. More ignorant, more poor, more fanatic, they give themselves up to every kind of trade and to all professions, even the very lowest. Few among them are physicians, droguemans, or men of business: not one is a cultivator. All trade to them is good if it yield a profit, however, trifling it may be. the rich practice usury, lend money on pledges at an interest of two or three percent by the month, and even more according to circumstances. They are brokers, bankers or traders. The Turkish customshouse officers make use of them for valuing goods and collecting the duties.

QUESTIONS

- Which groups did Olivier think well of? Which did he think poorly of?
- What, to Olivier, were attributes of an economic contributor?

Source: Guillaume-Antoine Olivier, *Travels in the Ottoman Empire, Egypt, and Persia*, translated from the French (London: T.N. Longman, O. Rees, T. Cadell, Jr., and W. Davies, 1801), 18–19.

6.5 THE GENERAL AGREEMENT ON TARIFFS AND TRADE (1948)

The United Nations proposed the GATT at its Conference on Trade and Employment after efforts to form an International Trade Organization failed. Twenty-three nations signed the agreement in 1947, and it took effect the following year. The Uruguay Round of Agreements in 1994 established the World Trade Organization (WTO) as GATT's successor. Although GATT successfully reduced tariffs from more than 22 percent to 5 percent in 1999, the agreement itself probably slowed that decrease by recognizing the importance of minimizing inequality between wealthy and poor nations.

PART IV TRADE AND DEVELOPMENT, Article XXXVI

2. There is need for a rapid and sustained expansion of the export earnings of the less-developed contracting parties.
3. There is need for positive efforts designed to ensure that less-developed contracting parties secure a share in the growth in international trade commensurate with the needs of their economic development.
4. Given the continued dependence of many less-developed contracting parties on the exportation of a limited range of primary products, there is need to provide in the largest possible measure more favorable and acceptable conditions of access to world markets for these products, and wherever appropriate to devise measures designed to stabilize and improve conditions of world markets in these products, including in particular measures designed to attain stable, equitable and remunerative prices, thus permitting an expansion of world trade and demand and a dynamic and steady growth of the real export earnings of these countries so as to provide them with expanding resources for their economic development.
5. The rapid expansion of the economies of the less-developed contracting parties will be facilitated by a diversification of the structure of their economies and the avoidance of an excessive dependence on the export of primary products. There is, therefore, need for increased access in the largest possible measure to markets under favorable conditions for

Source: *The General Agreement on Tariffs and Trade* (1948), 53–54, on https://www.wto.org/english/docs_e/legal_e/gatt47_e.pdf (consulted March 13, 2020).

processed and manufactured products currently or potentially of particular export interest to less-developed contracting parties.

6. Because of the chronic deficiency in the export proceeds and other foreign exchange earnings of less-developed contracting parties, there are important inter-relationships between trade and financial assistance to development. . . .

QUESTIONS

- What did this international agreement try to do?
- Do you think the provisions outlined here would work? Why or why not?

6.6 COVER CRITIQUES THE WTO

Jane Cover, a legal advisor for the National Lawyers Guild, helped to organize and then participated in the demonstrations in Seattle in November–December 1999. Her statements suggest the depth of concern and the effectiveness of grassroots organizing to build on the mass demonstrations that occurred in December 1997 in four Australian cities to protest proposed WTO regulations. Her emails suggest that trade is not always the panacea that many leaders claim it to be. Distrust of the authorities that signed them and that defended such trade pacts is also common among those discontented with trade agreements.

From: J. Cover

Sent: Thursday, December 02, 1999 1:44 p.m.

Dear Friends;

I'm forwarding some information about our riots out here that might not be included in the press coverage you are receiving in other parts of the country. Suffice it to say, this has shaken us up a lot, and it will take many Seattlites a long time to work through our frustration and anger with our local officials and our police department. You may not be aware that I am a legal observer at the protests and have seen many many civil rights violations over the past few days. The number of people who have been gassed, sprayed and shot at with rubber and plastic bullets numbers in the thousands. Don't be deceived by media reports suggesting that the police are responding to the shinanigans [sic] of hooligans and gang members. While of course those elements are taking advantage of the confusion, the vast majority of people out there in the streets are demonstrators committed to their cause and to nonviolence. Their courage in the face of police brutality is astounding.

In solidarity,

jane

From: J. Cover

Sent: Friday, December 03, 1999 2:34 p.m.

Hi Mark,

I must say, it's nice to be asked about the WTO issues. . . .

Civil liberty violations aside, I can give your question about what's wrong with the WTO a shot, and perhaps the rest of you can chime in with anything I've overlooked/misrepresented.

In my opinion, there are four big things wrong with the WTO. First, they are undemocratic and secretive. The WTO can rule that a country's laws and regulations are barriers to free trade, regardless of the fact that those laws were passed by the people or in the public interest. The decisions made by the WTO are heavily influenced by corporations who have access to the negotiations, while public citizens are excluded and have no vehicle to provide input. When I say they are influenced by corporations, I mean specifically that the advisory panels to the WTO are MADE UP OF CORPORATE INTERESTS, called "Industry Sector Advisory Committees". Proceedings are held behind closed doors (in the case of Seattle, the doors are guarded by rows of stormtroopers. . . .)

Source: Jane Cover, emails (December 2–3, 1999), http://depts.washington.edu/wtohist/testimonies/JaneCover.htm (consulted March 17, 2020).

Second, the WTO tramples on human rights. The WTO has ruled that it is: 1) illegal to ban a product because of the way it is produced (ie. Using child or prison labor) and 2) governments cannot ban products from companies who do business with vicious dictatorships (ie. Burma).

Third, the WTO is bad for your health. The South African government policy of encouraging the adoption of generic HIV drugs produced locally or imported from countries where they are cheaper is being challenged by the US (speaking for US drug companies) as a violation of free trade. To give another example, some European countries would rather not eat our hormone treated beef. The WTO has said that in order to avoid trade sanctions, or penalties, the countries need to produce scientific evidence that hormone treated beef is dangerous to human health (recall that normally, we require a product to be proven safe, not that it be proven dangerous . . .).

Finally, the WTO is bad for the environment. You may be familiar with the US Endangered Species Act regulations that bar the importation of tuna not caught with dolphin safe nets or shrimp with turtle safe nets. The WTO has ruled that these constitute barriers to free trade. The US has some options. We can stick to our guns and face trade sanctions (tariffs on our exports), pay a great big fine (paid with taxpayer dollars), or change our regulations. I'm not sure what has happened with the turtles, but in the case of the dolphins, the US has repealed its law. In another example, Venezuela challenged our Clean Air Act regulations requiring gas to be "clean". Because of the WTO ruling, our own standards for the Clean Air Act were relaxed in order to avoid sanctions or fines.

This is why the WTO is accused of being undemocratic, a hazard to people and our environment. Of course, there are other reasons why WTO is a big nightmare, but these are the kickers for me. To read more about it, go to www.globalexchange.org or nlg.org (national lawyers guild) or citizen.org (public citizen).

I have the impression that the ruckus out here has made some folks sit up and ask what all the fuss is about. With sustained pressure, we might be able to change the WTO. But we have a long row to hoe.

Jane

QUESTIONS

- What were Cover's main criticisms of the WTO?
- Are these critiques valid? Why or why not?

7

HUMANS AS PROPERTY
Slavery

7.1 MUNGO PARK, ON WAR AND SLAVERY IN WEST AFRICA (1799)

Mungo Park (1771–1806) was a Scots surgeon who explored the Niger River in West Africa on behalf of the British African Association. After his first expedition (1795–1797), he wrote *Travels in the Interior Districts of Africa*, describing his experiences. Published in 1799, the book became quite successful. Park was killed during his second trip. This excerpt illustrates his views on the treatment of African enslaved persons as well as his perspective on the role of war in acquiring humans both for labor in Africa and to be exported overseas.

The slaves in Africa, I suppose, are nearly in the proportion of three to one to the freemen. They claim no reward for their services, except food and clothing; and are treated with kindness or severity, according to the good or bad disposition of their masters. Custom, however, has established certain rules with regard to the treatment of slaves, which it is thought dishonorable to violate. Thus, the domestic slaves, or such as are born in a man's own house, are treated with more lenity than those which are purchased with money. The authority of the master over the domestic slave, as I have elsewhere observed, extends only to reasonable correction: for the master cannot sell his domestic, without having first brought him to a public trial, before the chief men of the place. But these restrictions on the power of the master extend not to the case of prisoners taken in war, nor to that of slaves purchased with money. All these unfortunate beings are considered as strangers and foreigners, who have no right to the protection of the law, and may be treated with severity, or sold to a stranger, according to the pleasure of their owners. There are, indeed, regular markets, where slaves of this description are bought and sold; and the value of a slave in the eye of an African purchaser, increases in proportion to his distance from his native kingdom; for when slaves are only a few days journey from the place of their nativity, they frequently effect their escape; but when one or more kingdoms intervene, escape being more difficult, they are more readily reconciled to their situation. On this account, the unhappy slave is frequently transferred from one dealer to another, until he has lost all hopes of returning to his native kingdom. . . .

Slaves of the second description, generally become such by one or other of the following causes, 1. Captivity. 2. Famine. 3. Insolvency. 4. Crimes. A freeman may, by the established customs of Africa, become a slave by being taken in war. War is, of all others, the most productive source, and was probably the origin of slavery. . . . [I]t is natural to suppose that the conquerors, finding it inconvenient to maintain their prisoners, would compel them to labor; at first, perhaps, only for their own support; but afterwards to support their masters. . . . The slaves which are thus brought

Source: Mungo Park, *Travels in the Interior Districts of Africa: Performed in the Years 1795, 1796, and 1797 with an Account of a Subsequent Mission to That Country in 1805* (London: John Murray, 1817), I: 436–41, 47–48.

from the interior, may be divided into two distinct classes; first, such as were slaves from their birth, having been born of enslaved mothers: secondly, such as were born free, but who afterwards, by whatever means, became slaves. Those of the first description are by far the most numerous; for prisoners taken in war (at least such as are taken in open and declared war, when one kingdom avows hostilities against another) are generally of this description. . . .

When a Negro has, by means like these, once fallen into the hands of his enemies, he is either retained as the slave of his conqueror, or bartered into a distant kingdom: for an African, when he has once subdued his enemy, will seldom give him an opportunity of lifting up his hand against him at a future period. A conqueror commonly disposes of his captives according to the rank which they held in their native kingdom. Such of the domestic slaves as appear to be of a mild disposition, and particularly the young women, are retained as his own slaves. Others that display marks of discontent, are disposed of in a distant country; and such of the freemen or slaves, as have taken an active part in the war, are either sold to the Slatees [African merchants], or put to death. War, therefore, is certainly the most general, and most productive source of slavery; and the desolations of war often (but not always) produce the second cause of slavery, famine; in which case a freeman becomes a slave to avoid a greater calamity.

QUESTIONS

- Do you think Park opposed or supported the slave system? Why do you think that?
- Does this account change how you think about the Atlantic slave trade? Why or why not?

7.2 YU HYŎNGWŎN, ON ABOLISHING SLAVERY
(c. 1650)

Scholar Yu Hyŏngwŏn (1622–1673) objected to the role of slavery in Korean society. His (exceptionally high) estimates of the percentage of the population that was enslaved hints at how prevalent the institution was, and how difficult it was to escape. He does not argue for the abolition of slavery, but rather for its restriction to legal limits as a way to jumpstart the local economy.

I have found that the name "slave" first appeared when criminals were confiscated and enrolled as slaves for a crime they had committed. . . . By the time of our Chosŏn dynasty, when our laws were formulated, they forced people into slavery, and once people were enslaved, there was no way for them to get out of slavery. It was for this reason that the size of the slave population has gradually increased to the point where 80 or 90% of the population are slaves while barely 10 or 20% are commoners.

(Note: Under the present law, the children of mixed slave/commoner marriages are supposed to adopt the status of their mother, but if the father is a slave and the mother a commoner, then the children adopt the father's status and become slaves. This means that once someone has become a slave, there is no way out for him or his descendants. In addition, because military service is even more onerous than slavery, many people marry their sons and daughters to private slaves, with the result that the commoner population is gradually getting smaller. Under this law, before a few hundred years pass the country definitely will have no commoners left at all. Even the 10 or 20% of the population that barely exist as commoners are only slaves who have run off to a distant place and gone into hiding or are the destitute offspring of *yangban* and their concubines.) . . .

It would be all right if we could continue the matrilineal succession law and apply it equally and uniformly. (Note: This means that if a child is born to a commoner woman, then that child becomes a commoner.) But if the government of a true moral king is put into practice, and he rectifies the various institutions of government and washes away all partiality and vulgarity, then it is clear that the law governing slavery would definitely have to be abolished. . . .

But in our country this slave law has been in existence for a very long time, and having slaves has become a long-established custom. All the scholar-officials rely on them, so much so that it would be difficult for their families if slavery were suddenly abolished. Any changes in this custom must come about gradually, with relations between the higher and lower orders of society gradually becoming warmer and the practice of hiring workers gradually increasing. Only after that takes place can you then abolish slavery.

Source: *Sources of Korean Tradition*, ed. Yŏng-ho Ch'oe, Peter H. Lee, and Wm. Theodore de Bary, 2 vols. (New York: Columbia University Press, 2000), II: 159–61.

(Note: What I mean by abolishing it, indeed, does not mean a sudden and total abolition of presently existing slaves. Just order that slavery stop with the slaves that exist at the present time. Those who are currently recognized as slaves will continue to be recognized as slaves until they die, but the law providing for the inheritance of slavery will be abolished. . . .)

QUESTIONS

- What did you learn about Korea's slave system from this document?
- What arguments did the author use to convince others to "abolish" slavery?

7.3 JAMES RAMSEY, ON WEST INDIAN SLAVERY (1784)

Scotsman James Ramsay (1733–1789) served in the British navy as a ship's surgeon. While serving in the Caribbean, he visited a slave ship. After an injury forced him to leave the Royal Navy, he entered the Anglican Church. He had a parish on Saint Christopher (now St. Kitts), where he became familiar with the normal workday on a plantation described here. Ramsay returned to England and became an influential abolitionist, encouraging others to investigate the facts of slavery in order to convince more people to oppose the slave trade and slavery itself.

[A]t four o'clock in the morning the plantation bell rings to call the slaves into the field. Their work is to manure, dig, and hoe, plow the ground, to plant, weed, and cut the cane, to bring it to the mill, to have the juice expressed, and boiled into sugar. About nine o'clock, they have half an hour for breakfast, which they take in the field. Again they fall to work, and, according to the custom of the plantation, continue until eleven o'clock, or noon; the bell then rings, and the slaves are dispersed in the neighborhood, to pick about the fences, in the mountains, and fallow or waste grounds, natural grass and weeds for the horses and cattle. The time allotted for this branch of work, and preparation of dinner, varies from an hour and a half, to near three hours. In collecting pile by pile their little bundles of grass, the slaves of low land plantations, frequently burnt up by the sun, must wander in their neighbor's grounds, perhaps more than two miles from home. . . .

At one, or in some plantations, at two o'clock, the bell summons them to . . . assemble to their field work. If the overseer thinks their bundles too small, or if they come too late with them, they are punished with a number of stripes [from whipping] from four to ten. Some masters, under a fit of carelessness for their cattle, have gone as far as fifty stripes, which eventually disable the culprit for weeks. . . .

About seven o'clock in the evening, or later, according to the season of the year, when the overseer can find leisure, they are called over by list, to deliver in their second bundles of grass; and the same punishment, as at noon, is inflicted on the delinquents. They then separate, to pickup, on their way to their huts, (if they have not done it, as they generally do, while gathering grass) a little brush wood, or dry cow-dung, to prepare some simple mess for supper, and to-morrow's breakfast. This employs them till near midnight, and then they go to sleep, till the bell calls them in the morning.

QUESTIONS

- What arguments did the author use to convince others of the immorality of the British slave system?
- Do you think contemporaries found his arguments effective? Why or why not?

Source: James Ramsay, *An Essay on the Treatment and Conversion of African Slaves in the British Sugar Colonies* (London: James Philips, 1784), 69–72.

7.4 GEORGIA SLAVE CODE (1848)

The U.S. state of Georgia published its laws regarding enslaved people in 1848. Note that many of the crimes and punishments apply also to free people of color, who might also have included Indigenous peoples. These rules suggest that lawmakers were concerned with subjugating enslaved persons and "keeping them in their place." The idea that these "crimes" could also apply to a free person suggests how difficult it was for people of color to truly escape their owners.

ART. 1. CRIMES, OFFENCES, AND PENALTIES.

SEC. I. CAPITAL OFFENCES.

1. Capital crimes when punished with death.—The following shall be considered as capital offences, when committed by a slave or free person of color: insurrection, or an attempt to excite it; committing a rape, or attempting it on a free white female; murder of a free white person, or murder of a slave or free person of color, or poisoning of a human being; every and each of these offences shall, on conviction, be punished with death. . . .

4. Punishment of slaves for striking white persons.—If any slave shall presume to strike any white person, such slave upon trial and conviction before the justice or justices, according to the direction of this act, shall for the first offence suffer such punishment as the said justice or justices shall in his or their discretion think fit, not extending to life or limb; and for the second offence, suffer death: but in case any such slave shall grievously wound, maim, or bruise any white person, though it shall be only the first offence, such slave shall suffer death. . . .

9. Punishment of free persons of color for inveigling slaves.—If any free person of color commits the offence of inveigling or enticing away any slave or slaves, for the purpose of, and with the intention to aid and assist such slave or slaves leaving the service of his or their owner owners, or in going to another state, such person so offending shall, for each and every such offence, on conviction, be confined in the penitentiary at hard labor for one.

10. Punishment for circulating incendiary documents.—If any slave, Negro, mustizoe [sic, a person of mixed racial or ethnic ancestry], or free person of color, or any other person, shall circulate, bring, or cause to be circulated or brought into this state, or aid or assist in any manner, or be instrumental in aiding or assisting in the circulation or bringing into this state, or in any manner concerned in any written or printed pamphlet, paper, or circular, for the purpose of exciting to insurrection, conspiracy, or resistance among the slaves, Negroes, or free persons of color of this state, against their owners or the citizens of this state, the said person or persons offending against this section of this act, shall be punished with death.

Source: William A. Hotchkiss, ed., *Codification of the Statute Law of Georgia*, 2nd ed. (Augusta, GA: Charles E. Grenville, 1848). Reprinted on https://racism.org/articles/citizenship-rights/slavery-to-reparations/slavery–2/118-laws-related-to-slavery/454-slavelaw (consulted February 10, 2020).

SEC. II. MINOR OFFENCES.

11. Punishment for teaching slaves or free persons of color to read.—If any slave, Negro, or free person of color, or any white person, shall teach any other slave, Negro, or free person of color, to read or write either written or printed characters, the said free person of color or slave shall be punished by fine and whipping, or fine or whipping, at the discretion of the court. . . .

16. Persons of color not allowed to preach or exhort without written license.—No person of color, whether free or slave, shall be allowed to preach to, exhort, or join in any religious exercise with any persons of color, either free or slave, there being more than seven persons of color present. They shall first obtain a written certificate from three ordained ministers of the gospel of their own order. . . .

17. Punishment for preaching or exhorting without license.—Any free person of color offending against this provision, to be liable on conviction, for the first offence, to imprisonment at the discretion of the court, and to a penalty not exceeding five hundred dollars, to be levied on the property of the person of color; if this is insufficient, he shall be sentenced to be whipped and imprisoned at the discretion of the court: Provided, such imprisonment shall not exceed six months, and no whipping shall exceed thirty-nine lashes. . . .

QUESTIONS

- What do you think Georgia's slave owners most feared?
- Why do you think they wanted to put these strictures into law? How did that strengthen the slave-owning system in Georgia?

7.5 A TREATY PROPOSED BY SLAVES (1790)

This "treaty" was proposed to Portuguese landowner Manoel da Silva Ferreira, whose plantation was near Bahia, Brazil, by his slaves "during the time they remained in revolt," around 1790. It suggests their wide range of tasks and demonstrates the high degree of independence, both personal and in terms of production, held by enslaved people. Designating the actions of these enslaved persons as a "revolt" also suggests some of the paranoia of slave owners and their desire to dominate.

My Lord, we want peace and we do not want war; if my Lord also wants our peace it must be in this manner, if he wishes to agree to that which we want.

In each week you must give us the days of Friday and Saturday to work for ourselves not subtracting any of these because they are Saint's days.

To enable us to live you must give us casting nets and canoes. . . .

Make a large boat so that when it goes to Bahia we can place our cargoes aboard and not pay freightage. . . .

The daily quota of sugarcane must be of five hands rather than six and of ten canes in each bundle. . . .

The present overseers we do not want, choose others with our approval. . . .

At each cauldron there must be one who tends the fire and in each series of kettles the same, and on Saturday there must be without fail work stoppage at the mill. . . .

We will go to work the cane field of Jabirú this time and then it must remain as pasture because we cannot cut cane in a swamp.

We shall be able to plant our rice wherever we wish, and in any marsh, without asking permission for this, and each person can cut jacaranda or any other wood without having to account for this.

Accepting all the above articles and allowing us to remain always in possession of the hardware, we are ready to serve you as before because we do not wish to continue the bad customs of the other *engenhos* [sugar mill and plantation].

We shall be able to play, relax and sing any time we wish without your hinderance nor will permission be needed.

QUESTIONS

- What strategies did the enslaved people use in an attempt to persuade?
- Do you think this "treaty" was likely to be accepted? Why or why not?

Quoted in Stanley Engerman, Seymour Drescher, and Robert Paquette, eds., *Slavery* (New York: Oxford University Press, 2001), 323–24.

7.6 BIOGRAPHY OF A RUNAWAY SLAVE (1964)

Esteban Montejo (1860–1973) was a Cuban enslaved person who escaped the plantation. He lived alone in the mountains in the years leading up to the Spanish–American War. This text was recorded by anthropologist Miguel Barnet (b. 1940), who published it in 1964. It suggests the pronatalist policies of slave owners and the comparison to stock raising.

At all the plantations there was an infirmary near the barracoons [barracks]. It was a large wooden house where they took the pregnant women. Children were born there and stayed there until they were six or seven years old, when they went to live in the barracoons to work like everyone else. . . . Sometimes the little *criollitos* wouldn't see their parents again because the master was the owner, and he could send them to another plantation. Then the nannies certainly would have to do everything. But who was going to worry about a child that wasn't even her own! In that same infirmary they stripped and bathed the children. The breed stock children cost some five hundred pesos.

The thing about the breed stock children was that they were born of strong, tall blacks. Tall blacks were privileged. The masters kept an eye out for them to mate with big healthy black women.

After they were together in a separate room in the barracoon, they were obliged to have sex, and the women had to bear good babies every year. I tell you it was like breeding animals. Well, if the woman didn't bear the way they liked, they separated them and put her out in the field again to work. The women who weren't like little rabbits were sunk because they had to go back to breaking their backs. Then they could choose a husband at will.

QUESTIONS

- Why do you think that slave owners sought to separate children from their parents?
- How does this document inform your sense of "agency" in communities of enslaved persons?

Source: Miguel Barnet, *Biography of a Runaway Slave* (1964), reprinted in *The Cuba Reader: History, Culture, Politics,* ed. Aviva Chomsky, Barry Carr, and Pamela Maria Smorkaloff (Durham, NC: Duke University Press, 2003), 63.

7.7 ELIZABETH HEYRICK, BOYCOTT SUGAR TO FREE THE SLAVES (1824)

Englishwoman Elizabeth Heyrick (1789–1831) was a militant abolitionist whose strong Christian beliefs combined with practical economics to bring slavery back into the forefront of public opinion after the abolition of the slave trade in 1807. Women made most of the household buying decisions and, in their hands, a boycott of plantation sugar by more than 300,000 households was an important weapon in building solidarity and undermining the economic argument in favor of continued slavery. Women were a vital part of the anti-slavery movement; their success encouraged them to push for other reforms.

The West Indian planter and the people of this country, stand in the same moral relation to each other, as the thief and the receiver of stolen goods. The planter refuses to set his wretched captive at liberty,—treats him as a beast of burden,—compels his reluctant unremunerated labor under the lash of the cart whip,—why?—because WE furnish the stimulant to all this injustice, rapacity, and cruelty,—by PURCHASING ITS PRODUCE. . . .

Is there nothing to be done, as well as said? Are there no tests to prove our sincerity,—no sacrifices to be offered in confirmation of our zeal?—Yes, there is one,— (but it is in itself so small and insignificant that it seems almost burlesque to dignify it with the name of sacrifice)—it is abstinence FROM THE USE OF WEST INDIAN PRODUCTIONS, sugar, especially, in the cultivation of which slave labor is chiefly occupied. Small, however, and insignificant as the sacrifice may appear,—it would, at once, give the death blow to West Indian slavery. When there was no longer a market for the productions of slave labor, then, and not till then, will the slaves be emancipated. . . .

We have no right, on any pretext of expediency or pretended humanity, to say—"because you have been made a slave, and thereby degraded and debased,—therefore, I will continue to hold you in bondage until you have acquired a capacity to make a right use of your liberty." As well might you say to a poor wretch, gasping and languishing in a pest house, "here will I keep you, till I have given you a capacity for the enjoyment of pure air." . . .

It had been well, for the poor oppressed African, had the asserters of his rights entered the lists against his oppressors, with more of the spirit of Christian combatants, and less of worldly politicians;—had they remembered, through the whole of the struggle, that it was a conflict of sacred duty, against sordid interests,—of right against might;—that it was, in fact, an holy war. . . .

Will the inhabitants of this benevolent, this Christian country, now want a stimulant to rouse their best exertions,—to nerve their resolutions against all participation with these human blood-hounds? Will the British public now want a "spirit stirring" incentive to

Source: Elizabeth Heyrick, *Immediate Not Gradual Abolition; or, An Inquiry into the Shortest, Safest, and Most Effectual Means of Getting Rid of West Indian Slavery* (London: Knight & Bagster, 1824), 4–5, 8, 18, 22.

prohibit, and to interdict,—henceforth, and forever,—the merchandize of slavery? Let the produce of slave labor,—henceforth, and forever,—be regarded as "the accursed thing," and refused admission into our houses;—or let us renounce our Christian profession, and disgrace it no longer, by a selfish, cold-hearted indifference which, under such circumstances, would be reproachful to savages.

QUESTIONS

- What strategies did Heyrick use to try to convince her audience of the need for a boycott?
- Was this essay successful in its use of rhetoric? Why or why not?

7.8 KING OSEI BONSU OF ASHANTI DEFENDS THE SLAVE TRADE (1820)

Osei Bonsu (r. 1804–1824) ruled Ashanti in West Africa when that state came to dominate the Gold Coast. He was frustrated by the unilateral British decision to stop trading in enslaved people and questioned the British justification that they were humanitarians on the basis of the need to distance war captives from his country to avoid uprisings. Osei Bonsu also wondered how the British could expect him to purchase their goods if they would not exchange them for enslaved persons.

"Now," said the king, after a pause, "I have another palaver, and you must help me to talk it. A long time ago the great king liked plenty of trade, more than now; then many ships came, and they bought ivory, gold, and slaves; but now he will not let the ships come as before, and the people buy gold and ivory only. This is what I have in my head, so now tell me truly, like a friend, why does the king do so?" . . . The king did not deem it plausible, that this obnoxious traffic should have been abolished from motives of humanity alone; neither would he admit that it lessened the number either of domestic or foreign wars.

Taking up one of my observations, he remarked, "the white men who go to council with your master, and pray to the great God for him, do not understand my country, or they would not say the slave trade was bad. But if they think it bad now, why did they think it good before? Is not your law an old law, the same as the Crammo [Muslim] law? Do you not both serve the same God, only you have different fashions and customs? Crammos are strong people in fetische [fetish], and they say the law is good, because the great God made the book; so they buy slaves, and teach them good things, which they knew not before. This makes everybody love the Crammos, and they go everywhere up and down, and the people give them food when they want it. . . . If the great king would like to restore this trade, it would be good for the white men and for me too, because Ashantee is a country for war, and the people are strong; so if you talk that palaver for me properly, in the white country, if you go there, I will give you plenty of gold, and I will make you richer than all the white men."

I urged the impossibility of the king's request, promising, however, to record his sentiments faithfully. "Well then," said the king, "you must put down in my master's book all I shall say, and then he will look to it, now he is my friend. And when he sees what is true, he will surely restore that trade. I cannot make war to catch slaves in the bush, like a thief. My ancestors never did so. But if I fight a king, and kill him when he is insolent, then certainly I must have his gold, and his slaves, and the people are mine too. Do not the white kings act like this? Because I hear the old men say, that before I conquered Fantee and killed the Braffoes and the kings, that white men came in great ships, and fought and killed many people; and then they took the gold and slaves to the white country: and sometimes they fought together. That is all the same as these black countries. The great God and the fetische made war for strong men everywhere, because then they can pay plenty of gold and

Source: Joseph Dupuis, *Journal of a residence in Ashantee* (London: Henry Colburn, 1824), 162–64.

proper sacrifice. When I fought Gaman, I did not make war for slaves, but because Dinkera [the king] sent me an arrogant message and killed my people, and refused to pay me gold as his father did. Then my fetische made me strong like my ancestors, and I killed Dinkera, and took his gold, and brought more than 20,000 slaves to Coomassy. Some of these people being bad men, I washed my stool in their blood for the fetische. But then some were good people, and these I sold or gave to my captains: many, moreover, died, because this country does not grow too much corn like Sarem, and what can I do? Unless I kill or sell them, they will grow strong and kill my people. Now you must tell my master that these slaves can work for him, and if he wants 10,000 he can have them. And if he wants fine handsome girls and women to give his captains, I can send him great numbers."

QUESTIONS

- What was Bonsu's commercial argument?
- Does this document change how you think about the African slave trade? Why or why not?

8

JOCKEYING FOR POSITION
Political Change, 1650–1775

8.1 TREATY OF KARLOWITZ (1699)

This Treaty ended a war between the Holy Roman Empire, the Venetian Republic, the Polish–Lithuanian Commonwealth, and the Russian Empire against the Ottoman Turkish Empire that began in 1683. The King of England and the leaders of the Dutch Republic mediated the agreement, which points to the growing importance of these prominent trading nations in international affairs. Separate documents were signed between the Turks and the Holy Roman Empire, Venice, and Poland. Russia fought on for another year to secure more territory in the Crimea. The excerpt below is adapted from the agreement between the Ottomans and the Poles. In addition to the territorial changes referred to in Chapter 8, the Treaty's articles call attention to the devastation caused by a generation of war, the enforced captivity of prisoners, and the steps needed to recover them, as well as to the (temporary) position of Poland as the protector of Roman Catholicism in Ottoman lands.

The Treaty between Augustus II. *King, and the Republic of* Poland *on one part, and* Mustapha Han *Sultan of the* Turks *on the other, by the Mediation of* William III. *King of* Great Britain, *and of the Lords the States General of the* United Netherlands *on the other, Concluded in a Tent at* Karlowitz, *in the County of* Szerem, *the 26th of* January 1699.

. . . [O]ut of a desire to stop the Effusion of human Blood, and to restore the Tranquility on both sides, which has been so long disturbed by a difference between the Kingdom of *Poland* and the Sublime Empire. . . a Peace was happily concluded on Terms of mutual obligation . . . by mutual Consent to be religiously observed forever between both Dominions. . . .

IV . . . the Viziers, Beglerbeys, and the Ham of Crimea Tartary, with the other Sultans, and the Weywood of Moldavia [terms for subordinate rulers or officials in the various areas] shall be expressly commanded by Royal Edicts, to be very diligent in observing and keeping Peace and Tranquility on the Frontiers, and that they do not injure the Subjects of Poland by carrying off their People, driving away their Cattle, or by hurting or molesting them in any other way. . . .

VII. The Roman Catholic Monks shall have their Churches, and the Exercise of their accustomed Functions throughout the Empire, without Molestation or Disturbance, according to the Edicts formerly granted them by the Sublime Empire and it shall be lawful for the Ambassador Extraordinary of Poland at the Resplendent Porte, to make any further Remonstrances as the head of Religion to the Imperial Throne.

VIII. Whereas Peace gives Life and Soul to Commerce, which, when regulated, reduces Provinces to a better State, the Merchants of both Dominions, who hereafter come and go, not through clandestine

Adapted from Samuel Whatley, ed., *A General Collection of Treatys of Peace and Commerce, Manifestos, Declarations of War, and other Publick Papers, from the End of the Reign of Queen Anne to the Year 1731*, Vol. IV (London: J. J. and P. Knapton et al., 1732), 290–322, reprinted on National University of Singapore, "Empire in Asia: A New Global History," http://www.fas.nus.edu.sg/hist/eia/documents_archive/karlowitz.php (consulted May 23, 2018).

Places but by Places of public Access, after they have paid the antient Duties for Goods imported and exported, shall not be molested with new Exactions and Demands. . . .

IX. The Prisoners and Captives taken by either side during the War shall be set at Liberty, paying their Ransom, which shall be settled according to the Laws, or according to the Oath that shall be made of it. . . .

QUESTIONS

- What were the signatories most concerned with?
- What issues can you foresee in the future enforcement of this treaty?

8.2 WILLIAM BOSMAN, THE MILITARY REVOLUTION AND ITS LIMITS IN WEST AFRICA (1700)

When he arrived in West Africa in 1688, William Bosman served as a trader's apprentice with the Dutch West India Company. He eventually rose to become the chief factor (head merchant) for the Company at Elmina, where more enslaved people embarked for the western hemisphere than from any other place. By September 1700, he had begun to write a series of 22 letters to a friend back in Holland that provide tremendous insight into this key site of cultural, political, and economic interaction between Africans and Europeans. In vain, he pointed out the potential dangers of European commercial practices.

Depicts it as a Description of their Military Arms:

The chief of these are Muskets or Carbines in the management of which they are wonderful dextrous. It is not unpleasant to see them exercise their Army; they handle their Arms so cleverly, discharging them [in] several ways, one sitting, the second creeping or lying, &c, that it is really to be admired [that] they never hurt one another.

Perhaps you wonder how the Negroes come to be furnished with Fire-arms, but you will have no reason when you know we sell them incredible quantities thereby obliging them with a Knife to cut our own Throats. But we are forced to it; for [if] we would not, there might be sufficient flow with that Commodity by the English, Danes, and Brandenburghers [Prussia]. And could we all agree together not to sell them any, the English and Zeelander [from another part of the Netherlands] interlopers would abundantly furnish them. And since that [firearms] and Gunpowder for some time have been the chief vendible [able to be sold] Merchandise here, we should have found but an indifferent Trade without our share in it.

It is indeed to be wished that these dangerous Commodities had never been brought here, or at least that the Negroes might be in a short time brought to be content with something else in their room [realm], but this in all appearance is never likely.

. . . I should tell you that some of them also are possessed of a few cannon . . . but they use them in a very slovenly manner. The King of Saboe [a region on the southern coast of West Africa] has a very small number, with which he has been in the field, but he never made use of them. Some of them, after once firing them, have suffered the Enemy to take them, as happened to the Comantyn [a coastal area to the west of Elmina]; after which those who took them were ignorant of the use of them, so that these Monarch's Cannons only serve by way of a Compliment and a Salutation of which the Blacks are very fond. . . .

Kings are obliged in this Country to preserve their Power by dint of force; wherefore the richer they are in Gold and Slaves, the more they are honored and esteemed; and without those they have not the least command over their Subjects, but, on the contrary,

Adapted from: William Bosman, *A New and Accurate Description of the Coast of Guinea*, trans. (London: J. Knapton, A Fell, R. Smith, D. Midwinter, W. Haws, W. Davis, Q. Straban, B. Lintolt, J. Round, V. & J. Walt, 1705), 184–85, 187–88, 191.

would not only be obliged to pray but pay their Underlings to execute their Commands. . . .

A King here is always very ready to be hired to the Assistance of any of his Neighbors in their Wars, because the greatest part of the Money agreed for falls to his share. After the receipt of which he is not much concerned whether the promised assistance be punctually ready at the appointed time or not. If he has received the Gold, it is enough. He always knows how to satisfy his Customers with one lie or another, in which they are so subtle that they will, unobserved, defraud even those who are very well upon their guard.

Though this is an advantageous sort of Trade, they are yet more fond of being Mediators between disagreeing Nations, for on this account they get Money from both Parties, and keep the Breach open as long as [they] possibly can, in order to get the most Money from each. It is upon these incomes that they chiefly subsist, for their Revenue is very inconsiderable. It is indeed true that they impose a Toll on all Goods passing through their Country, but the Collectors being always some of the Principal Men amongst them, make sure of the largest share of it, and collect so well for themselves that the King has very little of it.

QUESTIONS

- What were the "potential dangers" Bosman outlines?
- What might be the future effects of the king's actions he describes?

8.3 "TO LIVE AS THEY HAD": PEDRO NARANJO EXPLAINS THE PUEBLO REVOLT (1680)

The Spanish settled present-day New Mexico at the very end of the sixteenth century. Franciscan missionaries destroyed Indigenous religious images and objects, while and imposing Roman Catholicism. At the same time, the Spanish tried to turn the Native American population into European-style peasants who owed their overlords mandatory labor service. The Spanish also established control over scarce water resources. For three generations, the Indigenous population, who lived in villages of adobe homes, called pueblos, often located on hilltops or in remote valleys, slowly acclimated to these demands . . . or seemed to.

The Pueblo Revolt in 1680 was instigated by Popé, a resident of the Taos pueblo. As the document below shows, he was motivated by the desire to restore previous patterns of worship, which he claimed would lead to great prosperity. Eighty-year-old Pedro Naranjo from the Keresan pueblo was captured by the Spanish. He spoke "the Castilian language," though an interpreter was still used. Naranjo took "the oath in due legal form in the name of God, our Lord, and a sign of the cross." The use of the terms "devil" and "sorcerer" in the text remind us of the importance of the interpreter's worldview in trying to understand the views and values of a different culture.

"Declaration of Pedro Naranjo" [December 19, 1681]

Asked whether he knows the reason or motives which the Indians of this kingdom had for rebelling, forsaking the law of God and obedience to his Majesty, and committing such grave and atrocious crimes, and who were the leaders and principal movers, and by whom and how it was ordered; and why they burned the images, temples, crosses, rosaries, and things of divine worship, committing such atrocities as killing priests, Spaniards, women, and children. . . . [T]hey have planned to rebel on various occasions through conspiracies of the Indian sorcerers, and that although in some pueblos the messages were accepted, in other parts they would not agree to it. . . . . The pact which they had been forming ceased for the time being, but they always kept in their hearts the desire to carry it out, so as to live as they are living today.

Finally, in the past years, at the summons of an Indian named Popé who is said to have communication with the devil, it happened that in an estufa [meeting room] of the pueblo of Los Taos there appeared to the said Popé three figures of Indians who never came out of the estufa. They gave the said Popé to understand that they were going underground to the lake of Copala. He saw these figures emit fire from all the extremities of their bodies, and that one of them was called Caudi, another Tilini, and the other Tleume; and these three beings spoke to the said Popé, who was in hiding from the secretary, Francisco Xavier, who wished to punish him as a sorcerer. They told him to

Source: Adapted from Charles Wilson Hackett, *Revolt of the Pueblo Indians of New Mexico and Otermin's Attempted Reconquest, 1680–1682*, 2 vols. (Albuquerque: University of New Mexico Press, 1942), II: 245–49.

make a cord of maguey fiber and tie some knots in it which would signify the number of days that they must wait before the rebellion. He said that the cord was passed through all the pueblos of the kingdom so that the ones which agreed to it [the rebellion] might untie one knot in sign of obedience, and by the other knots they would know the days which were lacking; and this was to be done on pain of death to those who refused to agree to it. As a sign of agreement and notice of having concurred in the treason and perfidy they were to send up smoke signals to that effect in each one of the pueblos singly. The said cord was taken from pueblo to pueblo by the swiftest youths under the penalty of death if they revealed the secret.

. . . [T]wo days before the time set for its execution, because his lordship had learned of it and had imprisoned two Indian accomplices from the pueblo of Tesuque, it was carried out prematurely that night, because it seemed to them that they were now discovered; and they killed religious, Spaniards, women, and children. . . . Later this declarant saw that as soon as the Spaniards had left the kingdom an order came from the said Indian, Popé, in which he commanded all the Indians to break the lands and enlarge their cultivated fields, saying that now they were as they had been in ancient times, free from the labor they had performed for the religious and the Spaniards, who could not now be alive. He said that this is the legitimate cause and the reason they had for rebelling, because they had always desired to live as they had. . . .

Asked for what reason they so blindly burned the images, temples, crosses, and other things of divine worship, he stated that the said Indian, Popé, came down in person, and with him El Saca and El Chato from the pueblo of Los Taos, and other captains and leaders and many people who were in his train, and he ordered in all the pueblos through which he passed that they instantly break up and burn the images of the holy Christ, the Virgin Mary and the other saints, the crosses, and everything pertaining to Christianity, and that they burn the temples, break up the bells, and separate from the wives whom God had given them in marriage and take those whom they desired. In order to take away their baptismal

names, the water, and the holy oils, they were to plunge into the rivers and wash themselves with amole, which is a root native to the country, washing even their clothing, with the understanding that there would thus be taken from them the character of the holy sacraments. They did this, and also many other things which he does not recall, given to understand that this mandate had come from the Caydi and the other two who emitted fire from their extremities in the said estufa of Taos . . . because the God of the Spaniards was worth nothing and theirs was very strong, the Spaniard's God being rotten wood. . . . [H]e said likewise that the devil had given them to understand that living thus in accordance with the law of their ancestors, they would harvest a great deal of maize, many beans, a great abundance of cotton, calabashes, and very large watermelons and cantaloupes; and that they could erect their houses and enjoy abundant health and leisure. As he has said, the people were very much pleased, living at their ease in this life of their antiquity, which was the chief cause of their falling into such laxity. Following what has already been stated, in order to terrorize them further and cause them to observe the diabolical commands, there came to them a pronouncement from the three demons already described, and from El Popé, to the effect that he who might still keep in his heart a regard for the priests, the governor, and the Spaniards would be known from his unclean face and clothes, and would be punished. . . .

Asked what arrangements and plans they had made for the contingency of the Spaniards' return, he said that what he knows concerning the question is that they were always saying they would have to fight to the death, for they do not wish to live in any other way than they are living at present. . . . [H]e said that he has nothing more to say except that they should be always on the alert, because the said Indians were continually planning to follow the Spaniards and fight with them by night, in order to drive off the horses and catch them afoot, although they might have to follow them for many leagues. What he has said is the truth, and what happened, on the word of a Christian who confesses his guilt.

QUESTIONS

- Why do you think Popé's message was so effective?
- What message did Naranjo convey to his reader about the revolt?

8.4 PEACE TREATY—THE KING OF SPAIN AND THE SULTAN OF JOLO (1737)

This proposed treaty was ratified by King Philip V on June 9, 1742. This agreement applies equally to both parties: the Spanish colonial government in the Philippines was concerned deeply about raids by the Moros of Jolo and the return of captives and images looted from churches. The intervention of other Europeans was a factor in the diplomacy between these two states. The treaty provided for free trade, but that trade could only be carried on by a licensed merchant—illicit (or untaxed) trade was ruled out. The Spanish were also worried that the sultan would renege on the agreement. They recognized their own inability to do much about Jolo's changeable political position. Although Spain claimed the territory controlled by the Sultan of Jolo, this treaty demonstrates that the power relationships between colonial states and Indigenous peoples did not always favor Europeans.

Articles of peace proposed by the governor-general of the Philippines to the ambassadors representing Sultan Mujammad, King of Jolo.

1. The sultan, together with all his principal datos [officials] and vassals, and for the said ambassadors, must swear, in the form used by them, an unalterable peace and a firm and friendly faith to the Spaniards and natives of all the islands now subject, or which at any time hereafter may become subject to the Crown of Spain; and this Government for its part swears what is necessary that, through this means, the vassals of both kingdoms may hereafter enjoy a much-desired peace in consequence of the present treaty, which must be perpetual. This treaty cannot be broken on any pretext whatsoever so long as the party offended does not charge the other with the offense, informing the offender at the same time of the reasons for terminating the friendly relations; and both parties will, before commencing hostilities, be heard on the cause or complaint, which might prove ill-founded. The party that does not carry out the foregoing condition may be held to act in bad faith.

2. Those who are or may be hereafter the enemies of the Spanish nation must be considered by the Joloanos as their enemies, and vice-versa, so that both powers will make war together against whomsoever may be declared the enemy of either; but not against European nations, such as Hollanders, French, English, and others, since this Government has not power to declare war with them, but should any of said powers attempt extortionate demands on Joloanos or Spaniards, the parties not involved in the question will be obliged to continue neutral, nor will they under any pretext assist by furnishing men, arms, supplies, or other articles of war to the enemy of either of the contracting powers. The present articles of agreement to continue in full force and vigor with

Reprinted in *Hearings Before the Committee on the Philippines of the United States Senate (April 10, 1902)* 57th Congress, 1st Session, Part 3, Senate, Doc. No. 331 (Washington, DC: Government Printing Office, 1902), 2130–31.

regard to enemies other than those here mentioned.

3. Commerce is to be carried on free of duties between both Kingdoms by the subjects thereof, provided that said subjects that trade with said nations carried a stamped license signed by the Superior Government for its security, and vassals of the Sultan that go to Manila, or wish to go to any of the provinces of these islands to visit or trade, should also carry a license.

4. Should the vassals of one of the two contracting nations commence hostilities against the vassals of the other in time of peace, either on sea or land, the Sultan, as also this Government, shall be obliged, after the matter has been investigated, to indemnify the power offended, and severely chastise those who committed the offense.

5. Persons captured during war shall be returned by both parties, this being the main point on which the friendly relations and peace of both Kingdoms rest, and stability depends almost entirely on the observance of this article. If the Sultan restores in due time the church ornaments and furniture that have been in his Kingdom since past wars, he will prove his desire to bring about the reconciliation of which he speaks in his letters, and to which this Government has corresponded.

Acceptance and oath.

Manila, chamber of the royal palace, February 1, 1737.

Present, the governor-general of the Philippine Islands.

(Fernandez Valdes Tamon) and ambassadors of King of Jolo (6 in number).

Object of meeting: To solemnize articles of peace which were agreed to on the 22nd of last February, in the name of the King, princes, datos, and vassals of the said Kingdom of Jolo.

It was further agreed that the Sultan of Jolo should make a treaty of peace with the Sultan of Tamontaca, our friend, and establish peace, and be on friendly terms with other princes that may in the future join our Catholic arms. And, concerning the return of captives now in the Kingdom of Jolo, this city (esta ciudad) and other ports of the islands must, within four months, know and comply with what has been agreed to concerning said captives. . . .

QUESTIONS

- Do you think either party received an advantage in this treaty?
- Do you think this treaty could be enforced easily? Why or why not?

8.5 TREATY OF NERCHINSK (1689)

The Treaty of Nerchinsk was negotiated largely by Jesuits who acted as the agents of the Kangxi Emperor of China. The document was written in Latin. With only a few minor adjustments, this Treaty fixed the border between Russia and China until 1860. The Treaty of Nerchinsk marked a rare occasion where Russia gave up territory it had occupied. This was also the first time that China accepted the idea that another state could be their diplomatic equal—in other words they did not insist that their claim to control "all things under heaven" be acknowledged formally. The emphasis on raiders and on indicating the treaty line with stone markers also shows the fluidity of this border.

Treaty of Nerchinsk
Signed by Russia and China, 27 August 1689

1. The boundary between Russia and China is to be formed by the river Kerbechi, near the Shorna, which enters the Amur, and the long chain of mountains extending from its sources to the Eastern Ocean. The rivers or rivulets which flow from the southern slope of these mountains, as well as all territories to the south of them, will thus belong to China. The territories and rivers to the north of the said mountain chain remain with the Empire of Muscovy. The boundary is further to be found by the river Argun, which enters the Amur; the territories south of the said river belong to the Emperor of China, those to the north of it to the Empire of Muscovy. The towns or dwelling-houses at present situated to the south of the Argun shall be moved to the northern bank of the river.

2. The fortress built by the Russians at a place called Atbazeir shall be demolished, and the subjects of the Tsar residing there shall remove with their property to Muscovite territory. Hunters of either empire shall on no pretense cross the frontiers. If one or two persons cross the frontier to hunt, steal, or pilfer, they shall be arrested and given up to the nearest Imperial officers to be punished according to their deserts. In case, however, armed parties of ten or fifteen people cross the frontiers to hunt or plunder, or in case of any person being killed, a report shall be sent in to both emperors, and the parties found guilty shall be punished with death. On no account shall war be declared in consequence of any excess committed by private parties.

3. Everything which has occurred hitherto is to be buried in eternal oblivion.

4. Neither party shall receive fugitives or deserters from the date of this treaty. Subjects of either empire flying to the other shall be arrested and given up to the nearest authority on the frontier.

5. Subjects of Muscovy now in China, or Chinese now in the Empire of Muscovy, may remain where they are.

6. In consideration of this present treaty of peace and the reciprocal good understanding of the two empires, persons may pass from one empire to the other, provided they are furnished with passports, and they shall he permitted to carry on commerce and to sell or purchase at pleasure.

Source: Reprinted in Alexis Krause, *Russia in Asia: A Record and a Study, 1558–1899* (New York: Henry Holt, 1899), 330–31.

Copies of the above treaty, properly signed and sealed, shall be exchanged by the plenipotentiaries. The various articles of the treaty shall be engraved on stones in Tartaric, Chinese, Russian, and Latin, to be erected on the frontiers between the two empires as a permanent testimony to the good understanding between them.

QUESTIONS

- Why would each side agree to this Treaty? What do they gain?
- Do you think this Treaty could be enforced easily? Why or why not?

8.6 FREDERICK II, *POLITICAL TESTAMENT* (1752)

Intended solely for his heir, this first version of King Frederick II's *Political Testament* dates from 1752. It was revised in 1768, but only published in the twentieth century. Frederick II suggests how difficult it can be to forge a new polity from diverse parts as well as how to organize an effective and efficient government. His account also highlights some of the differences between Prussia and other absolutist states like France.

ON CERTAIN MAXIMS OF POLICY RELATING TO THE NOBILITY

An object of policy of the sovereign of this State is to preserve his noble class; for whatever change may come about, he might perhaps have one which was richer, but never one more valorous and more loyal. To enable them to maintain themselves in their possessions, it is necessary to prevent non-nobles from acquiring noble estates and to compel them to put their money into commerce, so that if some gentleman is forced to sell his lands, he may find only gentlemen to buy them.

It is also necessary to prevent noblemen from taking service abroad, to inspire them with an *esprit de corps* and a national spirit: this is what I have worked for, and why, in the course of the first war, I did everything possible to spread the name of "Prussian," in order to teach the officers that, whatever province they came from, they were all counted as Prussians, and that for that reason all the provinces, however separated from one another, form a united body.

It is right that a nobleman should prefer to devote his services to his own country, rather than to any other Power whatever. For this reason, severe edicts have been published against nobles who take service elsewhere without having obtained permission. But since many gentlemen prefer an idle and degraded life to service under arms, it is necessary to draw distinctions and to give preference to those who serve, to the exclusion of those who do not serve, and from time to time to collect together the young gentlemen, in Pomerania, in Prussia, and in Upper Silesia, to put them into cadet schools, and after, to post them to units. . . .

THAT A SOVEREIGN SHOULD CARRY ON THE GOVERNMENT HIMSELF

In a State such as this it is necessary for the sovereign to conduct his business himself, because he will, if he is wise, pursue only the public interest, which is his own, while a Minister's view is always slanted on matters that affect his own interests, so that instead of promoting deserving persons he will fill the places with his own creatures, and will try to strengthen his own position by the number of persons whom he makes dependent on his fortunes; whereas the sovereign will support the nobility, confine the clergy within due

Political Testament of Frederick II (1752), reprinted on German History in Documents and Images, vol. 2, "From Absolutism to Napoleon, 1648–1815," http://ghdi.ghi-dc.org/sub_document.cfm?document_id=3548 (consulted June 18, 2018).

limits, not allow the Princes of the blood to indulge in intrigues and cabals, and will reward merit without those considerations of interest which Ministers secretly entertain in all their doings.

But if it is necessary for the Prince to conduct the internal administration of his State himself, how much more necessary is it that he should direct his own [foreign] policy, conclude those alliances which suit his purposes, form his own plans, and take up his own line in delicate and difficult situations.

Finance, internal administration, policy and defense are so closely interlinked that it is impossible to deal with one of these branches while passing over the others. If that happens, the Prince is in difficulties. In France, the kingdom is governed by four Ministers: the Minister of Finance, who is called [the] *Contrôleur général* [Controller-General], and the Ministers of Marine, War, and Foreign Affairs. The four "kings" never harmonize or agree; hence all the contradictions which we see in the government of France: the one pulls down out of jealousy what the other has put up with skill; no system, no planning. Chance governs, and everything in France is done according to the pleasure of Court intrigues: the English know everything that is discussed in Versailles; no secrecy and, consequently, no policy.

A well-conducted government must have a system as coherent as a system of philosophy; all measures taken must be based on sound reasoning, and finance, policy, and military must collaborate toward one aim, the strengthening of the State and the increase of its power. But a system can be the product of only one brain; it must consequently be that of the sovereign's. Idleness, self-indulgence, or weakness are the causes which prevent a Prince from working on the noble task of creating the happiness of his peoples. Such sovereigns make themselves so contemptible that they become the butts and laughingstocks of their contemporaries, and in history books their names are useful only for the dates. They vegetate on thrones that they are unworthy to occupy, absorbed as they are in self-indulgence. A sovereign has not been raised to his high rank, the supreme power has not been conferred on him, to live softly, to grow fat on the substance of the people, to be happy while all others suffer. The sovereign is the first servant of the State. He is well-paid, so that he can support the dignity of his quality; but it is required of him that he shall work effectively for the good of the State and direct at least the chief affairs with attention. He needs, of course, help: he cannot enter into all details, but he should listen to all complaints and procure prompt justice for those threatened by oppression. A woman came to a King of Epirus with a petition; he snubbed her, telling her to leave him in peace. "And why are you King," she replied, "if not to procure justice for me?" A good saying, which Princes should always keep in mind.

QUESTIONS

- What, to Frederick II, were the most important aspects of a healthy political system?
- Do you agree that it is "necessary for the sovereign to conduct his business himself because he will, if he is wise, pursue only the public interest"? Why or why not?

8.7 MADAME DE SÉVIGNÉ, CONTROLLING THE NOBILITY (1671–1672)

Marie de Rabutin-Chantal became Marquise, or Madame de Sévigné, at her marriage (1626–1696). She was a famous letter-writer. This selection features two missives to her daughter, Françoise-Marguerite, the Countess de Grignon (1646–1705) that depict the "glories" of Louis XIV (r. 1643–1715) on the eve of and during a war against the Dutch (1672–1678). At the same time, de Sévigné reveals the financial control exercised by the King over the nobility, who were increasingly impoverished by the display needed to live at court. The second selection also makes clear that the desire for distinction prompted the nobility to lead from the front where they often died because of their valor.

[August 12, 1671] But listen to this example of the King's goodness and the pleasure of serving such a good master. He summoned the Field Marshal de Bellefonds to his private apartment and said, "Monsieur le Maréchal, I want to know why you wish to quit my service. Is it religion? Is it a desire to retire? Or is it the burden of your debts? If it is this last I want to straighten it out and go into the details of your affairs." The Field Marshal was very touched by this kindness. "Sire," he said, "it is my debts. I am ruined. I cannot watch the troubles of some of my friends who have helped me and whom I cannot satisfy." "Very well," said the King, "we must clear what is owing to them. I will give you 100,000 francs on your house at Versailles and a guarantee of 400,000 which will act as insurance in the event of your death. You will pay what is outstanding out of the 100,000, and that being so you can remain in my service." One would indeed have to be very hard-hearted not to obey a master who entered into his servants' interests with so much consideration. And the Field Marshal did not resist, so he is back in his place and has been showered with favors. All these details are true. . . .

[July 3, 1672] You must have had some very correct accounts that have shown you that the Ijssel was badly defended; the great miracle was to swim across it. Monsieur le Prince and his Argonauts were in a boat the squadron they attacked was asking for quarter when ill-fortune willed that M. de Longueville, who probably couldn't hear and was spurred on by furious ardor, leapon on to his horse that he had dragged after him and, wanting to be first, breached the barricade behind which they were entrenched and killed the first man who came to hand; but at the same moment he was run through five or six times. Monsieur le Duc followed him, Monsieur le Prince followed his son and all the others followed him. That is how the killing happened, which as you can see could have been avoided had they known these men's willingness to surrender. But everything is ordained by Providence. . . .

Adapted from Leonard Tancock, ed. and trans, *Madame de Sévigné: Selected Letters* (Hammondsworth: Penguin Books, 1982), 116–7, 146–7.

Don't forget to drop a little line to [Madame de] La Troche about her son's having distinguished himself and swum across the river—he was commended in the presence of the King as one of the bravest. It doesn't look as if any will defend themselves against such a victorious army. The French really are splendid. Nobody comes near them for acts of glory and courage, and there is no other river now that will act as a defense against their magnificent valor.

QUESTIONS

- How did Louis XIV "control" the nobility? Do you think such tactics were effective?
- What might be the future effects of such tactics?

9

MANUFACTURING A NEW WORLD ECONOMY, 1750–1914

9.1 CONDITIONS IN THE MINES (1842)

The British government responded to complaints about working conditions in the mines by appointing the Children's Employment Commission (Mines) headed by Lord Anthony Ashley-Cooper (1801–1885), seventh Earl of Shaftesbury. The Commission's *Report*, issued in 1842, led directly to the Mines and Collieries Act of 1842 that placed serious and enforceable limits on the employment of women and children in the mines of the United Kingdom. The quotations and references to the *Report* in this excerpt were published separately to address public opinion. They are not the most graphic or worst examples included in the more than 1,000 pages of testimony.

William Burnside, ten years old, coal bearer, same colliery [in Scotland]: "I gang with brother and sister; have done so for two months. I can fill one tub in the day; it takes me 17 journeys as my back gets sore. A tub holds near 5 cwt [560 pounds]. I follow sister with bits of coal strapped over my head and back. The works fatigues me muckle." (App. Pt. I, p. 447.)

Ellison Jack, a girl eleven years old, coal-bearer: "I have been working below three years on my father's account; he takes me down at two in the morning, and I come at one and two next afternoon. I go to bed at six at night to be ready for work next morning; the part of the pit I bear in the seams are much on the edge. I have to bear my burthen [*sic*] up four traps, or ladders, before I get to the main road which leads to the pit bottom. My task is four to five tubs; each tub holds 4¼ cwt. [476 pounds] I fill five tubs in 20 journeys. I have the strap when I did not do my bidding. Am very glad when my task is wrought, as it sore fatigues." (App. Pit. I, p. 446.) . . .

"George Foster has wrought a double shift of twenty-four hours three times in the Benton pit. About a year and a half ago he wrought three shifts at one time, going down at four o'clock one morning and staying thirty-six hours without coming up. . . . When lads say they stop double shift, they mean generally thirty-six hours. If, for instance, they are in the day shift, and are asked to stop for the night shift, then they stay their own shift for the next day;—their baits (meals) being sent down to them. *A great quantity of boys are doing this now*, from a scarcity of boys . . ."

Ephraim Riley, eleven years old: "Had three miles to walk to the pit; left home at five o'clock, winter and summer, and did not get home again until nine o'clock at night (16 hours); his legs and thighs hurt him so, with working so much, that he remains in bed on Sunday mornings." (App. Pt. II, p. 271.) . . .

John Greaves, collier: "Every boy has to clear away for two men, and if he do not do it they strap him. He dare not say much about it, for fear of their giving him more, and perhaps master turning him off. Most of the men wear a leather strap round them, which they can apply to the boys if need be." (App. Part I., p. 67.) . . .

Source: *The Condition and Treatment of the Children Employed in the Mines and Collieries of the United Kingdom: Carefully Compiled from the Appendix to the First Report of the Commissioners Appointed to Inquire into this Subject* (London: William Strange, 1842), 48, 55, 57–58, 60, 74, 80.

James Robinson, aged fourteen: "He worked at Hunt's Pitt, at Babbington, where he was so beaten that his father, on that account, took him away; the corporal there has kicked him when he was down down, pulled his ears and hair, and three coals at him; he dare not tell his masters then, or he believes the corporal would have killed him. His brothers, one ten, the other thirteen years old, now work at Hunt's, and are beaten until they can hardly get home, and dare not tell for fear of worse usage, and they and their father losing their work." (App. II, p. 308.) . . .

John Greaves, a collier, states: "The boys are not used so bad as they were; it is the butties' [miners] apprentices who are worst used. These lads are made to go where other men will not let their own children go. If they will not do it, they take them to the magistrates, who commit them to prison." (App. Pt. 1, p. 67.) . . .

Thomas Moorhouse, collier-boy at Halifax, says: "I don't know how old I am. Father is dead. I am a chance child. Mother is dead also; I don't know how long she has been dead; 'tis better na three years. I began to hurry when I was nine years old for William Greenwood. I was apprentices to him till I should be twenty-one; my mother apprenticed me. I lived with Greenwood; I don't know how long it was, but it was a goodish while. He was bound to find me in victuals and drink and clothes; I never had enough." (App. Pt. II, p. 118.) . . .

Margaret Harper, thirteen years old: "We hurry the carts on the railroads by pushing behind; I frequently draw with ropes and chains as the horses do; it is dirty, slavish work, and the water quite covers our ancles. I knock my head against the roofs, as they are not so high as I am, and they cause me to stoop, which makes my back ache." (App. Pt. I, p. 471.) . . .

Patience Kershaw says—"I wear a belt and chain at the workings to get the corves out. The getters are naked, except their caps; they pull off all their clothes. I see them at work when I go up. The boys take liberties with me sometimes; they pull me about. I am the only girl in the pit. There are 20 boys and 15 men. All the men are naked. I would rather work in the mill than in the coal pit." . . .

Sophia Lewis, twelve years old, labourer in the iron yard: "We have never been to any day-school: sister and I go to the Welsh Sunday-school, to learn the letters, (can scarcely tell one letter from the other in the Welsh primer.) Mr. Jones tell us that Jesus is our Lord, but does not know what he means by our Lord, nor who is God. There may be Commandments, but I never heard of any."

QUESTIONS

- Does this document shock you? Why or why not?
- Do you think the Report shocked the contemporary British public? Why or why not?

9.2 ANDREW URE, "THE PHILOSOPHY OF MANUFACTURES" (1835)

Andrew Ure (1778–1857) publicly rejected attempting to improve working conditions through legislative action, which had begun tentatively in 1833. A Scots medical doctor and chemist, he visited several model mills on behalf of industrial interests and proclaimed that reformers exaggerated the mistreatment of workers and that the government should therefore not intervene. He asserted that raising wages would lead to unemployment because entrepreneurs would not earn enough profit for them to maintain their enterprise. He also warned about "demagogues" who would mobilize "secret combinations" to resist the demands of factory owners, without considering whether children working 12-hour shifts would really behave in the way he described.

No master would wish to have any wayward children to work within the walls of his factory, who did not mind their business without beating, and he therefore usually fines or turns away any spinners who are known to maltreat their assistants. Hence, ill usage of any kind is a very rare occurrence. I have visited many factories, both in Manchester and in the surrounding districts, during a period of several months, entering the spinning rooms, unexpectedly, and often alone, at different times of the day, and I never saw a single instance of corporal chastisement inflicted on a child, nor indeed did I ever see children in ill-humour. They seemed to be always cheerful and alert, taking pleasure in the light play of their muscles,—enjoying the mobility natural to their age. The scene of industry, so far from exciting sad emotions in my mind, was always exhilarating. It was delightful to observe the nobleness with which they pieced the broken ends, as the mule carriage began to recede from the fixed roller-beam, and to see them at leisure, after a few seconds' exercise of their tiny fingers, to amuse themselves in any attitude they chose, till the stretch and winding-on were once more completed. The work of these lively elves seemed to resemble a sport, in which habit gave them a pleasing dexterity. . . . As to exhaustion by the day's work, they evinced no trace of it on emerging from the mill in the evening; for they immediately began to skip about any neighboring play-ground, and to commence their little amusements with the same alacrity as boys issuing from a school. It is moreover my firm conviction, that if children are not ill-used by bad parents or guardians, but receive in food and raiment the full benefit of what they earn, they would thrive better when employed in our modern factories, than if left at home in apartments too often ill-aired, damp, and cold.

QUESTIONS

- How did Ure portray child labor?
- Do these arguments seem similar to any modern economic arguments? Why or why not?

Source: Andrew Ure, *The Philosophy of Manufactures or an Exposition of the Scientific, Moral, and Commercial Economy of the Factory System of Great Britain* (London: Charles Knight, 1835), 300–01.

9.3 FRIEDRICH LIST, "THE NATIONAL SYSTEM OF POLITICAL ECONOMY" (1841–1844)

Friedrich List (1789–1846) was from Württemberg in the western German-speaking lands. A politician, journalist, professor, and entrepreneur, List's pointed critiques of the government ultimately forced him into exile in the United States. He was a leading advocate of the Zollverein, a German customs and commercial union that became the basis for industrialization. In this selection, he made clear that the ability of nations to defend themselves depended on their industrial power, and that free trade of the sort advocated by English economist Adam Smith benefited only those states that were already internationally competitive. To catch up, List stated, required a different, more statist approach to industrial development. List's ideas were influential among policymakers in many European and Asian states that sought to build industrial economies in the second half of the nineteenth century.

The productive powers of a nation are not only limited by the industry, thrift, morality, and intelligence of its individual members, and by its natural resources or material capital, but also by its social, political, and municipal laws and institutions, and especially the securities for the continued existence, independence, and power of the nationality. However industrious, thrifty, enterprising, moral, and intelligent the individuals may be, without national unity, national division of labor, and national co-operation of productive powers, the nation will never reach a high level of prosperity and power, or ensure to itself the lasting possession of its intellectual, social and material goods. . . .

At a time when technical and mechanical science exercise such immense influence on the methods of warfare, when all warlike operations depend so much on the condition of the national revenue, where successful defense depends on . . . whether it [the nation] can muster many or but few defenders of the country—at such times, more than ever before, must the value of manufactures be estimated from a political point of view. . . .

Adam Smith's doctrine . . . ignores the very nature of nationalities, [and] seems almost entirely to exclude politics and the power of the state, [it] presupposes the existence of a state of perpetual peace and of universal union. . . .

This system regards everything from the shopkeeper's point of view. The value of anything is wealth, according to it, so its sole object is to gain values. The establishment of powers of production, it leaves to chance, to nature, or to the providence of God (whichever you please), only the state must have nothing at all to do with it, nor must politics venture to meddle with the business of accumulating exchangeable values. It is resolved to buy wherever it can find the cheapest articles. . . .

We now see into what extraordinary mistakes and contradictions the [Smithite] school has fallen

Source: Friedrich List, "The National System of Political Economy (1841–1844)," in *The West in Global Context: From 1500 to the Present*, ed. George B. Kirsch, Frederick M. Schweitzer, Wolodymyr Stojko, and George L. Mahoney (Upper Saddle River, NJ: Prentice Hall, 1997), 137–42, 138–41.

in making material wealth or value of exchange the sole object of investigations. . . . As the individual chiefly obtains by means of the nation and in the nation mental culture, power of production, security, and prosperity, so is the civilization of the human race only conceivable and possible by means of the civilization and development of the individual nations.

QUESTIONS

- What was List's disagreement with Adam Smith?
- Do you think List's ideas would work? Why or why not?

9.4 JUAN BAUTISTA ALBERDI, PROPOSALS FOR THE ECONOMIC DEVELOPMENT OF ARGENTINA (1852)

Juan Bautista Alberdi (1810–1884) was an Argentine journalist and diplomat who sought to influence the creation of a new constitution and recognized that economic development was the best means of avoiding dictatorship in the future. This excerpt is from his *Bases and Points of Departure for the Political Organization of the Argentine Republic* (1852), in which he deliberately sought to imitate the United States. In it, he made a plea for mobilizing credit, building railroads, and enabling entrepreneurship by immigrants.

Our youth should be trained for industrial life, and therefore should be educated in the arts and sciences that would prepare them for industry. The South American type of man should be one formed for the conquest of the great and oppressive enemies of our progress: the desert, material backwardness; the brutal and primitive nature of this continent. . . .

Industry is the grand means of promoting morality. By furnishing men with the means of getting a living you keep them from crime, which is generally the fruit of misery and idleness. You will find it useless to fill the minds of youths with abstract notions about religion if you leave them idle and poor. . . .

The railroad offers the means of righting the topsy-turvy order that Spain established on this continent. She placed the heads of our states where the feet should be. For her ends of isolation and monopoly this was a wise system; for our aims of commercial expansion and freedom it is disastrous. . . . The railroad changes, reforms, and solves the most difficult problems without decrees or mob violence. . . .

Nor can you bring the interior of our lands within reach of Europe's immigrants, who today are regenerating our coasts, except with the powerful aid of the railroads. . . .

The means of securing railroads abound in these lands. Negotiate loans abroad, pledge your national revenues and properties for enterprises that will make them prosper and multiply. It would be childish to hope that ordinary revenues may suffice for such large expenditures; invert that order, begin with the expenditures, and you will have revenues. . . .

But you will not obtain loans if you do not have national credit—that is, a credit based on the united securities and obligations of all the towns of the state. With the credits of town councils and provinces you will not secure railroads or anything notable. . . . Dispersed and divided, expect nothing but poverty and scorn. . . .

Independent America is called upon to complete the work begun and left unfinished by the Spain of

---

Source: Juan Bautista Alberdi, "Proposals for the Economic Development of Argentina," in *Latin American Civilization: History and Society, 1492 to the Present*, ed. Benjamin Keen, 5th ed. (Boulder, CO: Westview Press, 1991), 283–86.

1450. . . . We need constitutions, we need a policy of creation, of settlement, of conquest of the solitude and the desert. . . .

The end of constitutional policy and government in America, then, is essentially economic. In America, to govern is to populate.

QUESTIONS

- Do you agree with Alberdi that "Industry is the grand means of promoting morality"?
- If, "to govern is to populate," how might a nation achieve such an ideal?

9.5 TREATMENT OF FACTORY WORKERS IN JAPAN

In Japan, more than 60 percent of factory workers in the early twentieth century were women. Silk factories were a major source of income. The profits of this sector were plowed back into heavy industry. The women and children who worked in these factories were subjected to harsh discipline and paid only a pittance for long days and poor conditions. The first excerpt comes from a 1906 government report into the prevalence of corporal punishment, and consists of conversations between investigators and women factory workers. The second excerpt is a poem that expresses despair over management's demands for profits.

Q: Do you get scolded?

A: We are taken to a room next to the office and are reprimanded there. We are also beaten. And, until we show a change of heart, we are kept there in the dark for several days.

Q: Are you fed?

A: No.

Q: Are there other forms of punishment?

A: If anyone steals something she is stripped naked and marched around the factory with a flag attached to her shoulders. They then take her to the dining hall and report her misdeed to everybody. . . . This spring a girl in the next room took *geta* [wooden clogs], which her roommate purchased for 70 sen. She was stripped naked, had the *geta* and a red flag bearing the words "*geta* thief" strapped to her shoulders, and was then marched around the factory.

Q: Do youngsters of seven and eight work only during the day or do they work at night, too?

A: They work at night, too. Since the supervisors are strict during the day, the children clean up the plant. But at night things are less closely supervised, so they don't do much cleaning. Even in the winter we wear only one unlined kimono. . . .

Q: Do they fall asleep in the factory?

A: If they fall asleep they are scolded and beaten.

Q: Do they get paid?

A: They are paid 8 sen. Then 7 sen is deducted for food, so they get only 1 sen.

Q: Are children charged 7 sen, too?

A: They are charged the same amount [for food as the adults].

Q: Are there many young children?

A: There are about ten workers who are seven or eight. There are many who are ten years old.

Source: Mikiso Hane, *Peasants, Rebels, and Outcasts: The Underside of Modern Japan,* 2nd ed. (Lanham, MD: Rowman and Littlefield, 2016 [1982]), 186–87.

My Factory

At other companies there are Buddhas and gods.
At mine only demons and serpents.
When I hear the manager talking,
His words say only "money, money, and time."
The demon overseer, the devil accountant,
The good-for-nothing chrysalis.

If you look through the factory's regulations,
You see that not one in a thousand lies unused.
We must follow the regulations;
We must look at the foreman's nasty face.

QUESTIONS

- Why do you think the factory owners practiced such a public form of corporal punishment for workers?
- What can these two documents teach us about debates surrounding industrialization in Japan?

Source: Patricia E. Tsurumi, *Factory Girls: Women in the Thread Mills of Meiji Japan* (Princeton, NJ: Princeton University Press, 1990), 98.

9.6 MACHINE-BREAKING IN SAXONY (1848)

In the 1840s, Saxony was one of the German-speaking areas undergoing rapid industrialization. Skilled labor resisted mechanization when possible with violence. The events in this account by the police occurred during the Revolutions of 1848, which empowered protestors and challenged authorities. Entrepreneurs regularly armed their workers against those who resented machine production. Similar events occurred over much of central and eastern Europe in the following decades, but have been far less well documented than similar occurrences in western Europe.

On 28 March 1848 it came to the notice of Jahn, the owner of a machine-made nail manufactory at Mittweida near Scheibenberg in the Erz Mountains that a nailmaker from Elterlein had been going about the district about the district around Mittweida and had incited the nailmakers there to "demolish" his manufactory stating that 1,500 nailmakers of the surrounding district would take part, who would "first assemble at Elterlein in order to destroy in the course of the following night the nail factory of Zimmermann and Leinbrock". Jahn thereupon began to make preparations to meet the calamity threatening; he hid the "firm's books, documents and cash box" in the cellar, sent a message to the District Governor for "the most urgent military assistance" and to the mayor for some volunteers. When news came from Elterlein that in the factory of Zimmermann and Leinbrock "all had been broken up and destroyed", Jahn called together his workmen and armed them with scythes and fire arms. In addition he got ready barrels of nails, cast iron articles and old machine parts to drop on the attackers from above. At 2 p.m.

began the attack on the nailmakers on the factory, for the defence of which Jahn had, to begin with, the support of the Schwarzenberg riflemen and about twenty men of the Volunteers [a militia]. After the nailmakers had been repulsed twice, and one woman had been shot in the fighting, the attackers withdrew in order to call up reinforcements. . . . When the nailmakers returned, the attacks were renewed and pursued with greater vigour. The latter succeeded in entering the factory first at one, and later at several points, whereupon Jahn saw the hopelessness of further resistance and fled from the attack of the nailmakers to Schneeberg. The destruction which Jahn found on his return to Mittweida, he described as follows: "the yard was full of stones . . .in the factory buildings nearly all the machines had been destroyed by axes and crowbars. Nothing of was left undamaged. . . . It is miraculous that the shooting, started by the way by the attackers . . . did not cause more injuries or deaths. The military asked for by Jahn arrived only after the riot. By the time of his return, they had, according to him, 'escorted 80 criminals to Zwickau.'"

QUESTIONS

- What does the extent of the damage reveal about debates surrounding industrialization in Saxony?
- What kind of changes do you think the protestors were reacting to?

Source: Sidney Pollard and Colin Holmes, eds. *Documents in European Economic History*, vol. 1, *The Process of Industrialization 1750–1870* (New York: St. Martin's Press, 1968), 530–31.

10

FROM SCARCITY TO SURPLUS
Modern Agriculture

10.1 OLAUDAH EQUIANO, AGRICULTURE AND FOOD IN GUINEA (1789)

Olaudah Equiano (1745–1797) was kidnapped from the Kingdom of Benin (Nigeria) in 1754 and spent twelve years as a slave in the Caribbean, where his name was changed to Gustavus Vassa. After purchasing his freedom, Equiano became an important abolitionist and published his autobiography in 1789. Although better known for his critique of slavery, this excerpt illustrates the varied diet and agricultural practices of this part of West Africa.

Our manner of living is entirely plain; for as yet the natives are unacquainted with those refinements in cookery which debauch the taste: bullocks, goats, and poultry, supply the greatest part of their food. These constitute likewise the principal wealth of the country, and the chief articles of its commerce. The flesh is usually stewed in a pan; to make it savoury we sometimes use also pepper, and other spices, and we have salt made of wood ashes. Our vegetables are mostly plantains, eadas, yams, beans, and Indian corn. . . . They are totally unacquainted with strong or spirituous liquours; and their principal beverage is palm wine. This is gotten from a tree of that name by tapping it at the top, and fastening a large gourd to it; and sometimes one tree will yield three or four gallons in a night. When just drawn it is of a most delicious sweetness; but in a few days it acquires a tartish and more spirituous flavour: though I never saw any one intoxicated by it. The same tree also produces nuts and oil. Our principal luxury is in perfumes; one sort of these is an odoriferous wood of delicious fragrance: the other a kind of earth; a small portion of which thrown into the fire diffuses a most powerful odour[D]. We beat this wood into powder, and mix it with palm oil; with which both men and women perfume themselves.

As we live in a country where nature is prodigal of her favours, our wants are few and easily supplied. . . .

Our land is uncommonly rich and fruitful, and produces all kinds of vegetables in great abundance. We have plenty of Indian corn, and vast quantities of cotton and tobacco. Our pineapples grow without culture; they are about the size of the largest sugar-loaf, and finely flavoured. We have also spices of different kinds, particularly pepper; and a variety of delicious fruits which I have never seen in Europe; together with gums of various kinds, and honey in abundance. All our industry is exerted to improve those blessings of nature. Agriculture is our chief employment; and every one, even the children and women, are engaged in it. Thus we are all habituated to labour from our earliest years. . . .

Our tillage is exercised in a large plain or common, some hours walk from our dwellings, and all the neighbors resort thither in a body. They use no beasts or husbandry; and their only

Source: Olaudah Equiano, *The Interesting Narrative of the Life of Olaudah Equiano; or Gustavus Vassa, the African. Written by Himself* (London: W. Cock, 1815 [1789]), 16–17, 19–21.

instruments are hoes, axes, shovels, and beaks, or pointed iron to dig with. Sometimes we are visited by locusts, which come in large clouds, so as to darken the air, and destroy our harvest. This however happens rarely, but when it does, a famine is produced by it.

QUESTIONS

- What adjectives would you use to describe eighteenth-century Guinea after reading the excerpt?
- What did Equiano mean by "where nature is prodigal of her favours, our wants are few and easily supplied"? Why might he say this in his autobiography?

10.2 GARCILASO DE LA VEGA, INKAN FARMING (1617)

This account was written by Garcilaso de la Vega (born Gómez Suárez de Figueroa, 1539–1616), a mestizo who spent most of his life in Spain but grew up hearing Andean oral tradition in the first generation after the conquest. He was an eyewitness to many practices and had access to detailed observations by others in writing his important ethnographic work on the Inka. This excerpt is from the volume that was published posthumously in 1617.

When the Inco [sic] had conquered any kingdom or province and established the form of government in its towns and the way of life of the inhabitants . . . he ordered that the agricultural land should be extended. This implies of course, the area under maize. For this purpose irrigation engineers were brought: some of these were extremely skilled. . . . These engineers made the necessary irrigation channels, according to the amount of land that could be turned to account. Because the country falls with the torrid zone, irrigation is necessary, and great attention is paid to this: not a grain of maize was sown unless channeled water was available. They also dug channels to water their pastures when the autumn rains were delayed: as they had an infinite quantity of flocks, they had to give their pastures the same attention as their grainlands. . . .

Having dug the channels, they levelled the fields and squared them so that the irrigation water could be adequately distributed. They built level terraces on the mountains and hillsides wherever the soil was good. . . . In order to make these terraces they would construct three walls of solid masonry, one in front and one at either end. These sloped back slightly (like all the Indian walls) so as to withstand the weight of earth with which they are filled to the level of the top of the walls. Above the first platform they built another smaller one, and above that still another still smaller. In this way the whole hill was gradually brought under cultivation, the platforms being [f]lattened out like stairs in a staircase, and all the cultivable and irrigable land being put to use. If there were rocky places, the rocks were removed and replaced by earth brought from elsewhere to form the terraces so that the space should not be wasted. The first platforms were large, according to the configuration of the place: they might be one or two or three hundred measures [could grow 1.6 bushels] broad and long. The second were smaller and they diminished progressively as they were higher up, until the last might contain only two or three rows of maize plants. This shows how industrious the Incas were in extending the area which could be planted with maize. A water channel was commonly brought fifteen or twenty leagues to water a few measures of soil, so that it should not be wasted. . . .

As a plough they use a stick two yards long: its front is flat and its back rounded, and it is about four fingers thick. It has a point to pierce the ground and, half a vara above it, a footrest made of two sticks tightly lashed to the main shaft. On this the Indian sets his foot and forcibly drives the plough in up to the footrest. They work in bands of seven or

Source: Garcilaso de la Vega, *Royal Commentaries of the Incas and General History of Peru*, part 2, trans. Harold V. Livermore (Austin, TX: University of Texas Press, 1966), 242–45.

eight, more or less, according to family or neighborhood groups. By all lowering their ploughs at once they can raise clods of earth so large that anyone who has not seen it could hardly credit it. It is remarkable to see them perform such a considerable task with such weak implements. . . . The women work opposite the men and help to lift the clods with their hands, turning the grass roots upwards so that they dry and die, and the harrowing requires less effort.

QUESTIONS

- What seems technologically advanced about the farming practices described in the excerpt?
- Why do you think the Inka immediately ordered that "agricultural land should be extended" after conquering an area?

10.3 GRIGGS, ENCLOSURE AND CROP ROTATION IN ESSEX (1794)

In the mid-1790s, England's Board of Agriculture sponsored county-wide surveys of the agricultural practices to demonstrate what progress had already been made and lobby for further parliamentary enclosures to break up common land and consolidate open fields. This report from Essex by a surveyor named Griggs assumed that elites deserved more control over agricultural practice because they were more innovative. It also shows the importance of secondary crops, local knowledge of how to manage crop rotation, and the importance of wheat.

Our waste lands, including the forest, may be estimated at full fifteen thousand acres; the greater part of which is as capable of producing corn, after a certain time for necessary improvements, as the adjoining lands, and would in most instances, it is presumed, be made profitable to the community could some method, such for instance, as passing a general act of parliament, to ascertain the rights of the lords of manors, tithe owners, and the several tenants, which, it is thought, might be done, by proportioning the tenant's claim to the nature and extent, or annual value of his tenements, held of the manor to which the waste belongs, and then enable the lord who is most frequently more enlightened, and better able to advance the various expenses of inclosing, and other necessary improvements, to purchase these rights. . . .

The most approved mode of treating the heavy land here, as in every other part of the county, is, to winter fallow it every third or fourth, and, in some parts, every second or third year, after which, in the eastern parts, oats or barley is sown, aud the land laid down with clover, trefoil and rye grass, and having lain one year, is again broke up soon after Michaelmas, and wheat is sown after which, if the land is clean and in good condition, the farmer takes a crop of beans and then fallows again. The next rotation frequently is wheat, beans, well hoed, and then wheat again; on the lighter lands are sown first turnips, for which, a fallow is always made, and the land manured. Barley-sown with clover, &c. which is fed the ensuing year, succeeds the crop of turnips, then wheat, upon the clover lay, and after that peas, but where the clover fails, a circumstance most unusual, the land is considered unfit for wheat, and peas are sown m its stead.

QUESTIONS

- What do you think of the argument that the lords should have had more control over agricultural practices?
- What do you think were the long-term effects of the enclosure movement in England?

Source: Messrs. Griggs, *General View of the Agriculture of the County of Essex* (London: C. Clarke, 1794), 9-10.

10.4 RACHEL CARSON, *SILENT SPRING* (1962)

Rachel Carson (1907–1964) was a marine scientist who worked for the U.S. Fish and Wildlife Service in Washington, DC when she decided to write about the effects of chemicals, especially the pesticide DDT on the environment. After years of research, when she published her findings, Carson was vilified by the chemical industry and farmers dependent on government programs that paid them not to produce in order to prop up prices. *Silent Spring* was an important inspiration for the environmental movement.

Since the mid-1940s over 200 basic chemicals have been created for use in killing insects, weeds, rodents, and other organisms described in the modern vernacular as "pests"; and they are sold under several thousand different brand names. These sprays, dusts, and aerosols are now applied almost universally to farms, gardens, forests, and homes—nonselective chemicals that have the power to kill every insect, the "good" and the "bad", to still the song of birds and the leaping of fish in the streams, to coat the leaves with a deadly film, and to linger on in soil—all this though the intended target may be only a few weeds or insects. Can anyone believe it is possible to lay down such a barrage of poisons on the surface of the earth without making it unfit for all life? They should not be called "insecticides", but "biocides". The whole process of spraying seems caught up in an endless spiral. Since DDT was released for civilian use, a process of escalation has been going on in which ever more toxic materials must be found. This has happened because insects, in a triumphant vindication of Darwin's principle of the survival of the fittest, have evolved super races immune to the particular insecticide used, hence a deadlier one has always to be developed—and then a deadlier one than that. It has happened also because, for reasons to be described later, destructive insects often undergo a "flareback", or resurgence, after spraying, in numbers greater than before. Thus the chemical war is never won, and all life is caught in its violent crossfire.

Along with the possibility of the extinction of mankind by nuclear war, the central problem of our age has therefore become the contamination of man's total environment with such substances of incredible potential for harm—substances that accumulate in the tissues of plants and animals and even penetrate the germ cells to shatter or alter the very material of heredity upon which the shape of the future depends.

Some would-be architects of our future look toward a time when it will be possible to alter the human germ plasm by design. But we may easily be doing so now by inadvertence, for many chemicals, like radiation, bring about gene mutations. It is ironic to think that man might determine his own future by something so seemingly trivial as the choice of an insect spray.

All this has been risked—for what? Future historians may well be amazed by our distorted sense of

Source: Rachel Carson, *Silent Spring* (Greenwich, CT: Crest Books, 1962), 13.

proportion. How could intelligent beings seek to control a few unwanted species by a method that contaminated the entire environment and brought the threat of disease and death even to their own kind? Yet this is precisely what we have done. We have done it, moreover, for reasons that collapse the moment we examine them. We are told that the enormous and expanding use of pesticides is necessary to maintain farm production. Yet is our real problem not one of *overproduction?* Our farms, despite measures to remove acreages from production and to pay farmers *not* to produce, have yielded such a staggering excess of crops that the American taxpayer in 1962 is paying out more than one billion dollars a year as the total carrying cost of the surplus-food storage program.

QUESTIONS

- What was Carson's central argument in 1962?
- Why do you think *Silent Spring* had such a significant impact on the United States after its publication?

10.5 JOHN P. GRANT, INDIGO CULTIVATION IN BENGAL (1860)

Sir John P. Grant (1807–1893) wrote this commentary on the work of a commission appointed to investigate conditions in the raising of indigo plants and the manufacture of dye in the British province of Bengal in India. He described the growing oppression of indigo farmers thanks to a cartel formed among the indigo manufacturers who used their authority to force tenant farmers to grow indigo for sub-market prices. This section discusses the economic pressures, but other parts of the text describe the use of manipulation of the judicial and tax systems, corporal punishment and even murder to intimidate the farmers. The commission was appointed after a peasant revolt against the indigo manufacturers occurred in 1859 which led to destruction of property and summary execution of some of the most oppressive industrialists. The government cracked down harshly, but also ruled that tenants could not be forced to grow indigo.

The improvement of the Police, which has checked affairs, has, as I believe, driven those to whom some means or other of forcing a cultivation unprofitable to the cultivators was a matter of necessity, to other methods of inducement more harassing, on the whole, than an occasional terrible example. The stoppage of all competition amongst Planters for Ryots [tenant farmers] must, of late years, very greatly have increased the weight bearing down the individual Ryot; and the withdrawal from him of such protection as he before obtained from Zemindars, not being Indigo Planters, must have had a like effect. There has been less friction, fewer stoppages, and less noise of late years, and the pressure of the machine must have been more effective in consequence. There is reason also to infer from the evidence that the demand, in some places at least, has been more severe of late upon the Ryot, in the quantity of Indigo cultivation required of him, and in the labor required in weeding and tending the crop, than was formerly the case. But the great aggravation of all is due to the late rise of prices. It is in evidence that all agricultural produce has risen in value, within the last three years or so, to double or very nearly double its former price, and that day labor, and the cost of the maintenance of cattle, has increased in price in the same way. As the single root of all that was at any time wrong in the Bengal Indigo system, is in the one fact that the Manufacturer did not pay the full cost of the plant; and as there has been no increase in the price paid for this one crop since the above-mentioned extraordinary rise of prices generally; here alone is a cause which must have doubled all the evil of the cultivation to the Ryot. The direct money loss was doubled: and as that was the cause of all the other evils, it seems reasonable to assume that they also were increased in the same ratio. No Planter pressed upon Ryots without an object; and his only possible object was to obtain Indigo plant, which would not be spontaneously grown for him at the price he gave. We may be sure that the pressure which is just enough to induce a Ryot to sacrifice ten Rupees, must be materially increased to induce him quietly to sacrifice twenty.

Source: John P. Grant, *Minute by the Lieutenant-Governor of Bengal on Report of the Indigo Commission* (Calcutta: Bengal Secretariat Office, 1861), 7.

QUESTIONS

- What was the message that Grant wanted to convey?
- What did Grant mean by "We may be sure that the pressure which is just enough to induce a Ryot to sacrifice ten Rupees, must be materially increased to induce him quietly to sacrifice twenty"? Why would this lead to a governmental response?

10.6 TOSHIE, VILLAGE LIFE IN TWENTIETH-CENTURY JAPAN (1935)

This exchange with a woman from the village of Kasé in Aomori prefecture was reported in 1935 in a local newspaper. It suggests the lived reality of differences in yield and how tenant farmers could easily fall into debt as well as how hard it was to escape despite help from the landlord, the community, and access to credit.

"How are you getting by these days?"

"We are renting two *tan* of rice fields, and we normally get six bales [about 360 kilograms] of rice per *tan*. Then we pay two balses [120 kilograms] per *tan* as rent, and five *tō* five *shō* [about thirty kilograms] for the fifty *tsubo* [165 square meters] our house is on. The rest we can eat. Then my husband does a little bit of day laboring, or helps with roof thatching, so up to now we have had just about enough to teat. But last year with the cold we only got three bales per *tan*, and this year with the floods we got nothing at all. So we don't have a grain of rice in the house, and if we don't get some help from the authorities there'll be nothing for it but to die of starvation."

"If you only got three bales last year how have you been eating until now?"

"The landlord reduced our rent, and so somehow or other we had rice to eat until March, and from then on we've been borrowing here and there, and eating pumpkin and potato and radish from our dry field, and my husband has been working five days a month or so for ¥0.70 per day, so we've just about been able to eat."

"What about loans?"

"Five or six years ago my husband was sick, so we borrowed money. Adding that to the money we've had to borrow to buy rice, the total comes to about one hundred yen."

"What kind of people have you borrowed from, and what interest do you pay?"

"We borrowed about seventy yen from some of the better-off people in this village. We also borrowed some money from a money-lender, and we're paying 15% interest per year. . . ."

"What are you eating these days?"

"Look for yourself."

"And she took the lid off the pot hanging from the ceiling and showed us. on examination, I saw that it was soup of barley with chopped radish leaves. The woman continued: "Right now I don't have a single grain of rice, so with the money my husband earned I'm buying the cheapest barley and making this kind of

Source: Simon Partner, *Toshié: A Story of Village Life in Twentieth-Century Japan* (Berkeley, CA: University of California Press, 2004), 47-47.

thing, and we're eating at least something, but when the snow comes there'll be no work for him, and even if he wants to do thatching, this year there was no straw, and even if we want to borrow more money, we can't pay back what we owe now so no one will lend it to us, so I'd just don't know what we'll do this winter."

QUESTIONS

- What factors made it so difficult for farmers to escape this cycle of poverty?
- What governmental actions might have alleviated the plight of tenant farmers?

10.7 JAN SLOMKA, SERFDOM IN DZIKOV, POLAND (c. 1900)

This account of village life in the Austrian section of Poland was written by Jan Slomka (1842–1932). Serfdom was abolished there only in 1848 and in the Kingdom of Poland ruled by Russia, the serfs only received their freedom in 1864. Slomka suggests the harsh labor expectations of even a "kindly" feudal master into the middle of the nineteenth century.

During serfdom days Dzikov belonged to the "demesne", i.e. to the lords of Dzikov. This had been long ago the home of the Counts Tarnowski. . . .

Towards the end of serfdom the total number of cottagers in Dzikov was forty-two, of whom twelve were owners, twenty-three tenants and seven day-labourers.

The first named had eighteen acres each, and did their dues six days a week for the lord of the manor, with team or yoke of oxen and implements, e.g. wagon, plough, harrows, disc, etc. for this they had in addition to the pasture used by the whole village, a special fifty acres near Zwierzyniets. . . . The tenants had six-acre lots in each case, and did their dues three days a week with hand tools—flail, sickle, hoe, spade, etc. The labourers had only huts, and were not bound to any dues at all. . . .

Every farmer had first to do his dues at the manor house, whether with his team or on foot. Only then could he work his own land, sowing and reaping at night. No excuse as to pressing needs at home was of any use. If one did not appear as ordered, at once the overseer would come. If he found the wife busy cooking he would throw a pail of water on the fire, or in winter would carry off the windows or the door.

In case that did not work, and men were needed for service, the overseer would come with his foremen and eject the farmer from home and homestead. Another would be put in his place. Nor was there any appeal anywhere, since that was the usage and at bottom the lord of the manor was owner of everything. His was both land and water, yes even the wind; since only he was allowed to build a wind-mill to grind corn.

Only when all his compulsory dues were done could the peasant sing the old song:

I'm not afraid the landlord will molest me,
My dues are done, I'll set me home and rest me!

Our Dzikov masters were esteemed as kindly and humane folk, yet no one dared go to the manor with any complaint about the manor servants: for the latter would find excuses and then afterward make trouble for us. the result that all gave up the thought of just dealing. Running away would have done no good, for elsewhere it was no better—rather worse.

QUESTIONS

- What were the expectations of serfs?
- Why did such a system persist for such a long time?

Source: Quoted in Alfred J. Bannan and Achilles Edelenyi, eds., *Documentary History of Eastern Europe* (New York: Twayne Publishers, 1970), 211-12.

10.8 JAIME WHEELOCK ROMÁN, A STRATEGY FOR DEVELOPMENT (1985)

Nicaraguan Jaime Wheelock Román (b. 1946) was one of the leaders of the Sandinista National Liberation Front that seized power in 1978. He became the minister of agricultural development and agrarian reform. He directed the seizure of land from the former dictator and his cronies and their redistribution to agricultural laborers. This excerpt is from a 1985 book outlining the difficulty of further Sandinista plans for agrarian reform in light of the ongoing proxy war waged by the United States against the Sandinista regime. This plan is a thoroughgoing rejection of neo-liberal economic policies: it also discusses the necessity of avoiding further ecological degradation.

First we have to modify the land tenure system. The implementation of this goal will confer domestic stability and peace, create a rational distribution of land, and establish a relationship between humans and land that will be more advantageous for production.

Second, in addition to agrarian reform, we must have a reform in the *use* of the land. For reasons outside of our control, our crops are not necessarily where they should be. a majority of those that are indispensable for life have been displaced to low-quality lands by crops that serve to feed the needs of other countries.

The best lands of Nicaragua, those that are optimum for the production of corn, beans, and sorghum, were occupied by agroexport crops until the triumph of the revolution. The indigenous farmers, who traditionally occupied the best lands in Nicaragua, were displaced by the large landlords. The latter, stimulated by the profit motive, were dedicated to the production of coffee, sugar, or cotton, depending on the epoch. . . .

Nicaragua in time had been converted into a producer of exports and an importer of manufactured products, to the extent that even food was imported.

The new strategy that we are implementing, from the point of view of agriculture, must reserve the lands of the Pacific lowlands for the production of food, employing intensive technology with annual row crops. . . . Considering what Nicaragua will consume over the next twenty years, we realize that we will need the entire Pacific region just to maintain the Nicaraguan diet at its present level. . . .

We need irrigation to produce cotton and corn in the same land in the same year. This is not only to increase the production of corn, but also to relocate its zone of production away from the mountainous regions where soil erosion has become a large problem. We are also bringing bean production into the Pacific region, similarly to stop the destruction of the fragile soils on which much of the production has been concentrated. We must produce these basic grains in the Pacific lowlands, but in order to do so

Source: Peter Rosset and John Vandermeer, eds., *Nicaragua: Unfinished Revolution. The New Nicaragua Reader* (New York: Grove Press, 1986), 482-83.

we must introduce irrigation. We are goint to have, year by year, the development of more irrigated croplands to produce both export goods and goods for internal consumption, the latter in terms of food for direct use of the population and in terms of inputs for agroindustry.

QUESTIONS

- What was Román's "strategy"?
- Do you think his proposals could work? Why or why not?

11

CREATION AND COLLAPSE
Revolutions and Political Change, 1775–1860

11.1 VOLTAIRE, TREATISE ON TOLERANCE (1763)

François-Marie Arouet (1694–1778), the son of a Parisian notary, wrote under the pen name Voltaire. The most famous and influential writer of his day, he was known for his epic poetry, travel and scientific writings, novels, plays, and histories, as well as a political pamphleteer. His *Treatise on Tolerance*, published in 1763 in response to the Calas Affair, focused on religion and the role of Enlightened philosophy in mitigating some of the more fervent aspects of Christian practice and stated that further progress was both possible and necessary. For Voltaire and the *philosophes*, religion was also a wedge issue that could help people see the need for tolerance in many other aspects of social life. The use of the comparative method was a common Enlightenment tactic, as was the call for people to make up their own minds instead of simply accepting what people in authority said.

But are this generation as barbaric as their fathers? Have not time, the progress of reason, good books, and the humanizing influence of society had an effect on the leaders of these people? And do we not perceive that the aspect of nearly the whole of Europe has been changed within the last fifty years?

Government is stronger everywhere, and morals have improved. The ordinary police, supported by numerous standing armies, gives us some security against a return to that age of anarchy. . . .

The rage that is inspired by the dogmatic spirit and the abuse of the Christian religion, wrongly conceived, has shed as much blood and led to as many disasters in Germany, England, and even Holland, as in France. Yet religious difference causes no trouble today in those States. The Jew, the Catholic, the Greek, the Lutheran, the Calvinist, the Anabaptist, the Socinian, the Memnonist, the Moravian, and so many others, live like brothers in these countries, and contribute alike to the good of the social body. . . .

Philosophy, the sister of religion, has disarmed the hands that superstition had so long stained with blood; and the human mind, awakening from its intoxication, is amazed at the excesses into which fanaticism had led it. . . .

I do not say that all who are not of the same religion as the prince should share the positions and honors of those who follow the dominant religion. In England the Catholics, who are regarded as attached to the party of the Pretender, are not admitted to office. They even pay double taxes. In other respects, however, they have all the rights of citizens. . . .

Let us get out of our grooves and study the rest of the globe. The Sultan governs in peace twenty million people of different religions; two hundred thousand Greeks live in security at Constantinople; the mufti himself nominates and presents to the emperor the Greek patriarch, and they also admit a Latin patriarch. The Sultan nominates Latin bishops for some of the Greek islands. . . . The annals of Turkey do not record any revolt instigated by any of these religions.

Source: Adapted from Voltaire, *Toleration and Other Essays*, trans. Joseph McCabe (New York: G. P. Putnam's Sons, 1912), 19–26, http://oll.libertyfund.org/titles/voltaire-toleration-and-other-essays (consulted July 14, 2018).

Go to India, Persia, or Tartary, and you will find the same toleration and tranquility. Peter the Great patronized all the cults in his vast empire. Commerce and agriculture profited by it, and the body politic never suffered from it. . . .

Toleration, in fine, never led to civil war; intolerance has covered the earth with carnage. Choose, then, between these rivals—between the mother who would have her son slain and the mother who yields, provided his life be spared.

I speak here only of the interest of nations. While respecting theology, as I do, I regard in this article only the physical and moral well-being of society. I beg every impartial reader to weigh these truths, verify them, and add to them. Attentive readers, who restrain not their thoughts, always go farther than the author.

QUESTIONS

- What did Voltaire mean by "tolerance"?
- Why did Voltaire consider the Ottomans as political models?

11.2 OLYMPE DE GOUGES, *DECLARATION OF THE RIGHTS OF WOMAN AND OF THE FEMALE CITIZEN* (SEPTEMBER 1791)

Under the pen name of Olympe de Gouges, Marie Gouze (1748–1793), a self–educated butcher's daughter, wrote a *Declaration* that largely paralleled the one promulgated for men. This demand for equality was endorsed by only a handful of people, even though free people of color and Jews were granted full citizenship. The French republic cracked down harshly on independent female political action in 1793. De Gouges shows that the concept of "equality" was in flux. That it took more than a century for most women to gain equal rights is a key limitation of both the practice of revolutionary politics and the legacy of the French Revolution. De Gouges was guillotined as a counterrevolutionary for defending King Louis XVI and Queen Marie-Antoinette.

Preamble.

Mothers, daughters, sisters, female representatives of the nation ask to be constituted as a national assembly. Considering that ignorance, neglect, or contempt for the rights of woman are the sole causes of public misfortunes and governmental corruption, they have resolved to set forth in a solemn declaration the natural, inalienable, and sacred rights of woman: so that by being constantly present to all the members of the social body this declaration may always remind them of their rights and duties; so that by being liable at every moment to comparison with the aim of any and all political institutions the acts of women's and men's powers may be the more fully respected; and so that by being founded henceforward on simple and incontestable principles the demands of the citizenesses may always tend toward maintaining the constitution, good morals, and the general welfare.

In consequence, the sex that is superior in beauty as in courage, needed in maternal sufferings, recognizes and declares, in the presence and under the auspices of the Supreme Being, the following rights of woman and the citizeness.

1. Woman is born free and remains equal to man in rights. Social distinctions may be based only on common utility.

2. The purpose of all political association is the preservation of the natural and imprescriptible rights of woman and man. These rights are liberty, property, security, and especially resistance to oppression.

3. The principle of all sovereignty rests essentially in the nation, which is but the reuniting of woman and man. No body and no individual may exercise authority which does not emanate expressly from the nation.

4. Liberty and justice consist in restoring all that belongs to another; hence the exercise of the natural rights of woman has no other limits than those that the perpetual tyranny of man opposes to

Source: These materials appeared originally in *The French Revolution and Human Rights: A Brief Documentary History,* translated, edited, and with an introduction by Lynn Hunt (Boston/New York Bedford/St. Martin's, 1996), 124–129 reproduced on http://chnm.gmu.edu/revolution/d/293/ (consulted July 16, 2018).

them; these limits must be reformed according to the laws of nature and reason.

5. The laws of nature and reason prohibit all actions which are injurious to society. No hindrance should be put in the way of anything not prohibited by these wise and divine laws, nor may anyone be forced to do what they do not require.

6. The law should be the expression of the general will. All citizenesses and citizens should take part, in person or by their representatives, in its formation. It must be the same for everyone. All citizenesses and citizens, being equal in its eyes, should be equally admissible to all public dignities, offices and employments, according to their ability, and with no other distinction than that of their virtues and talents.

7. No woman is exempted; she is indicted, arrested, and detained in the cases determined by the law. Women like men obey this rigorous law.

8. Only strictly and obviously necessary punishments should be established by the law, and no one may be punished except by virtue of a law established and promulgated before the time of the offense, and legally applied to women.

9. Any woman being declared guilty, all rigor is exercised by the law.

10. No one should be disturbed for his fundamental opinions; woman has the right to mount the scaffold, so she should have the right equally to mount the rostrum, provided that these manifestations do not trouble public order as established by law.

11. The free communication of thoughts and opinions is one of the most precious of the rights of woman, since this liberty assures the recognition of children by their fathers. Every citizeness may therefore say freely, I am the mother of your child; a barbarous prejudice [against unmarried women having children] should not force her to hide the truth, so long as responsibility is accepted for any abuse of this liberty in cases determined by the law [women are not allowed to lie about the paternity of their children].

12. The safeguard of the rights of woman and the citizeness requires public powers. These powers are instituted for the advantage of all and not for the private benefit of those to whom they are entrusted.

13. For maintenance of public authority and for expenses of administration, taxation of women and men is equal; she takes part in all forced labor service, in all painful tasks; she must therefore have the same proportion in the distribution of places, employments, offices, dignities, and in industry.

14. The citizenesses and citizens have the right, by themselves or through their representatives, to have demonstrated to them the necessity of public taxes. The citizenesses can only agree to them upon admission of an equal division, not only in wealth, but also in the public administration, and to determine the means of apportionment, assessment, and collection, and the duration of the taxes.

15. The mass of women, joining with men in paying taxes, have the right to hold accountable every public agent of the administration.

16. Any society in which the guarantee of rights is not assured or the separation of powers not settled has no constitution. The constitution is null and void if the majority of individuals composing the nation has not cooperated in its drafting.

17. Property belongs to both sexes whether united or separated; it is for each of them an inviolable and sacred right, and no one may be deprived of it as a true patrimony of nature, except when public necessity, certified by law, obviously requires it, and then on condition of a just compensation in advance.

POSTSCRIPT

Women, wake up; the tocsin of reason sounds throughout the universe; recognize your rights. The powerful empire of nature is no longer surrounded by prejudice, fanaticism, superstition, and lies. The torch of truth has dispersed all the clouds of folly and usurpation. Enslaved man has multiplied his force and needs yours to break his chains. Having become free, he has become unjust toward his companion. Oh women! Women, when will you cease to be blind? What advantages have you gathered in the Revolution? A scorn more marked, a disdain more conspicuous. During the centuries of corruption you only reigned over the weakness of men. Your empire is destroyed; what is left to you then? Firm belief in the injustices of men. The reclaiming of your patrimony founded on the wise decrees of nature; why should you fear such a beautiful enterprise? . . . Whatever the barriers set up against you, it is in your power to overcome them; you only have to want it. . . .

QUESTIONS

- Does this set of rights seem fair? Why or why not?
- Does the fact that de Gouges was executed for treason during the French Revolution change how you think of the French Revolution? Why or why not?

11.3 GIUSEPPE MAZZINI, *MANIFESTO OF YOUNG ITALY* (1831)

Giuseppe Mazzini (1805–1872) was a leading nationalist who sought to turn Italy into more than a "geographical expression." He participated in various secret societies that hoped to apply the lessons of the French Revolution to the Italian context. This document states the goals of a revolutionary society dedicated to uniting Italy through a popular uprising on behalf of liberal principles. It eventually counted more than 50,000 members under age 40. Mazzini played an important role in bringing about the Revolutions of 1848, but when these revolts were defeated, he was forced to spend most of the rest of his life in exile.

Great revolutions are the work rather of principles than of bayonets, and are achieved first in the moral, and afterwards in the material sphere. Bayonets are truly powerful only when they assert or maintain a right; rights and duties of society spring from a profound moral sense which has taken root in the majority. Blind brute force may create victors, victims, and martyrs, but tyranny results from its triumph, whether it crown the brow of prince or tribune, if achieved in antagonism to the will of the majority.

Principles alone, when diffused and propagated amongst the peoples, manifest their right to liberty, and by creating the desire and need of it, invest mere force with the vigor and justice of law. . . .

In Italy, as in every country aspiring towards a new life, there is a clash of opposing elements, of passions assuming every variety of form, and of desires tending in fact towards one sole aim, but through modifications almost infinite.

There are many men in Italy full of lofty and indignant hatred to the foreigner, who shout for liberty simply because it is the foreigner who withholds it.

There are others, having at heart the union of Italy before all things, who would gladly unite her divided children under any strong will, whether of native or foreign tyrant.

Others again, fearful of all violent commotions, and doubtful of the possibility of suddenly subduing the shock of private interests, and the jealousies of different provinces, shrink from the idea of absolute union, and are ready to accept any new partition diminishing the number of sections into which the country is divided.

Few appear to understand that a fatal necessity will impede all true progress in Italy, until every effort at emancipation shall proceed upon the three inseparable bases of unity, liberty, and independence. . . .

Love of country, abhorrence of Austria, and a burning desire to throw off her yoke, are passions now universally diffused, and the compromises inculcated by fear, or a mistaken notion of tactics and diplomacy, will be abandoned, and vanish before the majesty of the national will. In this respect, therefore, the question may be regarded as lying between tyranny driven to its last and most desperate struggle, and those resolved to bravely dare its overthrow. . . .

There is a class of men of civic ability and influence who imagine that revolutions are to be conducted with

Source: Adapted from Giuseppe Mazzini, *Life & Writings of Joseph Mazzini*, 6 vols. (London: Smith, Elder & Co., 1890 [1864–70]), I: 118–21, 123.

diplomatic caution and reserve, instead of the energy of an irrevocable faith and will. They admit our principles, but reject their consequences. They deplore extreme evils, yet shrink from extreme remedies, and would attempt to lead the peoples to liberty with the same cunning and artifice adopted by tyranny to enslave them.

Born and educated at a time when the conscience of a free man was a thing almost unknown in Italy, they have no faith in the power of a people rising in the name of their rights, their past glories, their very existence. They have no faith in enthusiasm, nor indeed in aught beyond the calculations of that diplomacy by which we have a thousand times been bought and sold, and the foreign bayonets by which we have been a thousand times betrayed.

They know nothing of the elements of regeneration that have been fermenting for the last half century in Italy, nor of that yearning after better things which is the heart's desire of our masses at the present day.

They do not understand that, after many centuries of slavery, a nation can only be regenerated through virtue, or through death. . . .

In the progress of revolutions, however, every error committed serves as a step towards truth.

QUESTIONS

- What did Mazzini advocate in the text?
- Why would these ideas have been considered dangerous?

11.4 CARL SCHURZ, "A LOOK BACK AT 1848"

Carl Schurz (1829–1906) was a student at Bonn's prestigious university in Prussia's western provinces (see Map 11.2) when the news of the overthrow of French King Louis-Philippe in February 1848 arrived. In these reminiscences of his youth, Schurz illuminated the hope, the sense of possibility, and the coming together of diverse groups into a single national whole. He also claimed that the views of these middle-class students reflected those of the people as a whole. High hopes and these false claims of solidarity made the defeat of the Revolutions of 1848 all the more demoralizing. Schurz fled the country; he emigrated to the United States and became first a journalist and then a general in the Union army during the Civil War. He was the first German-American to be elected to the Senate and was a stalwart of the new Republican Party.

"The French have driven away Louis Philippe and proclaimed the Republic!" . . .

Although it was still forenoon, the market was already crowded with young men talking excitedly. There was no shouting, no noise, only agitated conversation. What did we want there? This probably no one knew. But since the French had driven away Louis Philippe and proclaimed the republic, something of course must happen here, too. Some of the students had brought their rapiers along, as if it were necessary to make an attack or to defend themselves. We were dominated by a vague feeling as if a great outbreak of elemental forces had begun, as if an earthquake was impending of which we had felt the first shock, and we instinctively crowded together. Thus, we wandered about in numerous bands—to the *Kneipe* [pub or bar], where our restlessness, however, would not suffer us long to stay; then to other pleasure resorts, where we fell into conversation with all manner of strangers, to find in them the same confused, astonished, and expectant state of mind. . . .

The next morning there were the usual lectures to be attended. But how profitless! The voice of the professor sounded like a monotonous drone coming from far away. What he had to say did not seem to concern us. The pen that should have taken notes remained idle. At last we closed our notebooks with a sigh and went away, impelled by a feeling that now we had something more important to do—to devote ourselves to the affairs of the fatherland. And this we did by seeking again as quickly as possible the company of our friends, in order to discuss what had happened and what was to come. In these conversations, excited as they were, certain ideas and catchwords worked themselves to the surface, which expressed more or less the feelings of the people.

Now had arrived in Germany the day for the establishment of "German Unity," and the founding of a great, powerful, national German empire. First in line the convocation of a national parliament. Then the demands for civil rights and liberties, free speech, free press, the right of free assembly, equality before the law, a freely elected representation of the people with

Source: Adapted from Carl Schurz, *Reminiscences* (New York: Doubleday, 1908), I: 112–14, 116–17 on https://sourcebooks. fordham.edu/mod/1848schurz.asp (consulted July 20, 2018).

legislative power, responsibility of ministers, self-government of the communes, the right of the people to carry arms, the formation of a civic guard with elective officers and so on—in short, that which was called a "Constitutional form of government on a broad democratic basis."

Republican ideas were at first only sparingly expressed. But the word democracy was soon on all tongues, and many, too, thought it a matter of course that if the princes should try to withhold from the people the rights and liberties demanded, force would take the place of mere petition. Of course, the regeneration of the country must, if possible, be accomplished by peaceable means. . . . Like many of my friends, I was dominated by the feeling that at last the great opportunity had arrived for giving to the German people the liberty which was their birthright and to the German fatherland its unity and greatness, and that it was now the first duty of every German to do and to sacrifice everything for this sacred object. We were profoundly, solemnly, in earnest.

. . . In the great cities of Prussia there was a mighty commotion. Not only Cologne, Coblenz, and Trier, but also Breslau, Königsberg, and Frankfurt-am-der-Oder, sent deputations to Berlin to entreat the king. In the Prussian capital the masses surged upon the streets, and everybody looked for events of great import.

While such tidings rushed in upon us from all sides like a roaring hurricane, we in the little university town of Bonn were also busy preparing addresses to the sovereign, to circulate them for signature, and to send them to Berlin. On the 18th of March we too had our mass demonstration. A great multitude gathered for a solemn procession through the streets of the town. The most respectable citizens, not a few professors, and a great number of students and people of all grades marched in close ranks. At the head of the procession Professor Kunkel bore the tricolor—black, red, and gold—which so long had been prohibited as the revolutionary flag. Arriving in the market square, he mounted the steps of the city hall and spoke to the assembled throng. He spoke with wonderful eloquence, his voice ringing out in its most powerful tones as he depicted a resurrection of German unity and greatness and new liberties and rights of the German people, which now must be conceded by the princes or won by force by the people. And when at last he waved the black-red-gold banner, and predicted to a free German nation a magnificent future, enthusiasm without bounds broke forth. People clapped their hands; they shouted; they embraced one another; they shed tears. In a moment the city was covered with black, red, and gold flags, and not only the *Burschenschaft* [nationalist societies] but almost everybody wore a black-red-gold cockade on his hat.

QUESTIONS

- How did Schurz portray the Revolutions of 1848?
- Why was the rhetoric of republicanism so appealing, in Schurz's recollection?

11.5 COMMONWEALTH OF VIRGINIA, DECLARATION OF RIGHTS (1776)

Virginia's *Declaration of Rights*, adopted on June 12, 1776, both prefigured and encouraged the later adoption of a Bill of Rights, the first ten amendments to the U.S. Constitution, ratified in 1791. It is a more radical version of the American promise than that contained in other contemporary documents, but its authorship by George Mason and its passage by the slave owners in the Virginia Convention of Delegates undermines its universality.

I. That all men are by nature equally free and independent, and have certain inherent rights, of which, when they enter into a state of society, they cannot, by any compact, deprive or divest their posterity; namely, the enjoyment of life and liberty, with the means of acquiring and possessing property, and pursuing and obtaining happiness and safety.

II. That all power is vested in, and consequently derived from, the people; that magistrates are their trustees and servants, and at all times amenable to them.

III. That government is, or ought to be, instituted for the common benefit, protection, and security of the people, nation or community; of all the various modes and forms of government that is best, which is capable of producing the greatest degree of happiness and safety and is most effectually secured against the danger of maladministration; and that, whenever any government shall be found inadequate or contrary to these purposes, a majority of the community hath an indubitable, unalienable, and indefeasible right to reform, alter or abolish it, in such manner as shall be judged most conducive to the public weal.

IV. That no man, or set of men, are entitled to exclusive or separate emoluments or privileges from the community, but in consideration of public services; which, not being descendible, neither ought the offices of magistrate, legislator, or judge be hereditary.

V. That the legislative and executive powers of the state should be separate and distinct from the judicative; and, that the members of the two first may be restrained from oppression by feeling and participating the burthens of the people, they should, at fixed periods, be reduced to a private station, return into that body from which they were originally taken, and the vacancies be supplied by frequent, certain, and regular elections in which all, or any part of the former members, to be again eligible, or ineligible, as the laws shall direct.

VI. That elections of members to serve as representatives of the people in assembly ought to be free; and that all men, having sufficient evidence of permanent common interest with, and attachment to, the community have the right of suffrage and cannot be taxed or deprived of their property for public uses without their own consent or that of their representatives so elected, nor bound by any law to which they have not, in like manner, assented, for the public good.

VII. That all power of suspending laws, or the execution of laws, by any authority without consent of the representatives of the people is injurious to their rights and ought not to be exercised.

Source: http://avalon.law.yale.edu/18th_century/virginia.asp (consulted July 24, 2018).

VIII. That in all capital or criminal prosecutions a man hath a right to demand the cause and nature of his accusation to be confronted with the accusers and witnesses, to call for evidence in his favor, and to a speedy trial by an impartial jury of his vicinage, without whose unanimous consent he cannot be found guilty, nor can he be compelled to give evidence against himself; that no man be deprived of his liberty except by the law of the land or the judgement of his peers.

IX. That excessive bail ought not to be required, nor excessive fines imposed; nor cruel and unusual punishments inflicted.

X. That general warrants, whereby any officer or messenger may be commanded to search suspected places without evidence of a fact committed, or to seize any person or persons not named, or whose offense is not particularly described and supported by evidence, are grievous and oppressive and ought not to be granted.

XI. That in controversies respecting property and in suits between man and man, the ancient trial by jury is preferable to any other and ought to be held sacred.

XII. That the freedom of the press is one of the greatest bulwarks of liberty and can never be restrained but by despotic governments.

XIII. That a well regulated militia, composed of the body of the people, trained to arms, is the proper, natural, and safe defense of a free state; that standing armies, in time of peace, should be avoided as dangerous to liberty; and that, in all cases, the military should be under strict subordination to, and be governed by, the civil power.

XIV. That the people have a right to uniform government; and therefore, that no government separate from, or independent of, the government of Virginia, ought to be erected or established within the limits thereof.

XV. That no free government, or the blessings of liberty, can be preserved to any people but by a firm adherence to justice, moderation, temperance, frugality, and virtue and by frequent recurrence to fundamental principles.

XVI. That religion, or the duty which we owe to our Creator and the manner of discharging it, can be directed by reason and conviction, not by force or violence; and therefore, all men are equally entitled to the free exercise of religion, according to the dictates of conscience; and that it is the mutual duty of all to practice Christian forbearance, love, and charity towards each other.

Adopted unanimously on June 12, 1776, Virginia Convention of Delegates. Drafted by Mr. George Mason.

QUESTIONS

- Compare this to the Declaration of Independence and the U.S. Constitution. What seems similar and what appears different?
- In your mind, how could this document coexist with slave ownership?

11.6 LETTER FROM THE SLAVES OF MARTINIQUE, AUGUST 29, 1789

In the summer of 1789, rumors (unfounded) spread on the Caribbean island of Martinique that French King Louis XVI planned to abolish slavery, but that local officials would not implement his orders. These rumors arose before news arrived of the Parisian insurrection of July 14, 1789, much less the text of the *Declaration of the Rights of Man and Citizen*. Clandestine meetings were held. In this document, addressed to the governor of the island, enslaved persons expressed their concern that the mulattos (people of mixed European and African descent) were preventing emancipation. Some enslaved people revolted, unsuccessfully, that September, making clear that those in bondage shared fully in contemporary demands for liberty, equality, and fraternity.

Great General:

The entire Nation of the Black Slaves very humbly begs your august person to accept its respectful homage and to cast a humanitarian eye on the reflections it takes the liberty of presenting to you.

We are not unaware, Great General, of all the negative things that have been presented to you about us; we are painted in such a foul way that even the most solidly virtuous person would have reason to turn against us; but God, who sooner or later always stops the proud plans of men, this God who is so just knows what is deep inside us; he knows that we have never had any project but to patiently accept the oppression of our persecutors. This eternal God, who could no longer suffer so much persecution, must have given Louis XVI, the greatest of monarchs, the charge of delivering all the miserable Christians oppressed by their unjust fellow men. . . .

We have just learned with extreme desperation that the mulattos, far from taking care of their enslaved mothers, brothers, and sisters, have dared claim that we do not deserve to enjoy, as they do, the benefits that come from peace and liberty and are incapable of continuing the hard work that supports the merchants of the white nation and cannot provide any service to the state. This is a great absurdity, and this vile action must demonstrate to you the baseness of spirit of this proud nation and make you see the hate, the jealousy, and all the horror of the disdain this nation has for us. . . . It is not jealousy that forces us to complain about the mulattos, but the harshness they have shown in creating a plan for liberty for only themselves, when we are all of the same family. We do not know, Great General, if you have received the request of the mulattos, but you will receive it soon, and we are happy if we have the good fortune to have reached you before it. . . .

We end our reflections by declaring to you that the entire Nation of Black Slaves united together has a single wish, a singly desire for independence, and all the slaves with a unanimous voice send out only one cry, one clamor to reclaim the liberty they have gained through centuries of suffering and ignominious servitude.

Source: Laurent DuBois and John D. Garrigus, eds. *Slave Revolution in the Caribbean, 1789–1804: A Brief History with Documents* (New York: Bedford/St. Martin's, 2006), 66–67.

This is no longer a Nation that is blinded by ignorance and that trembles at the threat of the lightest punishments; its suffering has enlightened it and has determined it to spill to its last drop of blood rather than support the yoke of slavery, a horrible yoke attacked by the laws, by humanity, and by all of nature, by the Divinity and by our good King Louis XVI. We hope it will be condemned by the illustrious [Governor] Vioménil. Your response, Great General, will decide our destiny and that of the colony.

Please send it to the parish priests who will inform us about it at the announcements at the end of mass. We await it with the greatest impatience, but without leaving behind the respect that is due to your dignity, and the Nation asks you to believe it to be, [Great] Grand General, your most humble and obedient servant.

Signed,

The Entire Nation

29 August 1789

QUESTIONS

- What rhetorical strategies did the authors use to try to convince their audience?
- What connections to Enlightenment ideals do you see in this document?

11.7 SIMÓN BOLÍVAR, "LETTER FROM JAMAICA" (1815)

Venezuelan Simón Bolívar (1783–1830) was a criollo [a creole of solely Spanish descent] who fought for the liberation of Spain's colonies. He described how and why the Latin Americans declared their independence. After his troops were defeated, he went into exile in Jamaica, where he wrote this letter at the nadir of the struggle. Bolívar claimed that some parts of South America had already seized their freedom, in part because of the assistance of Indigenous groups, while others were mired in a bloody, devastating civil war. He called for unity as the best path to victory. Between 1818 and 1825, Bolívar won several notable victories that effectively liberated Venezuela, Bolivia, Colombia, Ecuador, Peru, and Panama. He served as president of several of those countries simultaneously.

Success will crown our efforts, because the destiny of America has been irrevocably decided; the tie that bound her to Spain has been severed. Only a concept maintained that tie and kept the parts of that immense monarchy together. That which formerly bound them now divides them. The hatred that the Peninsula has inspired in us is greater than the ocean between us. It would be easier to have the two continents meet than to reconcile the spirits of the two countries. The habit of obedience; a community of interest, of understanding, of religion; mutual goodwill; a tender regard for the birthplace and good name of our forefathers; in short, all that gave rise to our hopes, came to us from Spain. As a result there was born principle of affinity that seemed eternal, notwithstanding the misbehavior of our rulers, which weakened that sympathy, or, rather, that bond enforced by the domination of their rule.

At present the contrary attitude persists: we are threatened with the fear of death, dishonor, and every harm; there is nothing we have not suffered at the hands of that unnatural stepmother—Spain. The veil has been torn asunder. We have already seen the light, and it is not our desire to be thrust back into darkness. The chains have been broken; we have been freed, and now our enemies seek to enslave us anew. For this reason America fights desperately, and seldom has desperation failed to achieve victory.

Because successes have been partial and spasmodic, we must not lose faith. In some regions the Independents triumph, while in others the tyrants have the advantage. What is the end result? Is not the entire New World in motion, armed for defense? We have but to look around us on this hemisphere to witness a simultaneous struggle at every point.

The war-like state of the La Plata River provinces has purged that territory and led their victorious armies to Upper Peru, arousing Arequipa and worrying the royalists in Lima. Nearly one million inhabitants there now enjoy liberty.

The territory of Chile, populated by 800,000 souls, is fighting the enemy who is seeking her subjugation; but to no avail, because those who long ago put an end to the conquests of this enemy, the free and

Source: Simón Bolívar, "Letter from Jamaica" (1815), trans. Bertrand Lewis, Jr., ed. *Selected Writings of Bolivar* (New York: The Colonial Press Inc., 1951). Reproduced on https://library.brown.edu/create/modernlatinamerica/chapters/chapter-2-the-colonial-foundations/primary-documents-with-accompanying-discussion-questions/document-2-simon-bolivar-letter-from-jamaica-september-6-1815/ (consulted July 26, 2018).

indomitable Araucarias, are their neighbors and compatriots. Their sublime example is proof to those fighting in Chile that a people who love independence will eventually achieve it. . . .

With respect to heroic and hapless Venezuela, events there have moved so rapidly and the devastation has been such that it is reduced to frightful desolation and almost absolute indigence, although it was once among the fairest regions that are the pride of America. Its tyrants govern a desert, and they oppress only those unfortunate survivors who, having escaped death, lead a precarious existence. A few women, children, and old men are all that remain. Most of the men have perished rather than be slaves; those who survive continue to fight furiously on the fields and in the inland towns, until they expire or hurl into the sea those who, insatiable in their thirst for blood and crimes, rival those first monsters who wiped out America's primitive race. Nearly a million persons formerly dwelt in Venezuela, and it is no exaggeration to say that one out of four has succumbed either to the land, sword, hunger, plague, flight, or privation, all consequences of the war, save the earthquake. . . .

The role of the inhabitants of the American hemisphere has for centuries been purely passive. Politically they were nonexistent. We are still in a position lower than slavery, and therefore it is more difficult for us to rise to the enjoyment of freedom. . . .

When the French invasion, stopped only by the walls of Cadiz, routed the fragile governments of the Peninsula, we were left orphans. Prior to that invasion, we had been left to the mercy of a foreign usurper. Thereafter, the justice due us was dangled before our eyes, raising hopes that only came to naught. Finally, uncertain of our destiny, and facing anarchy for want of a legitimate, just, and liberal government, we threw ourselves headlong into the chaos of revolution. Attention was first given to obtaining domestic security against enemies within our midst, and then it was extended to the procuring of external security. Authorities were set up to replace those we had deposed, empowered to direct the course of our revolution and to take full advantage of the fortunate turn of events; thus we were able to found a constitutional government worthy of our century and adequate to our situation. . . .

Surely unity is what we need to complete our work of regeneration. The division among us, nevertheless, is nothing extraordinary, for it is characteristic of civil wars to form two parties, conservatives and reformers. The former are commonly the more numerous, because the weight of habit induces obedience to established powers; the latter are always fewer in number although more vocal and learned. Thus, the physical mass of the one is counterbalanced by the moral force of the other; the contest is prolonged, and the results are uncertain. Fortunately, in our case, the mass has followed the learned. . . .

QUESTIONS

- What rhetorical strategies did Bolivar use to try to convince his audience?
- Do you find the argument persuasive? Why or why not?

11.8 NATHANIEL ISAACS, KING SHAKA ENCOUNTERS EUROPEAN FIREARMS (1836)

Englishman Nathaniel Isaacs was in southeastern Africa searching for ivory. He and his fellow hunters and traders were on good terms with King Shaka of the Zulus, who saw them as sources of medicine and news about the outside world. The English also instructed the Zulus on the proper use of firearms. The Europeans needed Shaka's permission to trade, which helps to explain their willingness to accompany his military expedition against a rival. Although a brilliant tactician, Shaka did not understand the disadvantage of bladed weapons against massed musket fire. The Zulus would pay heavily in blood for their assumption that sufficient numbers of spears could overcome gunpowder weapons.

Early this morning we saw the king sitting outside his kraal with his warriors. Their conversation was mainly on the power of fire-arms. Shaka desired us, when we approached him, to go and shoot some vultures that they might see the effect of our arms. Jacob, having his musket with him, on hearing the command went out instantly and shot one of these carnivorous birds; the effect which this produced was astounding—they were at once, in a measure, paralysed. Jacob's fire had made the birds wild, and therefore, determining not to be outdone by him, we pursued them, but were stopped by a messenger from the king, who required our presence. We perceived him following, accompanied by a body of his people, and we soon found that his object was to try the effect of our fire-arms on another species of the animal creation. By this time a body of from 4,000 to 5,000 people had congregated, when the king halted, and the warriors formed a circle round him, at the same time enclosing us. Shaka addressed us, and asked "if our nation were as numerous as the body of men now about him."

We told him that it was, which he doubted, and then inquired "why we came so few at a time?" We replied that we were perfectly aware of his friendly disposition towards us, and consequently did not require to be numerous. He laughed, and asked me our mode of warfare, and said "he thought it would be no difficult matter to conquer us, as our muskets, when once discharged, took some time to reload, during which they might make a rush, and the losing a few men by the first discharge would be nothing to him who had so many." We now showed him the position of the square, one of us kneeling in front, and the other two in their respective positions, which proved to him that, according to the system of firing in that maneuver, the position was invulnerable to an irregular force. He saw it, but his warriors being inclined to flatter his military genius, observed that by charging in a body, in the way to which they usually resorted, especially under his

Source: Adapted from Nathaniel Isaacs, *Travels and Adventures in Eastern Africa*, 2 vols. (London: Edward Churton, 1836), I: 113–14, 128.

bold and judicious command, they thought it would more than overbalance the strength of our positions, and the force of our arms.

. . . [M]essengers had arrived from the king to request all the white people to proceed to him with their fire-arms immediately, to accompany him to war, as he had resolved on attacking Isseconyarna at his encampment. I walked up the beach with them, and sent the boat back for Mr. Hatton and our party. In the evening we all assembled and discussed the subject. Mr. Farewell observed, that, on a former occasion, he had refused to go when the king had sent for him; it was now however evident, from Shaka sending us a peremptory order to visit him, that he never took notice of a refusal. After some deliberation we agreed to go, as it would be better to accompany him to attack his foes, than excite him to approach and attack us as an enemy.

For several days we were engaged in making preparations for our march: our fire-arms occupied a good deal of our attention and care, so as to have them in proper condition for those active operations for which we were destined.

QUESTIONS

- How would you describe the worldview of Shaka?
- How would you describe the worldview of the English?

11.9 QUANG TRUNG EMPEROR, *EDICT ON ASCENDING THE THRONE* (1788)

Nguyen Hue, the middle Tay Son brother [discussed in the text], proclaimed himself the Quang Trung Emperor during Vietnam's campaign against China, which had intervened against Vietnam ostensibly to restore the previous figurehead emperor. This document suggests that he wished to portray himself as an ordinary person in extraordinary times who had been called by the people to rule. He also provided some tangible benefits of his accession to power both to the common people in the form of tax and forced labor relief, and to elites in the form of amnesty. Defeating a numerically superior Chinese force consolidated his position.

In the past, the Le house lost control of governing the country, and the land was divided between the Trinh clan and the former Nguyen. For more than two hundred years, the people's livelihoods were in disarray; rulers could only cling to false authority, while private families granted themselves fiefs. The pillars connecting Heaven and Earth fell and were not raised; never before had there been such a time. Furthermore, for these past few years, north and south have been at war and have sunk into a morass. I am a cotton-cloth [ordinary] person from Tay Son, without an inch of land to rely on and initially did not have imperial ambitions. Since in their hearts, the people abhor disorder, they longed for an enlightened ruler to benefit the age and settle the people. Therefore, I gathered together a righteous force. We assiduously cleared mountain and forest to aid my elder brother the king, and we rushed forward with our war horses, setting up our base on western ground. In the south, we pacified land belonging to Siam and Cambodia, and then we captured Phu Xuan and took Thank Long. Initially, I wanted to stamp out the rebellion, save the people from the midst of their distress, and then restore the country to the Le clan and return the land to my elder brother. I then could have roamed about in court robes and red slippers, only looking after the joys of the two territories.

But because of the vicissitudes of the times, it could not be as I wished.

No matter how I supported the Le family, the Le heir failed to take care of the gods of land and grain; he abandoned the country and fled. . . . My elder brother Nhac was weary of hard toil, so he was willing to maintain the one prefecture of Qui Nhon and consented to be called the western king. . . . Previously, civil officials and military officers inside and outside the court all wanted me to take the throne even earlier. . . . I truly fear that I am not worthy . . . I assent to Heaven and submit to man, I cannot stubbornly decline. Therefore, this year, on the twenty-second day of the eleventh month, I ascend the throne, and mark it as the first year of the Quang Trung reign.

For all of you common people, I think that of the rules disseminated by the throne for your observance; those concerning morality and law, humaneness, justice, equilibrium, and correctness are the main aspects

Source: George E. Dutton, Jayne S. Werner, and John K. Whitmore, eds., *Sources of Vietnamese Tradition* (New York: Columbia University Press, 2012), 218–19.

of humanity. Today, the people and I start anew, respecting the enlightened methods of the sages of the past in order to govern and civilize all under Heaven.

In every place in the thirteen circuits, the winter's ordinary labor and tax obligations shall be reduced 50% this year. For those affected by the rages of war, I will listen to the reports of the local administrator and waive all taxes.

Some officials of the old dynasty have been implicated in wrongdoing, and many have been reported several times. Except for those who committed serious crimes, the rest shall be pardoned.

QUESTIONS

- What word choices do you see that suggest that Nguyen "wished to portray himself as an ordinary person"?
- What was his view of hierarchy?

CHAPTER

12

"HAVES" AND "HAVE NOTS"

Power Relations and Imperialism, 1800–Present

12.1 MACGREGOR LAIRD AND R. A. K. OLDFIELD, STEAM IS POWER: EXPLORING THE NIGER RIVER (1832–1834)

Written by Macgregor Laird and R. A. K. Oldfield, the sole surviving officers of a British expedition on steamships into the interior of West Africa via the Niger River in 1832–1834, this account emphasizes the European faith in technology and links that faith not only to religious principles—notice the "gospel" reference—but also to the profits to be had and the growing British empire. These explorers create the impression that superior technology like the steam engine was a British birthright that would allow profits to be made and power to be gained.

We have the power in our own hands, moral, physical, and mechanical; the first based on the Bible; the second, upon the wonderful adaptation of the Anglo-Saxon race to all climates, situations, and circumstances,—a facility of constitution which has spread them from Hudson's Bay to the Gulf of Mexico—which is fast peopling Australasia, and which has changed the government of a hundred millions of people in the East; the third, bequeathed to us by the immortal Watt. By his invention every river is laid upon to us, time and distance are shortened. If his spirit is allowed to witness the success of his invention here on earth, I can conceive no application of it that would meet his approbation more than seeing the mighty streams of the Mississippi and the Amazon, the Niger and the Nile, the Indus and the Ganges, stemmed by hundreds of steam-vessels, carrying the glad tidings of "peace and good will towards men" into the dark places of the earth which are now filled with cruelty. This power, which has only been in existence for a quarter of a century, has rendered rivers truly "the highway of nations," and made easy what it would have been difficult, if not impossible, to accomplish without it. We are the chief repository of it: our mineral wealth, and the mechanical habits of our people, give us a superiority over all others in the application of it. Can there be a noble or more profitable application of it, than employing it to open up Central Africa? . . . By it the coast of Africa may be brought within a fortnight's sail from this country; by it her rivers may be explored and navigated in safety . . . by this Proteus-like power, will the oil from her palms, the sugar from her canes, the timber from her forests, be rendered more valuable and marketable.

QUESTIONS

- Is technological change a good thing for these authors?
- What future problems might be created by "opening up Central Africa"?

Source: Macgregor Laird and R. A. K. Oldfield, *Narrative of an Expedition into the Interior of Africa, by the River Niger, in the Steam-vessels Quorra and Alburkah in 1832, 1833, and 1834*, 2 vols. (London: Richard Bentley, 1837), II: 397–99.

12.2 FERDINAND DE LESSEPS, "REPORT TO HIS HIGHNESS THE VICEROY OF EGYPT" (MARCH 25, 1856)

In the aftermath of an assassination of the hereditary Ottoman Viceroy for Egypt, French diplomat and entrepreneur Viscount Ferdinand de Lesseps (1805–1894) lobbied his successor for the right to build a canal. With the support of the Ottoman sultan, de Lesseps was able to acquire permission in November 1854, during the Crimean War, which made France an Ottoman ally against Russia. De Lesseps had to raise an estimated 200 million francs to build the 110-mile-long canal and ports at either end. This Report proposes to found a journal to influence public opinion, illustrating the growing role of the press and public relations in imperialism. Of the 300 million francs ultimately spent building the canal, almost one-third was spent on promotion, politics, and incidentals. Here de Lesseps asserts the importance of Egypt and the benefits that would accrue to its government and people from the cooperation necessary to establish a canal. Events would prove this accommodating attitude to be temporary.

The unanimous welcome accorded to the scheme, the great and universal interests represented by it, seem to make it necessary for the enterprise of making the Suez Canal to have direct and constant communication with public opinion by a special, and in some sort an official, organ.

By means of such an organ, the company entrusted with managing this powerful element of civilisation and wealth for two worlds would have periodical and regular relations with its shareholders. While keeping public opinion on the alert, it would acquaint all with its progress and work. . . .

The organ of the International Company, if edited with intelligence and spirit, neither extravagant nor exclusively national, should become the organ of the whole commercial interest in the Mediterranean. It ought to cross the isthmus and unite the interests of East and West in its sheets.

Egypt would naturally become one of the chief objects of its interest and solicitude; for there can be no assured prosperity, and no security for the future of the Company, if Egypt is wretched and its position precarious. The Canal through the Isthmus of Suez is an event pregnant with political consequences to the ancient country of the Pharaohs. She will hold the key of the world; she will play an important role among the Powers; by the force of circumstances she will affect the equilibrium of Europe; she will compel nature to make her straits as important as those of the Dardanelles.

. . . Henceforth all nations will be interested in the prosperity and the future of Egypt. But intellectual intercourse must be established; Europe must know Egypt better; it must be made familiar with her efforts and difficulties in order to understand the obstacles she has already overcome and those she has yet to

Source: Ferdinand de Lesseps, *The Suez Canal: Letters and Documents Descriptive of Its Rise and Progress in 1854–1856*, trans. N. d'Anvers (London: Henry S. King & Co., 1876), 243–45.

conquer. Egypt in the future must become what she was in the past,—the leading Power of the East. The International Canal Company is henceforth answerable for the progress or decline of Egypt; there must be reciprocity of co-operation and defence between them.

A newspaper, the company's organ, would fail in its object if it did not understand that one of the chief objects of its publication is to help Egypt to develop her internal resources and make herself popular in the outer world. . . . It should always be a means of peace-making, of union, and of good-will to all; and should make a rule against admitting anything that would embitter, disturb, or divide the great interests which it is its aim to promote on behalf of industry and of peace.

QUESTIONS

- How did de Lesseps support his claims?
- Was this a form of imperialism? Why or why not?

12.3 WILLIAM HOWARD RUSSELL, ON MASSACRES IN INDIA (1858)

Irishman William Howard Russell (1820–1907), one of the first journalistic war correspondents, went to India soon after the revolt on behalf of the *London Times*. He visited Cawnpore, the site of the murder of British women and children and the far bloodier reprisals against both rebels and civilians taken by British forces. Russell recognized the cultural elements of British actions and suggested that racial attitudes were at the heart of the conflict.

I t was 6.30 in the morning, when Stewart, who has the art of compressing himself into a very small compass, woke me up "to look at Cawnpore." The scenes where great crimes have been perpetrated ever possess an interest, which I would not undertake to stigmatize as morbid; and surely among the sites rendered infamous forever in the eyes of British posterity, Cawnpore will be pre-eminent as the magnitude of the atrocities with which it is connected. But, though pre-eminent among crimes, the massacre of Cawnpore is by no means alone in any of the circumstances which mark turpitude and profundity of guilt. We who suffered from it think that there never was such wickedness in the world, and the incessant efforts of a gang of forgers and utterers of base stories have surrounded it with horrors that have been vainly invented in the hope of adding to the indignation and burning desire for vengeance which the naked facts arouse. Helpless garrisons, surrendering under capitulation, have been massacred ere now; men, women, and children have been ruthlessly butchered by the enemies of their race ere now; risings, such as that of the people of Pontus under Mithridates, of the Irish Roman Catholics against the Protestant settlers

in 1641, of the actors in the Sicilian vespers, of the assassins who smote and spared none on the Eve of St. Bartholomew, have been over and over again attended by inhuman cruelty, violation, and torture. The history of mediaeval Europe affords many instances of crimes as great as those of Cawnpore; the history of more civilized periods could afford some parallel to them in more modern times, and amid most civilized nations.

In fact, the peculiar aggravation of the Cawnpore massacres was this, that the deed was done by a subject-race—by black men who dared to shed the blood of their masters, and that of poor helpless ladies and children. Here we had not only a servile war and a sort of Jacquerie combined, but we had a war of religion, a war of race, and a war of revenge, of hope, of some national promptings to shake off the yoke of a stranger, and to re-establish the full power of native chiefs, and the full sway of native religions. There is a kind of God's revenge against murder in the unsuccessful issue of all enterprises commenced in massacre, and founded on cruelty and bloodshed. Whatever the causes of the mutiny and the revolt, it is clear enough that one of the

Source: William Howard Russell, *My Diary in India in the Year 1858-9*, 2 vols. (London: Routledge, 1860), I: 163–64.

modes by which the leaders, as if by common instinct, determined to effect their end was, the destruction of every white man, woman, or child who fell into their hands—a design which the kindliness of the people, or motives of policy, frustrated on many remarkable occasions.

QUESTIONS

- How did Russell describe the massacre?
- Why did he consistently compare the massacre to "mediaeval Europe"?

12.4 ROGER CASEMENT, REPORT ON CONGO (1903)

Irishman Roger Casement (1864–1916) was a British consul in Congo. He gathered evidence of the depredations inflicted on the Congolese by the Free State's officials to gather rubber. The Report touched off a major public scandal that forced the Belgian government to take control over the colony from Leopold II. Casement did another exposé of imperialist labor practices in Peru. He was executed during World War I for negotiating with Germany to support an armed revolt in Ireland.

The town of N* consists approximately of seventy-one K* houses, and seventy-three occupied by L*. These latter seemed industrious, simple folk, many weaving palm fiber into mats or native cloth; others had smithies, working brass wire into bracelets, chains, and anklets; some iron-workers making knives. . . . I then asked them to tell me why they had left their homes. Three of the men sat down in front of me, and told a tale which I cannot think can be true, but it seemed to come straight from their hearts. I repeatedly asked certain parts to be gone over again while I wrote in my note-book. The fact of my writing down and asking for names, &c, seemed to impress them, and they spoke with what certainly impressed me as being great sincerity.

I asked, first, why they had left their homes, and had come to live in a strange far-off country among the K*, where they owned nothing, and were little better than servitors. *AW*, when this question was put, women as well, shouted out, "On account of the rubber tax levied by the Government posts." . . .

I asked then how this tax was imposed. One of them, who had been hammering out an iron neck collar on my arrival, spoke first. He said: "I am N N. These other two beside me are O O and P P, all of us Y**. From our country each village had to take twenty loads of rubber. These loads were big: they were as big as this. . . ." (Producing an empty basket which came nearly up to the handle of my walking-stick.) "That was the first size. We had to fill that up, but as rubber got scarcer the white man reduced the amount. We had to take these loads in four times a-month."

Q. "How much pay did you get for this?"
A. (Entire audience.) "We got no pay! We got nothing!"

And then N N, whom I asked, again said:—
"Our village got cloth and a little salt, but not the people who did the work. Our Chiefs eat up the cloth; the workers got nothing. The pay was a fathom of cloth and a little salt for every big basket full, but it was given to the Chief, never to the men. It used to take ten days to get the twenty baskets of rubber—we were always in the forest and then when we were late we were killed. We had to go further and further into the forest to find the rubber vines, to go without food, and our women had to give up cultivating the fields and gardens. Then we starved. Wild beasts—the leopards—killed some of us when we were working away in the forest, and others got lost

Source: Roger Casement, *Correspondence and Report from His Majesty's Consul at Borna respecting the Administration of the Independent State of the Congo* (London: His Majesty's Stationary Office, 1904), 60–61.

or died from exposure and starvation, and we begged the white man to leave us alone, saying we' could get no more rubber, but the white-men and their soldiers said: 'Go! You are only beasts yourselves, you are nyama (meat).' We; tried, always going further into the forest, and when we failed and our rubber was short, the soldiers came to our towns and killed us. Many were shot, some had their ears cut off; others were tied up with ropes around their necks and bodies and taken away. The white men sometimes at the posts did not know of the bad things the soldiers did to us, but it was the white men who sent the soldiers to punish us for not bringing in enough rubber." . . .

[P P:] "We fled because we could not endure the things done to us. Our Chiefs were hanged, and we were killed and starved and worked beyond endurance to get rubber."

Q. "How do you know it was the white men themselves who ordered these cruel things to be done to you? These things, must have been done without the white man's knowledge by the black soldiers."

A. (P P): "The white men told their soldiers: 'You kill only women; you cannot kill men. You must prove that you kill men.' So then the soldiers when they killed us" (here he stopped and hesitated, and then pointing to the private parts of my bulldog—it was lying asleep at my feet), he said: "then they cut off those things and took them to the white men, who said: 'It is true, you have killed men.'"

Q. "You mean to tell me that any white man ordered your bodies to be mutilated like that, and those parts of you carried to him?"
P P, O O, and all (shouting): "Yes! many white men. D E did it."

Q. "You say this is true? Were many of you so treated after being shot?"

A. All (shouting out): "Nkoto! Nkoto!" (Very many! Very many!)

There was no doubt that these people were not inventing. Their vehemence, their flashing eyes, their excitement, was not simulated. Doubtless they exaggerated the numbers, but they were clearly telling what they knew and loathed. . . .

QUESTIONS

- According to the Report, how did the Belgians rule the Congo?
- What aspects are similar to traditional European imperialism? Different?

12.5 COUNT DE GOBINEAU, *THE INEQUALITY OF HUMAN RACES* (1855)

Joseph Arthur, Count de Gobineau (1816–1882) was a French diplomat. His *Inequality of Human Races* was published in four volumes in 1853–1855. In pseudoscientific terms, de Gobineau attributed the rise and fall of civilizations to racial characteristics. Social Darwinists endorsed much of de Gobineau's thinking because it justified imperialism. These views were also easily adopted by those who wanted to do more than dominate others. The Nazis, for example, took their interpretation of "survival of the fittest" literally.

If the human races were equal, the course of history would form an affecting, glorious, and magnificent picture. The races would all have been equally intelligent, with a keen eye for their true interests and the same aptitude for conquest and domination. Early in the world's history, they would have gladdened the face of the earth with a crowd of civilizations, all flourishing at the same time, and all exactly alike. . . .

Civilization is incommunicable, not only to savages, but also to more enlightened nations. This is shown by the efforts of French goodwill and conciliation in the ancient kingdom of Algiers at the present day as well as by the experience of the English in India, and the Dutch in Java. There are no more striking and conclusive proofs of the unlikeness and inequality of races. . . .

We come now to the white peoples. These are gifted with reflective energy, or rather with an energetic intelligence. They have a feeling for utility, but in a sense far wider and higher, more courageous and ideal, than the yellow races; a perseverance that takes account of obstacles and ultimately find a means of overcoming them; a greater physical power, an extraordinary instinct for order, not merely as a guarantee of peace and tranquility, but as an indispensable means of self-preservation. At the same time, they have a remarkable, and even extreme love of liberty, and are openly hostile to the formalism under which the Chinese are glad to vegetate, as well as to the strict despotism which is the only way of governing the negro. . . .

Such is the lesson of history. It shows us that all civilizations derive from the white race, that none can exist without its help, and that society is great and brilliant only so far as it preserves the blood of the noble group that created it, provided that this group itself belong to the most illustrious branch of our species.

QUESTIONS

- What was de Gobineau's argument?
- How would this document have been used to support imperialism? Or Nazism?

Sources: James R. Lehning and Megan Armstrong, eds., *Europeans in the World*, vol. 2, *Sources on Cultural Contact from 1650 to the Present* (Upper Saddle River, NJ: Prentice Hall, 2001), 106–10, 106–07 and Kevin Reilly, Stephen Kauffman, and Angela Bodino, eds., *Racism: A Global Reader* (Armonk, NY: M.E. Sharpe, 2003), 196–97.

12.6 NDANSI KUMALO, ON THE BRITISH CONQUEST OF THE NDBEBELE (1893)

Ndansi Kumalo (b. 1860?) was a Ndebele chief under King Lobengula until the British South Africa Company, headed by Cecil Rhodes, decided to appropriate their territory into what had modestly been named Rhodesia. This account was recorded from oral testimony in the 1930s and describes events between July and December 1893. The rebellion that occurred was a response to mistreatment and exploitation; it was swiftly defeated, but a more violent uprising took place three years later. The British destroyed resistance by dynamiting the caves where the Ndebele resistance attempted to hide.

We were terribly upset and very angry at the coming of the white men, for Lobengula had sent to the Queen in England and he was under her protection and it was quite unjustified that white men should come with force into our country. Our regiments were very distressed that we were not in a fit condition to fight for the king because of the smallpox.

[After a defeat in battle] Then the white people came to where we were living and sent word round that all chiefs and warriors should go into Bulawayo and discuss peace, for the King had gone and they wanted to make peace. The first order we got was, "When you come in, come in with cattle so that we can see that you are sincere about it." The white people said, "Now that your King has deserted you, we occupy your country. Do you submit to us?" What could we do? "If you are sincere, come back and bring in all your arms, guns and spears." We did so. . . .

So we surrendered to the white people and were told to go back to our homes and live our usual lives and attend to our crops. But the white men sent native police who did abominable things; they were cruel and assaulted a lot of our people and helped themselves to our cattle and goats. These policemen were not our own people; anybody was made a policeman. We were treated like slaves. They came and were overbearing and we were ordered to carry their clothes and bundles. They interfered with our wives and our daughters and molested them. . . . How the rebellion started I do not know; there was no organization, it was like a fire that suddenly flames up. We had been flogged by native police and then they rubbed salt water in the wounds. There was much bitterness because so many of our cattle were branded and taken away from us; we had no property, nothing we could call our own. We said, "It is no good living under such conditions; death would be better—let us fight." Our King gone, we had submitted to the white people and they ill-treated us until we became desperate and tried to make an end of it all. We knew that we had very little chance because their weapons were so much superior to ours. . . .

Source: Quoted in William H. Worger, Nancy L. Clark, and Edward A. Alpers, eds., *Africa and the West: A Documentary History*, vol. 1, *From the Slave Trade to Conquest, 1441–1905*, 2nd ed. (New York: Oxford University Press, 2010), 266–67.

I fought in the rebellion. . . . We took cover . . . and tried to ambush them. We were forced by the nature of our weapons not to expose ourselves. I had a gun, a breech-loader. They—the white men—fought us with big guns and Maxims and rifles.

QUESTIONS

- How did Kumalo portray the British?
- How does the situation compare to that of the Belgian Congo in Document 12.4?

13

NEW FORMS OF CONTROL

Decolonization and Economic Dominance, 1775–1914

13.1 MANUEL ABAD Y QUEIPO, ON THE DIVISIONS IN MEXICAN SOCIETY (1795)

Manuel Abad y Queipo (1751–1825) was a member of the Roman Catholic clergy who served as a judge for Indigenous people and earned a doctorate in canon law. He held several high-ranking positions in the hierarchy during the era leading up to and during the Mexican Revolution. Appointed a bishop twice, he was never confirmed by the papacy, ostensibly because he had been born out of wedlock. This document was part of a report made in 1795 that he gave to Prussian scientist and naturalist Alexander von Humboldt, who quoted it at length in his popular account of his five-year trip to Spain's American colonies. He believed that the mistreatment of Indigenous people was a major reason for the weakness of the Spanish Empire and identified the divisions within Mexican society as a potential source of violence.

The population of New Spain is composed of three classes of men, whites or Spaniards, Indians, and castes. I suppose the Spaniards to compose the tenth part of the whole mass. In their hands almost all the property and all the wealth of the kingdom are centered. The Indians and the castes cultivate the soil; they are in the service of the better sort of people; and they live by the work of their hands. Hence there results between the Indians and the whites that opposition of interests, and that mutual hatred, which universally takes place between those who possess all and those who possess nothing, between masters and those who live in servitude. Thus we see, on the one hand, the effects of envy and discord, deception, theft, and the inclination to prejudice the interests of the rich; and on the other, arrogance, severity, and the desire of taking every moment advantage of the helplessness of the Indian. I am not ignorant that these evils everywhere spring from a great in equality of condition. But in America they are rendered still more terrific, because there exists no intermediate state: we are rich or miserable, noble or degraded by the laws or the force of opinion (*infame de derecho y hecho.*)

In fact, the Indians and the races of mixed blood (*castas*) are in a state of extreme humiliation. The colour peculiar to the Indians, their ignorance, and especially their poverty, remove them to an infinite distance from the whites, who occupy the first rank in the population of New Spain. The privileges which the laws seem to concede to the Indians are of small advantage to them, perhaps they are rather hurtful. Shut up in a narrow space of 600 varas (500 metres) of radius, assigned by an ancient law to the Indian villages, the natives may be said to have no individual property, and are bound to cultivate the common property (*bienes de communidad*). This cultivation is a load so much the more insupportable to them, as they have now for several years back lost all hope of ever being able to enjoy the fruit of their labour.

The law prohibits the mixture of cast[e]s; it prohibits the whites from taking up their residence in Indian villages; and it prevents the natives from establishing

Source: Manuel Abad y Queipo, *Informe del Obisbo y Cabildo eclesiastico de Valladolid de Mechoacan al Rey sobre Jurisdiccion y Ymundides del Clero Americano* (October 25, 1795), quoted in Alexander von Humboldt, *Political Essay on the Kingdom of New Spain*, trans. John Black, 2 vols. (London: Longman, Hurst, Rees, Orme, and Brown, 1811), I: 189–94.

themselves among the Spaniards. This state of insulation opposes obstacles to civilization. The Indians are governed by themselves; all their subaltern magistrates are of the copper coloured race. In every village we find eight or ten old Indians who live at the expense of the rest, in the most complete idleness, whose authority is founded either on a pretended elevation of birth, or on a cunning policy transmitted from father to son. These chiefs, generally the only inhabitants of the village who speak Spanish, have the greatest interest in maintaining their fellow citizens in the most profound ignorance; and they contribute the most to perpetuate prejudices, ignorance, and the ancient barbarity of manners. . . .

The cast[e]s, descendants of negro slaves, are branded with infamy by the law; and are subjected to tribute. This direct impost imprints on them an indelible stain: they consider it as a mark of slavery transmissible to the latest generations. Among the mixed race, among the mestizos and mulattoes, there are many families, who from their colour, their physiognomy, and their cultivation, might be confounded with the Spaniards; but the law keeps them in a state of degradation and contempt. Endowed with an energetic and ardent character, these men of colour live in a constant state of irritation against the whites; and we must be astonished that their resentment does not more frequently dispose them to acts of vengeance.

QUESTIONS

- In the excerpt, how were racial divisions maintained in Spanish American society?
- What factors made the experiences of Indigenous people and different castes especially difficult?

13.2 VISCOUNT PALMERSTON, ON THE LIMITATIONS ON MORALS IN ECONOMIC MATTERS (1841)

At the time of this speech, Henry John Temple, Viscount Palmerston (1784–1865; prime minister 1855–58; 1859–65) was a member of the Whig Party and the foreign secretary of the United Kingdom. Palmerston dominated British foreign policy in this era. Here, he ridiculed the proposal to lower the tariff on foreign sugar. Since sugar from the colonies was not subject to this duty, it was hoped that this measure would increase the consumption of sugar and raise tax revenues. His irony does not detract from his depiction of how British entrepreneurs made a mockery of prohibitions on commodities produced by enslaved people.

. . . [W]e ought not to consume the produce of slave labour—Well if that principle is to be adopted, apply it honestly, faithfully, and throughout. Prohibit the importation of the enormous quantities of cotton which are brought every year from the United States of North America. Prohibit the tobacco; prohibit the rice which you bring from thence and which is all the produce of slave labour. [Cheers and cries of oh! oh!] The Hon. Gentlemen opposite laugh and cry Oh! at the very idea of such a thing—they shrink from such an application of their principle—they know that such an application of their principle would deprive of employment some millions of their fellow countrymen, and would bring them to utter ruin. They say it would not be expedient to do this—expedient indeed! A pretty principle this to take stand upon, the practical application of which is to depend on comparative expediency. [Cheers]. . . .

We say to the Brazilians we can supply you with cotton goods cheaper and better than any you can get elsewhere, will you buy them? By all means, reply the Brazilians, and we will pay you for your goods by our sugar and our coffee. No, say we, your sugar and coffee are produced by slave labour, we are men of principle, and our consciences will not allow us to consume the produce of slave labour, we cannot take your sugar and your coffee—Well then, anybody would imagine that the transaction ended here; that we sent our manufactures to some free labour market, and left the Brazilians to eat and drink their sugar and coffee, or to dispose of them as best they may.

No such thing; we are men of principle, but we are also men of business, and we try to help the Brazilians out of their difficulty. We say to them, it is true that we cannot consume your slave labour sugar and coffee; but close by us, and near at hand live some forty millions of industrious thriving Germans who are not so conscientious as we are; take your sugar to them; they will buy it of you, and you can pay us for our cottons with the money you will thus receive; and though we cannot take your sugar and coffee, we shall not scrapie to take the money you have sold them for. But the Brazilians represent that there will be some difficulty in this. The Germans. they say, live on the other side of

Source: *Speech of the Right Honourable Viscount Palmerston in the House of Commons, on Wednesday, May 19, 1841 on Lord Sandon's Resolution* (London: J. Ridgway, 1841), 5–8.

the Atlantic, we must send them our sugar in ships; now our ships are few in number, and are ill fitted to cope with the waves of the great ocean; what shall we do! Our reply is ready— Do not let this disturb you, we have plenty of ships, and they are quite at your service—[cheers.]

It is true that slave labour produce would contaminate our warehouses, our shops, and our tables; but our ships are different things, and they shall carry your sugar for you. But the Brazilians have another difficulty; indeed there is no end to their difficulties. They tell us that the Germans are particular in their own way about these matters, and have a fancy for refined sugar.—That it is not easy to refine sugar in Brazil, and that the Germans do not like the trouble of refining it themselves. Our desire to oblige is inexhaustible, we again step in with an expedient: Come never mind, we will help you here also; we will not only carry your sugar, but we will refine it for you too. It is sinful indeed to consume slave labour sugar, but there can be no harm in refining it, which, in fact, is to cleanse it from part of its original impurity—[cheers.]

Accordingly. we refine the sugar, and to be sure we think we have done. Not a bit. The Brazilians are at us again. The fact is, say they, we produce a great deal of sugar; more than the Germans will buy, at least at a remunerating price; what are we to do with our surplus? Well, our goodness is infinite; having carried the Brazilians on so far. We are determined not to leave them till we have seen them safe home; we have a remedy, we tell them, for this also; we ourselves will buy your surplus. It cannot indeed be consumed at home, because the people of this kingdom are the inhabitants of the mother country, and are men of conscience; but we will send it to the West Indies, and to Australia; the people who live in those parts are only Negroes and Colonists and what right can they have to consciences; your slave labour sugar can do them no harm: and now, that you may not plague us any more about these matters, we tell you at once, that if ever the price of our own sugar shall rise above a certain amount, we will then buy more of your slave labour sugar, and eat it ourselves.

QUESTIONS

- How did British entrepreneurs actively evade attempts to limit commodities produced by enslaved people?
- Why did Palmerston oppose this proposal?

13.3 SALOMÉ UREÑA DE HENRIQUEZ, "16TH OF AUGUST"

In this poem, Dominican poet, educator, and feminist Salomé Ureña de Henriquez (1850–1897) commemorated "Restoration Day," when the republic regained its full independence after a Spanish invasion from 1861 to 1865. This elegy to liberty and secular ideals underscores the refusal of the Dominican people to accept the recolonization of their country and provides a warning against similar efforts by other countries.

Reclined luxuriantly
On her bed of floating seaspray
Heedless of the thick fog
In which the sky enveloped her glories
Quisqueya [a Taino word for the island], aban-
    doned [was] indifferent
To the sound of the waves that lulled her to sleep.
And in her fleeting lethargy,
She did not see the ambition for shiny metal
Of the giant hydra,
Sacrificing honor and patriotism,
A future of high hopes,
To sink—oh Lord!—into the deep abyss.
Such a fatigued athlete,
She lost her liberty, the true currency;
The sad tropic breeze
Folded its spotless wings,
So as not to ruffle, not to stir,
The foreign flag of Castille.
The tall palm tree laid low
Turns its brow upward to grow free;
The chest of the gallant
Trembles with secret pain;
Quisqueya, the same, apparently calm,

Was lulled asleep by the sound of the waves.
More, out of sheer arrogance,
The Iberian dictated servitude and death
By law to the sturdy people,
and Quisqueya shook off her swoon
to squeeze her delicate bosom
into the armor of Pelagius. [a theologian who
    supported temporal law over religious
    authority]
Rising up indignantly,
seeking the motto written with her blood;
and upon her rousing call,
sensing the insult to her fortune,
she made the legions tremble that in Granada
saw the crescent at their feet.
The magnificent multicolored flag
showed itself in this contest of the Cross;
in pursuit of eternal fame
a thousand of the faithful gathered in its
    shadow,
whose triumph immortalized the moment,
as the echoes of the old country died away.
And the cry of victory rang from valley to
    mountain,

Source: Salomé Ureña de Henriquez, "16th of August," trans. Eric Paul Roorda, in *The Dominican Republic Reader: History, Culture, Politics*, ed. Eric Paul Roorda, Lauren Derby, and Raymundo Gonzálo (Durham, NC: Duke University Press, 2014), 228–30.

and in vain, in vain Spain
tried to stifle it with her ferocity:
but Quisqueya dug a grave for her pride
on the fields of glory.
And such a fierce example
and warning perhaps to other nations,
how the land of banners,
uncertain, laid low, and vanquished,
turned the tables on the terrified Iberian,
sent packing by his hosts aroused to war.
Honor, eternal glory

of August to those giant champions,
who in unequal contests,
struggling with the faith of patriotism,
returned greatness to their history,
teaching a hard lesson to despotism!
For them today the Homeland lifts to her brow
a wreath of a thousand laurels,
with ardent affection,
bathed by the sun of hope,
in pursuit of new light, of new life,
to reach an intrepid future.

QUESTIONS

- What is the message of the poem?
- Which stanza stands out the most? Why does it stand out to you?

13.4 JEAN PIERRE BOYER, HAITI'S RURAL CODE (1826)

This law was passed in July 1826. It sought to institute or reinstitute a type of forced labor reminiscent of that imposed by earlier Haitian leaders from Toussaint-L'Ouverture, to Dessalines, to Christophe. The new law put the military in charge of enforcing obedience on the population, which had few means of protecting itself, but the army was neither strong enough nor competent enough to make the system work. This rural code shows the desperation of the elite to find workers to revive the export economy and the lengths they were willing to go to. Former slaves and the descendants of enslaved persons refused to tolerate this kind of control for such a small percentage of the benefit.

Art. 1.—AGRICULTURE being the principal source of prosperity in a state, shall be specially protected and encouraged by the civil and military authorities. . . .

Art. 3.—It being the duty of every citizen to aid in sustaining the state, either by his active services or by his industry, those who are not employed in the civil service, or called upon for the military service; those who do not exercise a licensed profession; those who are not employed in felling timber for exportation; in fine, those who cannot justify their means of existence, shall cultivate the soil.

Art. 4.—Citizens whose employment is agriculture shall not be permitted to quit the country to inhabit the towns and villages, without a permission from the justice of peace of the commune they desire to quit, and of the commune in which they desire to establish themselves. . . .

Art. 6.—Military enlistments, which can only be made by order of the President of Haiti, shall never be made of citizens attached to agriculture, unless by express command of the chief of state, alleging imminent danger. . . .

Art. 38.—The labourers attached to any plantation labouring for one quarter of the produce, shall have assigned to them for their personal use a garden for provisions, which they shall cultivate during their hours and days of rest. . . .

Art. 57.—Each individual entitled to share shall be inscribed upon list in one of three classes, according to his strength and activity, and the time he has worked.

The monies to be shared shall be divided into quarter shares, half shares and shares. The drivers and headmen shall be entitled to three shares each.

Source: *Code rural of Haiti as issued by president Boyer and printed in Port-au-Prince in 1826* (London: Printed by order of the House of Commons, 1827), https://archive.org/details/haticopyofcoderu00grea/page/n2 (consulted July 11, 2019).

Sugar-boilers, and chief carter, and other head-men, two shares each.

Good working men and women of the first class, a share and half each.

Those or the second class, a share each.

Those of the third class, three quarters of a share each.

Children from twelve to sixteen years of age, and elderly people, half a share.

Children from nine to twelve, and weak infirm people, a quarter share each.

Any monies remaining over and above the shares paid to each person shall be divided among those who have shown the most steadiness and activity in their labour. . . .

Art. 60.—Proprietors farmers and overseers, are forbidden to give permission to any labourer to travel in the commune, or to absent himself from his domicile and work, for more than eight days. . . .

Art. 61.—Proprietors, farmers or overseers, shall employ the labourers with whom they have contracted in agricultural labour, or labour relating to agriculture *only*. They shall treat their labourers as parents would their children. . . .

Art. 123.—The commandant of each military district, having the general inspection of the cultivation of the district entrusted to him, unites in his own person all the authority necessary for enforcing agriculture. . . .

Art. 188.—Gangs of labourers upon estates shall be obedient to their drivers, jobbers, sub-farmers, farmers, proprietors and managers or overseers, whenever they are called upon to execute the labour they have bound themselves to perform.

Art. 189.—Every act of disobedience or insult on the part of a workman, commanded

to do any work to which he is subjected, shall be punished by imprisonment, according to the exigency of the case, at the discretion of the justice of peace of the commune.

Art. 190.—Saturdays and Sundays and holidays being at the disposal of the labourers, they shall not on working days abandon their work, to indulge in dancing or feasting, either by day or by night. Such delinquents shall be subject to imprisonment for three days for the first offence, and for six days, in case of a repetition of the offence.

QUESTIONS

- How did the Code justify this labor system?
- Which portions of the Code seem especially unfair to you? Why?

13.5 JOSÉ MARTÍ, *OUR AMERICA* (1891)

Cuban José Julián Martí y Pérez, known as José Martí (1853–1895), was an intellectual who wrote this essay while in political exile in the United States. He articulated a national identity for the island during its struggle for independence against Spain. Martí expressed a populist vision of anti-racial and anti-imperialist nation in which people would work together within Cuba and across the hemisphere. His fears of U.S. aggression and the dangers of racial division ultimately proved accurate. Martí attempted to organize a revolution, but U.S. authorities seized all the supplies and munitions that he and his Cuban Revolutionary Party had accumulated, leading to the collapse of his efforts and his own death. Popular at the time, Martí became an icon across Latin America because of the powerful, positive vision of Cuban and "American" identity he articulated.

Good government is nothing more than the balance of the country's national elements. . . .

Thrown out of gear for three centuries by a power which denied men the right to use their reason, the continent disregarded or closed its ears to the unlettered throngs that helped bring it to redemption, and embarked on a government based on reason—a reason belonging to all for the common good, not the university brand of reason over the peasant brand. The problems of independence did not lie in a change of forms but in change of spirit.

It was imperative to make common cause with the oppressed, in order to secure a new system opposed to the ambitions and governing habits of the oppressors. . . . Our America is saving itself from its enormous mistakes—the pride of its capital cities, the blind triumph of a scorned peasantry, the excessive influx of foreign ideas and formulas, the wicked and unpolitical disdain for the aboriginal race. . . .

If a Republic refuses to open its arms to all, and move ahead with all, it dies. . . .

The scorn of our formidable neighbor, who does not know us, is Our America's greatest danger. . . . Nations should have a pillory for whoever stirs up useless hatred, and another for whoever fails to tell them the truth in time.

There can be no racial animosity, because there are no races. . . . The soul, equal and eternal, emanates from bodies of different shapes and colors. Whoever foments and spreads antagonism and hatred between the races, sins against humanity. But as nations take shape among other different nations, there is a condensation of vital and individual characteristics of thought and habit, expansion and conquest, vanity and greed which could—from the latent state of national concern, and in the period of internal disorder, or the rapidity with which the country's character has been accumulating—be turned into a serious threat for the weak and isolated neighboring countries, declared by the strong country to be inferior and perishable.

Source: José Martí, "Our America," in *The Cuba Reader: History, Culture, Politics,* ed. Aviva Chomsky, Barry Carr, and Pamela Marie Smorkaloff (Durham, NC: Duke University Press, 2003), 122–27.

. . . [T]he present generation is carrying industrious America along the road enriched by their sublime fathers; from Rio Grande to the Strait of Magellan, the Great Semí [a Taino deity], astride its condor, spreading the seed of the new America over the romantic nations of the continent and the sorrowful islands of the sea!

QUESTIONS

- What was Martí's main message?
- Why do you think Martí became an "icon" after his death?

13.6 ALEXANDROS YPSILANTIS, PROCLAMATION OF REVOLT (1821)

Alexandros Ypsilantis (1792–1828) headed a secret society dedicated to Greek independence. He was a high-ranking Russian cavalry officer from a prominent family. This proclamation, issued on February 24, 1821, in the Danubian Principalities (Moldavia and Wallachia) was intended to spark a general uprising of the Greek Orthodox peoples throughout the Balkans. Clearly, Ypsilantis acted upon the belief that "Greek" meant all followers of Greek Orthodoxy, not just those who either spoke Greek or were ethnic Greeks. Ypsilantis and the Enlightened members of the secret society also expected outside help based on the European heritage of classical Greek thought. The hope for elections and a popular government took a long time to reach fruition.

Fight for Faith and Motherland! The time has come, O Hellenes. Long ago the people of Europe, fighting for their own rights and liberties, invited us to imitation. . . .

Our brethren and friends are everywhere ready. The Serbs, the Souliots and the whole of Epirus, bearing arms, await us. Let us then unite with enthusiasm. The Motherland is calling us!

The enlightened peoples of Europe are occupied in restoring the same well-being, and full of gratitude for the benefactions of our forefathers towards them, desire the liberation of Greece. We, seemingly worthy of ancestral virtue and of the present century, are hopeful that we will achieve their defense and help. Many of these freedom-lovers want to come and fight alongside us. . . . Our cowardly enemy is sick and weak. Our generals are experienced, and all our fellow countrymen are full of enthusiasm. Unite then, O brave and magnanimous Greeks! Let national phalanxes be formed, let patriotic legions appear and you will see those old giants of despotism fall by themselves, before our triumphant banners. . . .

Turn your eyes, O fellow countrymen, and behold our miserable state! See here the ruined churches! There, our children seized for the shameless use of the shameless hedonism of our barbarous tyrants! Our houses stripped bare, our fields laid waste, and ourselves miserable slaves!

It is time to overthrow this insufferable yoke, to liberate the Motherland, to throw down the [Turkish Muslim] Crescent from the clouds, in order to raise up the syambol by which we always conquer, I mean the Cross, and thus rid the Motherland and our Orthodox faith from the impious scorn of the heathen.

Among ourselves the most noble is he who bravely defends the rights of the Motherland and works for it

Source: Richard Clogg, ed. and trans., *The Movement for Greek Independence 1770–1821: A Collection of Documents* (London: Macmillan, 1976), 201–03.

in a beneficial way. The nation assembled will elect its rulers, and to this highest parliament all our acts will yield. . . .

Let us then once again, O brave and magnanimous Greeks, invite Liberty to the classical land of Greece! . . .

QUESTIONS

- How did Ypsilantis portray each side in the revolution to come?
- Do you find the argument persuasive? Why or why not?

14

PRIVATION AND POWERLESSNESS IN AN AGE OF PLENTY

Political Change, 1860–1945

14.1 HAILE SELASSIE, SPEECH (1936)

Haile Selassie I (regent 1916–1930; emperor 1930–1974) came to power in part because of his commitment to defending Christianity against Islam. He took the name "Might of the Trinity" to mark that view. A progressive who sought to improve the lives of his people, Selassie recognized that international organizations like the League of Nations were a possible means of allowing smaller, weaker states to resist the demands of the great powers. When Fascist Italy invaded in 1935, he led a spirited resistance, but was forced out of Ethiopia the following year. He addressed the League in June 1936, asking for the body and especially the other great powers to maintain collective security by observing international law. He was ignored, and British assistance came only after 1939. Ethiopian exiles helped Britain push out Italy and restore Selassie in 1941.

I, Haile Selassie I, Emperor of Ethiopia, am here today to claim that justice which is due to my people, and the assistance promised to it eight months ago, when fifty nations asserted that aggression had been committed in violation of international treaties.

There is no precedent for a Head of State himself speaking in this assembly. But there is also no precedent for a people being victim of such injustice and being at present threatened by abandonment to its aggressor. Also, there has never before been an example of any Government proceeding to the systematic extermination of a nation by barbarous means, in violation of the most solemn promises made by the nations of the earth that there should not be used against innocent human beings the terrible poison of harmful gases. . . .

The very refinement of barbarism consisted in carrying ravage and terror into the most densely populated parts of the territory, the points farthest removed from the scene of hostilities. The object was to scatter fear and death over a great part of the Ethiopian territory. These fearful tactics succeeded. Men and animals succumbed. The deadly rain that fell from the aircraft made all those whom it touched fly shrieking with pain. All those who drank the poisoned water or ate the infected food also succumbed in dreadful suffering. In tens of thousands, the victims of the Italian mustard gas fell. . . .

In October, 1935. the 52 nations who are listening to me today gave me an assurance that the aggressor would not triumph, that the resources of the Covenant would be employed in order to ensure the reign of right and the failure of violence. . . .

It is not merely a question of the settlement of Italian aggression. It is collective security: it is the very existence of the League of Nations. It is the confidence that each State is to place in international treaties. It is the value of promises made to small States that their integrity and their independence shall be respected and ensured. It is the principle of the equality of States on the one hand, or otherwise the obligation laid upon small Powers to accept the bonds of vassalship. In a word, it is international morality that is at stake. Have the signatures appended to a Treaty value only in so far as the signatory Powers have a personal, direct and immediate interest involved?

Source: Haile Selassie, "Speech" (June 1936), https://www.mtholyoke.edu/acad/intrel/selassie.htm (consulted January 1, 2019).

Faced by numerous violations by the Italian Government of all international treaties that prohibit resort to arms, and the use of barbarous methods of warfare, it is my painful duty to note that the initiative has today been taken with a view to raising sanctions. Does this initiative not mean in practice the abandonment of Ethiopia to the aggressor? On the very eve of the day when I was about to attempt a supreme effort in the defense of my people before this Assembly does not this initiative deprive Ethiopia of one of her last chances to succeed in obtaining the support and guarantee of States Members? Is that the guidance the League of Nations and each of the States Members are entitled to expect from the great Powers when they assert their right and their duty to guide the action of the League? Placed by the aggressor face to face with the accomplished fact, are States going to set up the terrible precedent of bowing before force?

QUESTIONS

- How did Selassie portray European colonization?
- How did he try to appeal to his audience at the League of Nations?

14.2 KANG YUWEI, "MEMORIAL TO THE EMPEROR" (1898)

As a scholar and government official, Kang Yuwei (1858–1927) was deeply engaged in the project of reforming China, building its wealth, and facing up to international challenges. He saw the need for change as imperative and mobilized both historical and contemporary arguments in favor of a reform program modeled on Meiji Japan. Kang sent a "Comprehensive Consideration of the Whole Situation" to the Guangxu Emperor (r. 1875–1908) in late January 1898, which led to Kang being put in charge of reform efforts. The program was undermined by court factions; after 100 days, Kang was ousted by the Dowager Empress Cixi (1835–1908) and the Emperor became a virtual prisoner for the rest of his life. In China, elites were powerful enough to prevent radical change, but not strong enough to remake the country and make it competitive.

A survey of all states in the world will show that those states that undertook reforms became strong while those states that clung to the past perished. . . . [I]f we can change, we can preserve ourselves; but if we cannot change, we shall perish. Indeed if we can make a complete change, we shall become strong, but if we only make limited changes, we shall still perish. . . .

Our present trouble lies in our clinging to old institutions without knowing how to change. In an age of competition between states, to put into effect methods appropriate to an era of universal unification and laissez-faire is like wearing heavy furs in summer or riding a high carriage across a river. . . .

It is a principle of things that the new is strong but the old weak; that new things are fresh but old things rotten; that new things are active but old things static.

If the institutions are old, defects will develop. Therefore there are no institutions that should remain unchanged for a hundred years. Moreover, our present institutions are but unworthy vestiges of the Han, Tang, Yuan, and Ming dynasties; they are not even the institutions of the [Manchu] ancestors. In fact, they are the products of the fancy writing and corrupt dealings of petty officials rather than the original ideas of the ancestors. . . .

Although there is a desire to reform, yet if the national policy is not fixed and public opinion not united, it will be impossible for us to give up the old and adopt the new. . . .

Your Majesty knows that under the present circumstances reforms are imperative and old institutions must be abolished. I beg Your Majesty to make up your mind and to decide on the national policy. . . .

Source: Kang Yuwei, "Memorial," in *Sources of Chinese Tradition: From 1600 through the Twentieth Century*, ed. Wm. Theodore de Bary and Richard Lufrano, 2nd ed., vol. 2 (New York: Columbia University Press, 2000), 269–70.

. . . [China should] take the Meiji Reform of Japan as the model for our reform. The time and place of Japan's reform are not remote and her religion and customs are somewhat similar to ours. Her success is manifest; her example can be easily followed.

QUESTIONS

- What did Yuwei mean by "reform"?
- What would a system based on Meiji Reform have entailed?

14.3 KING PRAJADHIPOK'S ABDICATION STATEMENT (1935)

King Prajadhipok, also known as Rama VII (1925–1935), was educated in Britain and served in the British army. He was a reformer who recognized the shortcomings of the monarchy's absolute power. Like so many leaders, Prajadhipok had no effective response to the Great Depression of 1929 and admitted his own ignorance of financial matters. When the 1932 military coup sought to make him a constitutional monarch, he accepted the role in particular since he had already planned to institute a constitution. In this statement, he explained that he could no longer accept the things being done in his name.

I tried to assist in maintaining good order so that this important change could be made as smoothly as possible, but my efforts were without avail, because the new leaders failed to establish real political freedom, nor did they truly listen to the wishes of the people. From the two Constitutions it can be seen that the power to carry out various policies rested solely with the People's Party and their supporters, not with the elected representatives of the people. . . . Also, some members of the People's Party favoured making radical changes in the economic policy of the country. This caused a split within the People's Party, leading, upon the recommendation of the government then in power, to the closing of the Assembly and the suspending of some sections of the Constitution, which resulted in political unrest. . . .

Because the People's Party did not establish real political freedom and the people had no opportunity to express their opinions before important policy decisions were made, a rebellion broke out, with Thai killing Thai. . . .

I feel that the government and its party employ methods of administration incompatible with individual freedoms and the principles of justice. I am unable to agree to any person or any party carrying on such a government in my name. . . .

I deeply regret that I am no longer able to serve my people and my country in accordance with the hopes and intentions which I inherited from my forefathers.

QUESTIONS

- What is the tone of the speech?
- Was this speech revolutionary? Why or why not?

Source: Benjamin Batson, *The End of the Absolute Monarchy in Siam*, ASAA Southeast Asia Publications Series (Singapore: Oxford University Press, 1984), 315–7.

14.4 E. Y. HARBURG AND JAY GORNEY, "BROTHER, CAN YOU SPARE A DIME?" (1932)

Written by E. Y. Harburg and Jay Gorney, the lyricist and composer respectively, this song appeared as part of a musical review entitled *Americana* on October 5, 1932. Popular primarily for this song, the review had 77 performances on New York's Broadway stage. It is often considered the anthem of the Depression in the United States. Both Harburg and Gorney had long careers in music. The themes relate to an unfulfilled American Dream: joblessness and poverty were powerful responses to the Depression.

They used to tell me I was building a dream,
And so I followed the mob
When there was earth to plough or guns to bear
I was always there right on the job.
They used to tell me I was building a dream
With peace and glory ahead
Why should I be standing in line
Just waiting for bread?
Once I built a railroad,
Now it's done
Brother, can you spare a dime?
Once I build a tower, to the sun.
Brick and rivet and lime,

Once I built a tower,
Now it's done,
Brother, can you spare a dime?
Once in khaki suits
Gee, we looked swell
Full of that Yankee Doodle-de-dum.
Half a million boots went sloggin' thru Hell,
I was the kid with the drum.
Say, don't you remember, they called me Al
It was Al all the time
Say, don't you remember I'm your Pal?
Buddy, can you spare a dime?

QUESTIONS

- In the song, what had changed from the past to the present?
- Is there any hope for the future in the lyrics?

Source: Diane Ravitch, ed., *The American Reader: Words that Moved a Nation*, 2nd ed. (New York: Perennial, 2000), 467–8.

14.5 A. MITCHELL PALMER, *THE CASE AGAINST THE "REDS"* (1920)

A. Mitchell Palmer (1872–1936), attorney general of the United States from 1919 to 1921, was convinced that the Bolshevik Revolution augured a conspiracy by communists to overthrow the U.S. government. He sought peacetime use of the Espionage Act of 1917 and the Sedition Act of 1918 to attack anyone suspected of revolutionary sympathies. Government agents arrested thousands of people in 33 cities on January 2, 1920. Known as the Palmer Raids, these efforts discredited both the attorney general and the U.S. government, but, as this document makes clear, Palmer believed that only strict measures could protect the government against aliens and criminals.

Like a prairie-fire, the blaze of revolution was sweeping over every American institution of law and order a year ago. It was eating its way into the homes of the American workman, its sharp tongues of revolutionary heat were licking the alters of the churches, leaping into the belfry of the school bell, crawling into the sacred corners of American homes, seeking to replace marriage vows with libertine laws, burning up the foundations of society. . . .

In this conclusion we did not ignore the definite standards of personal liberty, of free speech, which is the very temperament and heart of the people. The evidence was examined with the utmost care, with a personal leaning toward freedom of thought and word on all questions. . . .

By stealing, murder, and lies, Bolshevism has looted Russia not only of its material strength, but of its moral force. A small clique of outcasts from the East Side of New York has attempted this, with what success we all know. Because a disreputable alien—Leon Bronstein, the man who now calls himself Trotsky—can inaugurate a reign of terror from his throne room in the Kremlin; because this lowest of all types known to New York can sleep in the Tsar's bed, while hundreds of thousands in Russia are without food or shelter, should Americans be swayed by such doctrines? . . .

My information showed that communism in this country was an organization of thousands of aliens, who were direct allies of Trotsky. Aliens of the same misshapen caste of mind and indecencies of character, and it showed that they were making the same glittering promises of lawlessness, of criminal autocracy to Americans that they had made to the Russian peasants. . . .

One of the chief incentives for the present activity of the Department of Justice against the "Reds" has been the hope that American citizens will themselves become voluntary agents for us, in a vast organization for mutual defense against the sinister agitation of men and women aliens, who appear to be either in the pay or under the criminal spell of Trotsky and Lenin. . . .

Every scrap of radical literature demands the overthrow of our existing government. All of it demands obedience to the instincts of criminal minds, that is, to the lower appetites, material and moral. The whole

Source: A Mitchell Palmer, *The Case Against the "Reds,"* first published in *The Forum* 64 (Feb. 1920), 173–180. Reprinted on https://www.marxists.org/history/usa/government/fbi/1920/0200-palmer-redscase.pdf (consulted December 22, 2018).

purpose of communism appears to be a mass formation of the criminals of the world to overthrow the decencies of private life, to usurp property that they have not earned, to disrupt the present order of life regardless of health, sex, or religious rights. By a literature that promises the wildest dreams of such low aspirations, that can occur to only the criminal minds, communism distorts our social law.

QUESTIONS

- How did Palmer justify these raids?
- Why was "Bolshevism" so dangerous, in Palmer's mind?

14.6 MARIANO CASANOV, "GOD DISTRIBUTES HIS GIFTS UNEQUALLY" (1893)

Mariano Casanova (1833–1908) was a Jesuit theology professor who became archbishop of Santiago, Chile, in 1886. A dedicated opponent of the institution of compulsory, lay, primary education, secular marriage, and a free press, Casanova was leery of the statement in *Of New Things*, the 1891 papal encyclical by Pope Leo XIII that "Its [the Roman Catholic Church's] desire is that the poor should rise above poverty and wretchedness, and should better their condition in life; and for this it strives." [paragraph 23]. He believed that inequality and thus hierarchy was necessary to God's plan. His defense of elites in this 1893 pastoral letter shows that the Roman Catholic Church did not always speak with one voice, complicating its message and impact.

Socialism establishes as a right the equal distribution of wealth among all citizens, and as a consequence the abolition of property. War on the rich! . . . The simple enunciation of this doctrine is enough to persuade one that its acceptance would bring about the ruin of society such as God established it. In effect, the redistribution of wealth would destroy the unequal social conditions on which society is founded. In order for society to subsist it requires relationships of necessity among members, to the point that each member, to satisfy his own needs, relies on the competition and services of the rest. Therefore, the rich need the poor, and the poor the rich; the worker needs industry for his salary, and industry needs the worker to give impulse to production. . . . [T]he inequality of conditions is not the work of man but of nature, or rather, of god, who distributes his gifts unequally. As well as not having equal talent, equal strength, nor equal nobility, not all have the same fortune. And out of this inequality social harmony results, this variety in unity that is like the hallmark of divine works. Property, be it inherited or acquired, is a right as sacred as that which every man has to the fruits of his work, of his strengths or his talents. And the day that this right disappears, all stimulus to work will be lacking, and consequently, progress in all laws of human activity will be stopped.

Socialist doctrine, then, is antisocial, because it tends to overturn the bases which God, author of society, has established. And it is not in the hands of man to correct what God has done. God as sovereign lord of all that exists, has distributed wealth according to his approval, and prohibits committing an offense against it in his seventh commandment. But he has not left the poor without compensation. If he has not given them wealth, he has given them the means to acquire subsistence with a job that, if it

Source: Mariano Casanova, "Pastoral Letter," in *The Chile Reader: History, Culture, Politics*, ed. Elizabeth Quay Hutchison, Thomas Miller Klubock, Nara B. Milanich, and Peter Winn (Durham, NC: Duke University Press, 2014), 228–9.

overwhelms the body, makes the soul rejoice. If the poor have less wealth, in exchange they have few necessities: they are happy in their own poverty. If the rich have greater goods, they have in exchange more anxieties in their souls, more desires in their hearts, more grief in life.

QUESTIONS

- What was Casanova's main argument against socialism?
- What are the social implications of his view?

14.7 WOODROW WILSON, THE 14 POINTS (1918)

President Woodrow Wilson (1915–1921) delivered this peace plan, the 14 Points, to a joint session of Congress on January 8, 1918. Both within the U.S. and without, it was perceived by many as overly optimistic, unrealistic, and hypocritical for a country with both an empire and high tariffs. Explicitly anti-imperialist, Wilson called for open diplomacy and for peoples to be consulted on who should govern them, a principle known as national self-determination, yet also demanded sea access for Poland and Serbia. Wilson asked for assistance to Russia, despite the outbreak of the Bolshevik Revolution, and for Germany to renounce its goal of "mastery." To implement these somewhat contradictory goals, Wilson advocated a "general association of nations," which later became the League of Nations. To achieve this dream, Wilson participated in the postwar Versailles Peace Conference, thus becoming the first sitting U.S. president to leave the country. He also drove himself so hard attempting to convince the American people to accept the treaty that he experienced a debilitating stroke.

It will be our wish and purpose that the processes of peace, when they are begun, shall be absolutely open and that they shall involve and permit henceforth no secret understandings of any kind. The day of conquest and aggrandizement is gone by; so is also the day of secret covenants entered into in the interest of particular governments and likely at some unlooked-for moment to upset the peace of the world. . . .

We entered this war because violations of right had occurred which touched us to the quick and made the life of our own people impossible unless they were corrected and the world secure once for all against their recurrence. What we demand in this war, therefore, is nothing peculiar to ourselves. It is that the world be made fit and safe to live in; and particularly that it be made safe for every peace-loving nation which, like our own, wishes to live its own life, determine its own institutions, be assured of justice and fair dealing by the other peoples of the world as against force and selfish aggression. All the peoples of the world are in effect partners in this interest, and for our own part we see very clearly that unless justice be done to others it will not be done to us. The programme of the world's peace, therefore, is our programme; and that programme, the only possible programme, as we see it, is this:

I. Open covenants of peace, openly arrived at, after which there shall be no private international understandings of any kind but diplomacy shall proceed always frankly and in the public view.

II. Absolute freedom of navigation upon the seas, outside territorial waters, alike in peace and in war. . . .

III. The removal, so far as possible, of all economic barriers and the establishment of an equality of trade conditions among all the nations. . . .

IV. Adequate guarantees given and taken that national armaments will be reduced to the lowest point consistent with domestic safety.

V. A free, open-minded, and absolutely impartial adjustment of all colonial claims, based upon a

Source: Woodrow Wilson, "14 Points Speech" (January 8, 1918), http://avalon.law.yale.edu/20th_century/wilson14.asp (consulted January 12, 2019).

strict observance of the principle that in determining all such questions of sovereignty the interests of the populations concerned must have equal weight with the equitable claims of the government whose title is to be determined.

VI. The evacuation of all Russian territory and such a settlement of all questions affecting Russia. . . . The treatment accorded Russia by her sister nations in the months to come will be the acid test of their good will, of their comprehension of her needs as distinguished from their own interests, and of their intelligent and unselfish sympathy.

VII. Belgium, the whole world will agree, must be evacuated and restored. . . .

VIII. All French territory should be freed and the invaded portions restored. . . .

IX. A readjustment of the frontiers of Italy should be effected along clearly recognizable lines of nationality.

X. The peoples of Austria-Hungary, whose place among the nations we wish to see safeguarded and assured, should be accorded the freest opportunity to autonomous development.

XI. Rumania, Serbia, and Montenegro should be evacuated; occupied territories restored; Serbia accorded free and secure access to the sea; and the relations of the several Balkan states to one another determined by friendly counsel along historically established lines of allegiance and nationality; and international guarantees of the political and economic independence and territorial integrity of the several Balkan states should be entered into.

XII. The Turkish portion of the present Ottoman Empire should be assured a secure sovereignty, but the other nationalities which are now under Turkish rule should be assured an undoubted security of life and an absolutely unmolested opportunity of autonomous development, and the Dardanelles should be permanently opened as a free passage to the ships and commerce of all nations under international guarantees.

XIII. An independent Polish state should be erected which should include the territories inhabited by indisputably Polish populations, which should be assured a free and secure access to the sea, and whose political and economic independence and territorial integrity should be guaranteed by international covenant.

XIV. A general association of nations must be formed under specific covenants for the purpose of affording mutual guarantees of political independence and territorial integrity to great and small states alike.

In regard to these essential rectifications of wrong and assertions of right we feel ourselves to be intimate partners of all the governments and peoples associated together against the Imperialists. . . .

For such arrangements and covenants we are willing to fight and to continue to fight until they are achieved; but only because we wish the right to prevail and desire a just and stable peace such as can be secured only by removing the chief provocations to war, which this programme does remove. . . . We wish her [Germany] only to accept a place of equality among the peoples of the world,—the new world in which we now live,—instead of a place of mastery.

QUESTIONS

- Which of the points strike you as the most revolutionary?
- What do you think the effects of Wilson's 14 Points might have been on colonized peoples?

14.8 ADOLF HITLER, DEALING WITH THE MASSES (1925)

Adolf Hitler (1889–1945) believed in both his own superiority and the gullibility of the general population. In this excerpt from his 1925 autobiography *Mein Kampf*, written when he was only 36 and had not yet achieved much either politically or personally, Hitler outlines his views on the simplicity and gullibility of the masses, who he believed both wanted and needed to be told what to do. He also emphasized the success of a "big lie," which, he asserted, was that the Jewish people were a religious community rather than a "race." These tactics were fundamental to Nazi public discourse and education; they focused on indoctrinating young people and underlay their plans to remake humanity. Although *Mein Kampf* was a runaway best-seller, contemporaries were stunned when Hitler and the Nazis attempted to put their principles into practice. An overwhelming majority of the world's inhabitants were not "people," according to the Nazis' racial dogma.

Propaganda. Here the art of propaganda consists in putting a matter so clearly and forcibly before the minds of the people as to create a general conviction regarding the reality of a certain fact, the necessity of certain things and the just character of something that is essential. . . . [P]ropaganda . . . must appeal to the feelings of the public rather than to their reasoning powers.

All propaganda must be presented in a popular form and must fix its intellectual level so as not to be above the heads of the least intellectual of those to whom it is directed. Thus its purely intellectual level will have to be that of the lowest mental common denominator among the public it is desired to reach. . . .

Propaganda must not investigate the truth objectively and, in so far as it is favorable to the other side, present it according to the theoretical rules of justice; yet it must present only that aspect of the truth which is favorable to its own side.

The Big Lie. All this was inspired by the principle— which is quite true in itself—that in the big lie there is always a certain force of credibility; because the broad masses of a nation are always more easily corrupted in the deeper strata of their emotional nature than consciously or voluntarily; and thus in the primitive simplicity of their minds they more readily fall victims to the big lie than the small lie, since they themselves often tell small lies in little matters but would be ashamed to resort to large-scale falsehoods. It would never come into their heads to fabricate colossal untruths, and they would not believe that others could have the impudence to distort the truth so infamously. Even though the facts which prove this to be so may be brought clearly to their minds, they will still doubt and waver and will continue to think that there may be some other explanation. For the grossly impudent lie always leaves traces behind it, even after it has been nailed down, a fact which is known to all expert liars in this world and to all who conspire together in the art of lying. These people know only too well how to use falsehood for the basest purposes.

From time immemorial. however, the Jews have known better than any others how falsehood and calumny can be exploited. Is not their very existence

Source: Adapted from Adolf Hitler, *Mein Kampf*, trans. James Murphy (London: Hurst and Blackett, 1939 [1925]), Book 1, Chapters 6 and 10, http://gutenberg.net.au/ebooks02/0200601.txt (consulted January 26, 2019).

founded on one great lie, namely, that they are a religious community, whereas in reality they are a race? And what a race! One of the greatest thinkers that mankind has produced has branded the Jews for all time with a statement which is profoundly and exactly true. He (Schopenhauer) called the Jew "The Great Master of Lies". Those who do not realize the truth of that statement, or do not wish to believe it, will never be able to lend a hand in helping Truth to prevail.

QUESTIONS

- What was the art of propaganda, in Hitler's mind?
- What was the "Big Lie"? Why was it so significant to Hitler?

14.9 ARMENIAN SURVIVORS BEAR WITNESS (1993)

These three brief excerpts illustrate three phases of the genocide that began in 1915. The Armenian community faced increasing violence as men were beaten and robbed of their possessions before being murdered. Those who were deported experienced horrific conditions, illustrating that this was a road to nowhere: deportation was intended to be a death march. These remembrances also suggest that in the initial phases, the violence was personal. Clearly, the Armenians' neighbors now thought differently about them than they had not long before. This shift reflects an important aspect of how governments get populations to go along with their plans.

A survivor from Jibin:

"The next day they gathered up other influential men in the church, including my father and his brothers, and began beating them in the churchyard. We were young; I was only about six years old. We used to go and see our fathers get beaten, and we would cry. One of my father's best [Turkish] friends, who used to come to our house several times a week, was now beating my dad and saying to him that he wanted all of his belongings. My poor father, being exhausted, said that he would do that. So right there in the courtyard, this man brought the papers, and my father signed, saying that he had indeed sold all his belongings to Ismail Beg."

A Konia survivor recalled:

"They asked all the men and boys to separate from the women. There were some teen boys who were dressed like girls and disguised. They remained behind. But my father had to go. He was a grown man with a mustache. As soon as they separated the men, a group of armed men came from the other side of a hill and killed all the men right in front of our eyes. They killed them with bayonets at the end of their rifles, sticking them in their stomachs. Many of the women could not take it, and they threw themselves in the River Euphrates, and they, too, died. They did this killing right in front of us. I saw my father being killed."

Another Armenian survivor described the journey:

"[W]e left everything behind. There were crowds from every street, all going to the same place. We walked and walked until dark, and I noticed how all the people coming from different directions would end up on the same road. There were gendarmes [police] on both sides of the road to make sure that no one swerved from his line or fell behind. . . . Anyone who would fall behind would be shot on the spot. They took us through desolate places, through the

Source: Donald E. Miller and Lorna Touryan Miller, eds., *Survivors: An Oral History of the Armenian Genocide* (Berkeley, CA: University of California Press, 1993), 69, 80–2.

deserts and mountain paths, so we would not be near any of the cities where we would get water or food. We got wet at night by the dew and were scorched by the sun during the day. I remember going and going."

QUESTIONS

- What common themes emerge from these stories?
- Why did former friends do such things to their neighbors?

14.10 PRIMO LEVI, DEHUMANIZATION (1958)

A Jewish Italian, Primo Levi (1919–1987) was captured along with the resistance and sent to one of the labor camps that were part of the Auschwitz complex. His training in chemistry helped him survive. These passages are from *If This Is a Man?*, which was translated as *Survival in Auschwitz*, illustrate the dehumanization imposed on the inmates by the Nazi design. The first excerpt took place not long after Levi's arrival, when he was shaved of all body hair while waiting to be tattooed as number 174517. The second excerpt takes place after a "selection," where the Germans sent those who could no longer work to the gas chambers. After the war, Levi married and had children as well as a long and productive career as a chemist and literary figure. He committed suicide in 1987.

Then for the first time we become aware that our language lacks words to express this offence, the demolition of a man. In a moment, with almost prophetic intuition, the reality was revealed to us: we had reached the bottom. It is not possible to sink lower than this; no human condition is more miserable than this, nor could it conceivably be so. Nothing belongs to us anymore; they have taken away our clothes, our shoes, even our hair; if we speak, they will not listen to us, and it they listen, they will not understand. They will even take away our name: and if we ant to keep it, we will have to find in ourselves the strength to do, to manage somehow so that behind the name something of us, of us as we were, still remains. . . .

Imagine now a man who is deprived of everyone he loves, and at the same time of his house, his habits, his clothes, in short of everything he possesses: he will be a hollow man, reduced to suffering and needs, forgetful of dignity and restraint, for he who loses all often easily loses himself. He will be a man whose life and death can be lightly decided with no sense of human affinity, in the most fortunate of cates, on the bases of a pure judgment of utility. It is in this way that one can understand the double sense of the term "extermination camp". . . .

I see and hear old Kuhn praying aloud, with his beret on his head, swaying backwards and forwards violently. Kuhn is thanking God because he was not chosen [to be killed].

Kuhn is out of his senses . . . . Can Kuhn fail to realize that next time it will be his turn?

Does Kuhn not understand that what has happened today is an abomination, which no propitiatory prayer, no pardon, no expiation by the guilty, which nothing at all in the power of man can ever clean again?

If I was God, I would spit at Kuhn's prayer.

QUESTIONS

- What did Levi mean by "the demolition of a man"?
- What did he mean by "If I was God, I would spit at Kuhn's prayer"?

Source: Primo Levi, *Survival in Auschwitz: The Nazi Assault on Humanity*, trans. Stuart Woolf (New York: Touchstone, 1996 [1958]), 22–23, 118.

CHAPTER

15

"MACHINES AS THE MEASURE OF MEN"?

The Changing Basis of Industrial Power, 1914–Present

15.1 GEORGES RENARD, WAR PROFITEERING (1917)

French professor Georges Renard (1876–1943) wrote a critical survey of the economic repercussions of the Great War in 1917. It made clear that workers were being charged high rents and prices. While many took advantage of wartime desperation to sell and to consume and small businesses sought to capitalize on their opportunities, military suppliers were the chief profiteers.

Where workers have been called *en masse* to work in the war industries, at Bourges, Firminy and Châtellerault, they were charged at first large sums for board and lodging and even if they earned quite high wages, they were able to keep only a small amount in their own pockets.

It is also important not to forget the small workshops which the war has brought into being or made to prosper; those concerned with producing sleeping bags, woolen goods, sweaters, balaclavas, stoves for the trenches, bullet shields, first aid equipment, and those making mourning clothes and funeral wreaths; photographers, besieged by crowds of mothers, sisters, fiancées and friends eager to send their portraits to some absent loved one. . . . Street hawkers who plastered their illustrated postcards on the windows of disused shops and whose gaily colored displays will always remain one of the most picturesque aspects of Parisian life during the Great War; toy dealers offering peaceful cannons or multi-coloured lead soldiers; sellers of candles and ex-voto for novenas, through which people implored heaven for miracles, victory of the safety of a loved one. . . .

One could easily give many more examples of cheap-jacks, whose business has found a favourable soil. But their profits are only trifles when compared with those amassed by the large-scale profiteers. I refer to those who have supplied the state, who have obtained contracts with the commissariat. . . . In spite of a more active surveillance than has existed before, the practice has not been checked. Whether it is a question of meat, or fodder, horses or oats, explosives or vegetables, clothes or barbed wire, the profits have been considerable, especially at first, when the urgency of the situation did not allow any discussion of the proposed conditions of sale.

QUESTIONS

- What are the main problems Renard is outlining?
- What might the government have done to ameliorate these problems?

Source: Sidney Pollard and Colin Holmes, eds., *Documents of European Economic History*, vol. 3, *The End of the Old Europe 1914–1939* (New York: St. Martins, 1973), 7–8.

15.2 JOHN SCOTT, *BEHIND THE URALS* (1942)

Inspired by socialist ideals, U.S. college student John Scott (1912–1976) went to the Soviet Union in 1932 at the height of industrialization. He spent a decade there, about half of that working in Magnitogorsk, the USSR's "city of steel" in the Ural Mountains, before returning to the United States. He published this memoir of his experiences in 1942 before going to work for the U.S. government. Scott spent most of his career as a staunchly anti-Soviet journalist. In this excerpt, Scott exposed the difficulty of conditions and how unsuited many of the workers were for their tasks, but also their dedication to the job of building socialism in this remote area.

The big whistle on the power house sounded a long, deep, hollow six o'clock. All over the scattered city-camp of Magnitogorsk, workers rolled out of their beds or bunks and dressed in preparation for their day's work. . . .

It was January, 1933. The temperature was in the neighborhood of thirty-five below. A light powdery snow covered the low spots on the ground. . . .

It was two miles to the blast furnaces, over rough ground. There was no wind, so our noses did not freeze. I was always glad when there was no wind in the morning. It was my first winter in Russia and I was not used to the cold. . . .

By the time the seven o'clock whistle blew, the shanty was jammed full of riggers, welders, cutters, and their helpers. It was a varied gang, Russians, Ukrainians, Tartars, Mongols, Jews, mostly young and almost all peasants of yesterday, though a few, like Ivanov, had long industrial experience. . . . Khaibulin, the Tartar, had never seen a staircase, a locomotive, or an electric light until he had come to Magnitogorsk a year before. His ancestors for centuries had raised stock on the flat plains of Kazakhstan . . . [After the Revolution, t]hey had attended meetings of the Soviet, without understanding very clearly what it was all about, but through all this their lives had gone on more or less as before. Now Shaimat Khaibulin was building a blast furnace bigger than any in Europe. He had learned to read and was attending an evening school, learning the trade of electrician. He had learned to speak Russian, he read newspapers. His life had changed more in a year than that of his antecedents since the time of Tamerlane. . . .

It was just about nine-fifteen when I finished [welding] one side of the pipe and went around to start the other. The scaffold was coated with about an inch of ice, like everything else around the furnaces. The vapor rising from the large hot-water cooling basin condensed on everything and formed a layer of ice. . . . I was just going to start welding when I heard someone sing out, and something swished down past me. It was a rigger who had been working at the very top.

He bounced off the bleeder pipe, which probably saved his life. Instead of falling all the way to the ground, he landed on the main platform about fifteen feet below me . . . [t]hree of us took him and carried him down to the first-aid station. . . .

Source: John Scott, *Behind the Urals: An American Worker in Russia's City of Steel* (Bloomington, IN: Indiana University Press, 1973 [1942]), 9–10, 15–21.

I was making my way unsteadily back to the bleeder pipe on No. 3 when Kolya [superviser] hailed me. "Don't bother to go up for a while, the brushes burnt out on the machine you were working on. They won't be fixed for half an hour or so." I went toward the office with Okya and told him about the rigger. I was incensed and talked about some thorough checkup on scaffoldings. Kolya could not get interested. He pointed out there was not enough planking for good scaffolds, that the riggers were mostly plowboys who had no idea bout being careful, and that at thirty-five below without any breakfast in you, you did not pay as much attention as you should.

"Sure, people will fall. But we're building blast furnaces all the same, aren't we?" and he waved his hand toward No. 2 from which the red glow of flowing pig iron was emanating.

QUESTIONS

- What does the line "Sure, people will fall. But we're building blast furnaces all the same, aren't we?" indicate about Soviet objectives?
- Was Magnitogorsk a place of opportunity or not?

15.3 JI YUN, "HOW CHINA PROCEEDS WITH THE TASK OF INDUSTRIALIZATION" (1953)

This account by journalist Ji Yun appeared in the official newspaper of the Chinese Communist Party, *The People's Daily*, in May 1953. It detailed the Central Committee's decision to follow a Soviet model of industrialization based on top-down five-year plans focused on iron and steel production. This plan represents the high point of Soviet influence on Chinese policy.

The five-year construction plan, to which we have long looked forward, has now commenced. Its basic object is the gradual realization of the industrialization of our state. Industrialization has been the goal sought by the Chinese people during the past one hundred years. From the last days of the Manchu dynasty to the early years of the republic, some people had undertaken the establishment of a few factories in the country. But industry as a whole has never been developed in China. . . . It was just as Stalin said: "Because China did not have its own heavy industry and its own war industry, it was being trampled upon by all the reckless and unruly elements. . . ."

We are now in the midst of a period of important changes, in that period of transition, as described by Lenin, of changing "from the stallion of the peasant, the farm hand, and poverty, to the stallion of mechanized industry and electrification."

We must look upon this period of transition to the industrialization of the state as one equal in importance and significance to that period of transition of the revolution toward the fight for political power. . . .

It was through the implementation of the policies of the industrialization of the state andthe collectivization of agriculture that the Soviet Union succeeded in building up, from an economic structure complicated with five component economies, a unified socialist economy; in turning a backward agricultural nation into a first-class industrial power of the world; in defeating German fascist aggression in World War II; and in constituting itself the strong bastion of world peace today.

We are looking upon the Soviet Union as our example in the building of our country. Soviet experiences in the realization of industrialization are of great value to us. . . . The foundation of socialism is large industrial development. Lenin said, "There is only one real foundation for a socialist society, and it is large industry. If we do not possess factories of great size, if we do not possess a large industrial structure with the most advanced equipment, then we shall generally not be able to talk of socialism, much less in the case of an agricultural country."

Accordingly, in order to enable our state to progress victoriously toward socialism, we must construct large industries. . . . Numerous facts have proved that it is futile to attempt the enforcement of socialism on the foundations of small agriculture or small handicrafts.

Source: William Theodore de Bary and Richard Lufrano, eds., *Sources of Chinese Tradition: From 1600 through the Twentieth Century*, 2nd ed., vol. 2 (New York: Columbia University Press, 2000), 455–56.

Industry must first be developed to provide possibilities for the collectivization and mechanization of agriculture, for the socialist reform of agriculture.

At the same time, only with industrialization of the state may we guarantee our economic independence and nonreliance on imperialism.

QUESTIONS

- What did this five-year plan try to achieve?
- Why did Yun admire the Soviet Union so much?

15.4 EDUARDO GALEANO, *OPEN VEINS OF LATIN AMERICA* (1973)

Uruguayan Eduardo Galeano (1940–2015) wrote novels and articles for a variety of leftist publications, but was best known for writing about soccer. He was a transnational, investigative journalist who focused on U.S. imperialism in Latin America and the ways that economic inequality was perpetuated in the region. In 1973, he was jailed and then exiled when the military seized power. The book that this excerpt is taken from was banned in Uruguay, Chile, and Argentina. Galeano fled right-wing death squads and resided in Spain, where he wrote his most famous works, until his return to Uruguay in 1985 during democratization. His example of using journalism to write about long-standing issues of political economy was a powerful model for others fighting against censorship and oppression in Latin America.

The end of World War II found European interests in full retreat from Latin America, and U.S. investments triumphantly advancing. . . . At the present time $1 of every $3 invested in Latin America is invested in industry. . . .

In return for insignificant investments, the affiliates of giant corporations jump over customs barriers erected—paradoxically—against foreign competition, and take over the internal industrializing process. They export factories or, not infrequently, corner and devour those already existing. For this they can rely on the enthusiastic aid of most local governments and on the power of extortion with which international credit organizations endow them. . . .

Thus the dynamism of U.S. factories south of the Río Grande is much more intense than that of Latin American industry in general. The figures for the three biggest countries are eloquent: with an index of 100 in 1961, Argentina's industrial product amounted to 112.5 in 1965, while in the same period sales by U.S.-affiliated concerns rose to 166.3. For Brazil the equivalent figures are 109.2 and 120; for Mexico, 142.2 and 186.8. . . .

Furthermore, the investments that turn Latin American factories into mere cogs in the giant corporations' machinery do not in any way alter the international division of labour. There is no change in the system of intercommunicating arteries through which capital and merchandise circulate between poor countries and rich countries. Latin America continues exporting its unemployment and poverty: the raw materials that the world market needs, and on whose sale the regional economy depends. Unequal exchange functions as before: hunger wages in Latin America help finance high salaries in the United States and Europe. Brazil, despite its industrialization, continues substantially dependent on coffee exports, Argentina on sales of meat; Mexico exports very few manufactures. . . .

We find that the new model does not make its colonies more prosperous, although it enriches their poles of development; it does not ease social and regional tensions, but aggravates them; it spreads

Source: Eduardo Galeano, *Open Veins of Latin America: Five Centuries of the Pillage of a Continent*, trans. Cedric Belfrage (London: Latin American Bureau, 1997 [1973]), 205–07.

poverty even more widely and concentrates wealth even more narrowly; it pays wages twenty times lower than in Detroit and charges prices three times higher than in New York; it takes over the internal market and the mainsprings of the productive apparatus. . . .

QUESTIONS

- How had international corporations affected Latin America, in Galeano's mind?
- What kind of system do you think Galeano would have preferred?

15.5 JEFFREY BALLINGER, "THE NEW FREE-TRADE HEEL: NIKE'S PROFITS JUMP ON THE BACKS OF ASIAN WORKERS" (1992)

U.S. labor organizer, Jeffrey Ballinger (b. 1953) published an initial account of conditions in Nike's overseas factories in 1991 when he was working in Indonesia on behalf of the AFL–CIO, a major U.S. labor federation. Based on the reports of others, this piece was published in *Harper's Magazine* in August 1992 and received wide attention. He founded a non-governmental organization, Press for Change, to oppose sweatshop practices, especially among sneaker and apparel makers.

Her only name is Sadisah, and it's safe to say that she's never heard of Michael Jordan. Nor is she spending her evenings watching him and his Olympic teammates gliding and dunking in prime time from Barcelona. But she has heard of the shoe company he endorses—Nike, whose logo can be seen on the shoes and uniforms of many American Olympic athletes this summer. Like Jordan, Sadisah works on behalf of Nike. You won't see her, however, in the flashy TV images of freedom and individuality that smugly command us to JUST DO IT!—just spend upward of $130 for a pair of basketball shoes. Yet Sadisah is, in fact, one of the people who is doing it—making the actual shoes, that is, and earning paychecks such as this one in a factory in Indonesia.

In the 1980s, Oregon-based Nike closed its last U.S. footwear factory, in Saco, Maine, while establishing most of its new factories in South Korea, where Sung Hwa Corp. is based. Sung Hwa is among many independent producers Nike has contracted with. Nike's actions were part of the broader "globalization" trend that saw the United States lose 65,300 footwear jobs between 1982 and 1989 as shoe companies sought non-unionized Third World workers who didn't require the U.S. rubber-shoe industry average of $6.94 an hour. But in the late 1980s, South Korean laborers gained the right to form independent unions and to strike. Higher wages ate into Nike's profits. The company shifted new factories to poorer countries such as Indonesia, where labor rights are generally ignored and wages are but one seventh of South Korea's. (The Sung Hwa factory and others like it are located in Tangerang, a squalid industrial boomtown just outside Jakarta.) Today, to make 80 million pairs of shoes annually, Nike contracts with several dozen factories globally, including six in Indonesia. Others are in China, Malaysia, Thailand, and Taiwan. By shifting factories to cheaper labor pools, Nike has posted year after year of growth; in 1991 the company grossed more than $3 billion in sales—$200 million of which Nike attributes to Jordan's endorsement—and reported a net profit of $287 million, its highest ever. . . . Sadisah worked 63 hours of overtime during this pay period, for which she received an extra 2 cents

Source: Jeffrey Ballinger, "The New Free-Trade Heel: Nike's Profits Jump on the Backs of Asian Workers," *Harper's Magazine* (August 1992), 46–47.

per hour. At this factory, which makes mid-priced Nikes, each pair of shoes requires .84 manhours to produce; working on an assembly line, Sadisah assembled the equivalent of 13.9 pairs every day. The profit margin on each pair is enormous. The labor costs to manufacture a pair of Nikes that sells for $80 in the United States is approximately 12 cents. . . [while] the daily wage for seven and a half hours of work, which in Sadisah's case is 2,100 Indonesia rupiah—at the current rate of exchange, $1.03 *per day*, That amount, which works out to just under 14 cents per hour, is less than the Indonesian government's figure for "minimum physical need." A recent International Labor Organization survey found that 88 percent of Indonesian women working at Sadisah's wage rates are malnourished. And most workers in this factory—over 80 percent—are women. With seldom more than elementary-school educations, they are generally in their teens or early twenties, and have come from outlying agricultural areas in search of city jobs and a better life. Sadisah's wages allow her to rent a shanty without electricity or running water.

Here are Sadisah's net earnings for a month of labor. She put in six days a week, ten and a half hours per day, for a paycheck equivalent to $37.46—about half the retail price of one pair of the sneakers she makes. . . .

QUESTIONS

- How did free trade affect Sadisah?
- Do stories such as this affect your own consumption habits? Why or why not?

15.6 MARIA HENGEVELD, NIKE'S HYPOCRISY (2016)

Dutch journalist Maria Hengeveld was a graduate student at the University of Cambridge and contributes to the website "Africa is a Country." This excerpt was published by *Slate* in 2016 and was supported by The Nation Institute in New York. It is based on her master's thesis at Columbia University, for which she interviewed Nike workers about working conditions and wages.

Just as Nike has worked hard in recent years to elevate the status of women on the field and court, it's been successful doing the same in the world of global philanthropy. Ever since the Nike Foundation launched the "Girl Effect" campaign in 2008—arguing that empowering and preparing girls to work is the key to lifting the developing world out of destitution—the company has left its brand all over the global anti-poverty field. The idea: that liberating girls from oppressive social norms and cultures, keeping them healthy and in school, will unleash their earning potential and "break the cycle of global poverty." . . .

But what effect has the Girl Effect had on Nike's own supply chain? Of the estimated million-plus workers who cut, stitch, sew, glue, label, and package shoes, sports fashion, and collegiate apparel for Nike contractors (including for Nike brands Converse and Hurley), almost a third work in Vietnam, the single largest host to Nike manufacturing in the world. With at least 75 contracted factories there, Nike is a major driver of employment in the country. About 80 percent of workers in Nike's Vietnam factories are women and girls; some may be as young as 16, the minimum age for certain factory work in Nike's Code of Conduct. Many migrate from poor rural areas in the central and northern provinces of the country to industrial parks in the south. According to Nike, they are often "the first women in their family to work in the formal economy."

Over four weeks in January, I interviewed 18 women, 23 to 55 years old, who currently or recently produced, labeled, and packaged Nike shoes and apparel at five different factories within 30 miles of Ho Chi Minh City, Vietnam. . . .

Although they may be unfamiliar with Nike's global campaign, the goal of the women I spoke with sounds a lot like the Girl Effect—to raise themselves and their families out of poverty. Each of the 18 women, however, reported pay so low they could not even meet the basic needs of their families, let alone save money or contribute to their communities. . . . They told me that they would need to earn between three to four times their current salaries to offer their families a basic level of economic security. The average monthly wage for manufacturing in Vietnam was $200 in 2015. Their stories highlighted something the Girl Effect campaign is silent about: the importance of a living wage.

I also found evidence that Nike's contract factories breach basic Girl Effect tenets of freedom from exploitation and harassment, security, safety, and Nike's own Code of Conduct, put in place to prohibit, among other things, harassment, abuse, and nonconsensual

Source: Maria Hengeveld, "Nike Boasts of Empowering Women Around the World, While The Young Women Who Make Its Products in Vietnam are Intimidated, Belittled, and Underpaid" (August 26, 2016), https://slate.com/business/2016/08/nikes-supply-chain-doesnt-live-up-to-the-ideals-of-its-girl-effect-campaign.html (consulted April 8, 2020).

overtime. Women who worked in different factories told remarkably similar stories of being subjected to arbitrary punishments—such as financial penalties and threats of dismissal for making manufacturing mistakes, not working quickly enough, or coming in late, along with intimidation and ongoing humiliation by managers. . . .

Nike's talk of empowerment notwithstanding, these women feel helpless in the face of these conditions. "We have voices," a 32-year-old pregnant worker, who receives a small hazardous work bonus for her work in the gluing section and fears the effects of chemicals on her unborn baby, told me. "But we can't really speak."

QUESTIONS

- How do you think Nike would have justified the "Girl Effect," given narratives such as those in the excerpt?
- Compare this document to Document 15.5. Had labor conditions changed?

PAYING FOR IT ALL
Taxation and the Making of the Modern World

16.1 GUILLAUME-ANTOINE OLIVIER, OTTOMAN TAXES IN THE GREEK ISLANDS (1790S)

Guillaume-Antoine Olivier (1756–1814) was an entomologist sent by the French government as part of a scientific expedition to the Ottoman Empire, Egypt, and Persia from 1793 to 1798. As part of that voyage, he visited various Greek islands under Ottoman control. The first paragraph concerns Santorini; the rest is about the large island of Crete. These excerpts illustrate the different modes of tax collection, including tax-farming, and the reproduction and maintenance of many aspects of feudalism. It also shows the expectation that people had to pay mandatory "gifts" to the government.

Santorin[i] pays about 55,000 piastres impot [tax], including the land-tax, the karatch, the duty of two parats per oke, at which the wine is taxed, and the customary presents, every year, at the time of the arrival of the captain-pacha's fleet in the archipelago. The land-tax ought to be no more than a tenth of the produce, as it was settled at the time of the surrender of the island; but the waiwode, who farms this duty from the Porte [Ottoman government], has for a long time past levied on private individuals a fifth, without the latter ever having been able to bring their just remonstrances to a hearing. . . .

The island of Crete is divided into three pachaliks or governments. . . . All three [pachas or leaders], in their turn and in their provinces, art to superintend the collection of the impost [taxes], and the safety of the places which are intrusted to them. They are also bound to cause justice to be done. . . .

The pachaliks are divided into a certain number of districts, and each district comprises, in its extent, a certain number of villages, some of which belong to the imperial mosques, some to the sultana-mother; and the greater number under the name of *Malikiane-Agassi* [or *Mukata'a*], are granted for life to agas or lords, in consideration of a sum of money, more or less great, paid into the imperial treasury before the firman [grant] of investiture, and an annual quit-rent, which is carried into the coffers of the treasurer of Candia, for the maintenance of the fortresses and the pay of the troops of the country.

All land-owners, Greeks or Mussulmans, pay to the aga, to the mosque, or to the sultan, a seventh of the produce of their lands. They are also obliged to carry their olives to the mills which the agas alone have the right to cause to be constructed. Oil pays a seventh; and, what becomes a very important object to the lord, the crusts, or miry waters, which remain as an indemnification for the workmen whom he places at the mill for the extraction of the oil, and for the horses that he furnishes for the pressing of the olives.

QUESTIONS

- Briefly, describe the taxation system depicted in the excerpt.
- Does this system strike you as fair? Why or why not?

Source: Guillaume-Antoine Olivier, *Travels in the Ottoman Empire, Egypt, and Persia, Undertaken by Order of the Government of France, during the First Six Years of the Republic* (London: T.N. Longman and O. Rees, T. Cadell Jun. and W. Davies, 1801), 176, 202–03.

16.2 MONGKUT, "THE ESTABLISHMENT OF THE KINGDOM" (1851)

Mongkut of Siam was also known as Rama IV (r. 1851–1868). He spent 27 years as a Buddhist monk before becoming King. This document set forth his views on taxation, describing what had been taxable under previous dynasties and illuminating the role of the royal family in expediting trade. Only after their commercial needs had been filled could others purchase many valuable goods. His predecessor had simplified and eliminated some taxes, but Mongkut here wonders how to tax foreign trade so that the burden did not fall too heavily on the people. Despite these concerns, he signed a series of unequal treaties with European powers that ended the royal monopoly and vastly lowered the tax on foreign goods; they also vastly expanded the economy as people rushed to grow cash crops to afford to buy luxuries. Tax policy shaped economic development.

The duties and taxes of the Dynasty which established T'onaburi as the capital, and of the two reigns preceding the present, were of ten kinds: 1. Distilleries. 2. Fisheries. 3. Grain producers. 4. Large gardens. 5. Fields on which were cultivated short lived plants. 6. Petty traders and dealers. 7. Gambling establishments. 8. Birds nests collected on the Western Coast. 9. Lead. 10. Vessels. These were the only sources of income. There are a variety of other articles that are prohibited, others are not allowed to trade in them—to wit, Elk's horns, Elephant's tusk, cardamums, good and bastard and Gambage. The gatherers of these articles could sell them only to the king, who purchased them and stored them in the royal warehouses for exportation. Sapanwood, Redwood, and Black Pepper others could not purchase till after the king had bought enough for his Junks. When there was enough for them, the prohibition was removed and then they could sell to others. These prohibitions and this pre-purchasing by the king in this way, terminated with the close of the third reign. After this taxes were established and levied, certain articles that were taxable in the third reign, or that had come down from former times, if they were small items, have, in the present reign been abolished. Such as taxes on bricks and on coolies (hawlers and drawers) and other taxes have been substituted in their place. In employments in which many are engaged or in the taxes which have been established by the late sovereign, if they were sources of vexation and of prolific litigation, they have, in some instances been suspended. . . .

In the Singapore papers also there are frequent insinuations. They praise imports as tending to prosperity. They praise exports as tending to prosperity. These are subjects to which I have but an imperfect knowledge. In what way will they be advantageous to the country? It is said imports tend to prosperity because it will be an advantage to the inhabitants who purchase foreign articles. Its tendency [is] to relate the price of articles. Exports tend to prosperity because it is an

Source: Samuel J. Smith, ed., *The Siam Repository* (Bangkok: Smith's Place, 1869), 111–12.

advantage to foreign merchants. It is proposed to abolish taxes on vessels. If this is done, is it the designated substitute in their stead inland taxes? If not, will not the rulers of the land become overburdened with poverty? If it be allowed to recollect duties from ships, is it to be collected on land? What is has been customary to receive from foreigners, as the duties on rice, four ticals per coyan, shall it be distributed and collected directly from the cultivators? If this is done, will it not be an oppression among ourselves? This item is included in the treaty with every foreign power and all have agreed to it. A change would be attended with much difficulty. Those who suppose the King a fool to be led, throw out all their conceived speculations hoping to incite him.

QUESTIONS

- Why do you think the King prohibited trade in certain items?
- Do Mongkut's concerns about foreign trade make sense to you? Why or why not?

16.3 ETHIOPIAN TAX FORM FOR MILITARY REQUISITION (1922)

This document, dated Genbot 11 1914 (Ethiopian calendar) or May 19, 1922, has been preserved by historian Richard Pankhurst. It was used for a plot of 80–100 acres. The lord received one-third of the produce, and the landlord collected an additional tithe. This tax form suggests the different level of exaction based on how many soldiers and of what ranks claimed the right of military requisition as well as the minimal financial return.

Concerting the allocation of soldiers' Provisions

To be given to the cultivator, and the soldier and which serves as land certificate for the owner of the land.

Name of *wātadär* (i.e. soldier) receiving provisions. . . . .

The *wana aläqa* (i.e. chief head). . . . .

Of the *šambäl* (i.e. captain). . . . .
Number. . . . .

Of the *méto aläqa* (i.e. lieutenant). . . . .
Of the *amsa aläqua* (i.e. sergeant). . . . .
Quantity of provision. . . . .
Wäräda (i.e. district) of the *agär* (i.e. country). . . .
Mälkäñña (i.e. lord) under whom (the soldier) is billeted. . . . .
Čeqa šum (i.e. local chief). . . . .
Name of the *balä märét* (i.e. landlord). . . . .

The *awaj* (i.e. decree). . . . .
People eligible to share the land. . . . .
Type of land for taxation. . . . .
Sämon (i.e. church land), name of church. . . . . . .
The tax. . . . .
Person who holds formerly *yänegus mätkaya* (i.e. king's planting land). . . .
Gänzäb (i.e. money) paid by the *balä rest* (i.e. owner) of the land: one *alad* (i.e. half dollar).
Gänzäb (i.e. money) paid by the *tekeläñña* (noble) for the *Negus* (i.e. King): one *rub* (i.e. ½ of a dollar).
Gänzäb (i.e. money) paid by the *wātadär* (i.e. soldier) for the allocation of provisions: two *mähaleq* (i.e. 2-16ths. of a dollar).
. . . . day 191. . . . Year of Mercy
Magistrate's name. . . . . Clerk's name. . . . .

QUESTIONS

- Who was intended to benefit from such a tax policy?
- Does this system seem similar to any other system you have encountered in your study of world history?

Source: Richard Pankhurst, "Ethiopian Tax Documents of the Early Twentieth Century," *Journal of Ethiopian Studies* 11:2 (1973): 157–66, 159–60.

16.4 CORDELL HULL, "SPEECH ON THE INCOME TAX" (1913)

Cordell Hull (1871–1955) of Tennessee gave this speech to the House of Representatives on April 26, 1913. It was published in *The Commoner* (May 16, 1913). In the aftermath of the ratification of the Sixteenth Amendment to the Constitution two months earlier, Hull set out the case for implementing a graduated income tax on the grounds of equity and fairness. The description of how the wealthy escaped many taxes was closely linked to his frustrations that the process had taken so long after the Supreme Court ruled in 1895 that a tax on income was unconstitutional. Congress passed a Revenue Act, setting a 1 percent tax on corporations and on personal income over $3,000 while lowering the tariff from 40 percent to 26 percent.

The general uprising throughout the country in behalf of this tax is due to the longstanding dissatisfaction with existing tax conditions and to the belief which long since became a conviction, that the masses were being grossly discriminated against through the agency of our tax laws. Every citizen realizes that the general government is obliged to secure revenues to defray its necessary expenses. . . .

During recent years there has been a general agitation and demand in almost every state in the union and almost every country in the world for intelligent, fair, and practical reforms and readjustments of their tax systems, to the end that every citizen may be required to contribute to the wants of the state or government in proportion to the revenue he enjoys under its protection. To this end the doctrine of equality of sacrifice or ability to pay is being universally invoked. A glance at the fiscal history of all countries shows a constant struggle on the part of the wealthy and more powerful classes to shift the chief weight of government taxation to the shoulders and backs of those weaker, poorer, and less able to protect themselves from the injustice and oppression inflicted by disproportionate tax burdens. This conflict has been and is today being waged in the United States.

All taxes in this country, whether for national or state and local purposes fall upon the American people; however, the gross inequalities and injustices resulting from tax evasion by those most able to pay and the shifting of the tax burden to those least able to pay is seen alike in connection with both national and local taxation. . . .

[A special tax commission found:] 1. That the richer a person grows the less he pays in relation to his property or income.

2. Experience has shown that under the present system personal property practically escapes taxation for either local or state purposes. . . .

The small property owner, who can not hide his property nor shift his tax burdens, constantly feels the crushing weight of taxation, while the rich investor in securities, the money lender, and the wealthy business

Source: Cordell Hull, "Speech on the Income Tax" (May 16, 1913), https://chroniclingamerica.loc.gov/data/batches/nbu_carson_ver02/data/46032385/00237284926/1913051601/0737.pdf (consulted May 19, 2020).

and professional men cover up most of their taxable property, as well as much of their city realty, when the assessor comes around. . . .

Our system of high protective-tariff taxation violates every canon of taxation and is outrageous in its operation and effects. It is conceived upon the idea that the people should be taxed, not according to their ability to pay, but according to their needs, and, practically, their poverty. No civilized or humane people can long tolerate this system of diabolical extortion. . . .

The experience of all countries with respect to every form of taxation has resulted in the universal conclusion that the fairest and most just of all taxes is that which is levied upon the citizen according to ability to pay, and that this result can best be accomplished by imposing a tax on net incomes.

Fifty-two countries and states have taken this step, and wherever given a reasonable trial this form of tax has never been repealed, save in the United States.

QUESTIONS

- What was Hull's main argument?
- Do you agree with his argument?

16.5 "EVIDENCE OF MRS. TAYLOR IN SIERRA LEONE ON THE HUT TAX WAR" (1888)

In the nineteenth century, African resistance to European rule often centered on taxes. A common levy imposed in much of Africa was the so-called Hut Tax, which required Africans to pay for the privilege of living in their own houses. This was a variant of the tactics used to mobilize labor by obliging people to work for Europeans to earn money to pay taxes applied across the western hemisphere and South Asia. It was a de facto forced labor tax. The tax and its enforcement spawned a revolt in Britain's West African colony of Sierra Leone in 1887–1889. As part of an investigation into the causes of the conflict, commissioner Sir David Chalmers (1820–1899) gathered this testimony.

My name is Nancy Violette Taylor. I am a Sierra Leonean. We lived at Bolian on the Mapelle River, Kassi Lake. The policeman's treatment gave rise to this war. When they were sent to collect the tax, they used to ill-use the natives and took their wives. The policemen went to Kabomp and met a man with his wife and daughter. They beat the man and assaulted the wife and daughter, and threatened his daughter with a knife if she cried out. In the town where we were, Captain Carr spent three days. The police caught all the fowls in the town.

Q. Did nobody complain to Captain Carr?

All the people ran away while Captain Carr was there, till he had left. Captain Carr asked for the Head Chief. He said he would burn the town if the headman did not come. Mr. Smith brought the man to the town, and he promised to pay the tax in a week's time. The next day a messenger, Williams, came to say he must pay in three days' time. He asked Mr. Schlenker to lend him the money.

We were afterwards caught by the war-boys, and I was with them for six weeks. On 29th April a sudden attack was made on Bolian. We went away in a boat, my husband, myself, a constable, and several others. In less than half an hour we got to a town, and over 200 people came on us with cutlasses, sticks and guns. They rushed on the policeman, W. J. Caulker, and chopped him and killed him and took his gun, and then threw him into the sea. They took the other two men and laid them side by side on the ground and chopped them to pieces. They killed my husband at my feet.

I asked them, "Why do you punish Sierra Leoneans so?" They say, "You pay the hut tax." They say, "The Sierra Leonneans with Bai Burreh had not paid the tax, so we did not kill them." They said we were lucky not to be caught before, as the Head Chief had, just the day before, said that no more women were to be killed. They said to me afterwards, "The government say we must not keep slaves, not have women palaver, nor pledge human beings." We say, 'All right.' They come, last of all, and say we must pay for these dirty huts.

"The Government look on us as a lazy people, but the whole of us will die before we pay his tax. We will

Source: Leon E. Clark, ed., *Through African Eyes: Cultures in Change*, vol. IV, *The Colonial Experiences: An Inside View* (New York: Praeger, 1970), 40–41.

kill Captain Carr, and then the Governor will come; we will kill the Governor, and then the Queen will come herself. The policemen catch our big men and flog them. If they have not anyone to fight for them they must fight for themselves."

It was one of the one of the war-boys who told me all this.

QUESTIONS

- What does Taylor mean that "the policeman's treatment gave rise to this war"?
- How did those rebelling describe their rebellion?

16.6 ENGLAND'S "ACT FOR THE RELIEF OF THE POOR" (1601)

"The Poor Relief Act 1601" (43 Eliz 1 c 2) followed up on a measure enacted four years earlier that created Overseers of the Poor. It made each parish—the unit of local government in rural areas—responsible for taxing and spending on helping the poor, establishing a place for them to live, and punishing those who would not pay. The Act demonstrates how taxes were assessed and collected; it was in force until 1834.

. . . Overseers of the poor of the same Parish . . . with the consent of two or more Justices of Peace, as is aforesaid, for setting to work of the children whose parents . . . be thought [un]able to keep and maintain their children. And also for setting to work all such persons married or unmarried, having no means to maintain them, or no ordinary and daily trade of life to get their living by, and also to raise weekly or otherwise (by taxation of every Inhabitant, Parson, Vicar, and other, and of every occupier of Lands, Houses, Tithes impropriate, or Propriations of Tithes, Coalmines, or saleable underwoods in the said Parish, in such competent sum and sums of money as they think fit) a convenient stock of Flax, Hemp, Wool, Thread, iron, and other necessary ware and stuff to set the poor on work, and also competent sums of money, for, and towards the necessary relief of the lame, impotent, old, blind, and such other among them being poor, and not able to work, and also for the putting out of such children to be apprentices, to be gathered out of the same Parish, according to the ability of the same parish, and to do and execute all other things, as well for the disposing of the said stock, as otherwise concerning the premises, as to them shall seem convenient. . . .

And be it also enacted, that if the said Justices of peace do perceive that the Inhabitants of any Parish are not able to levy amongst themselves sufficient sums of money for the purposes aforesaid: that then the said two Justices shall and may tax, rate and assess, as aforesaid, any other of other Parishes, or out of any Parish within the Hundred where the said Parish is, to pay such sum and sums of money to the Churchwardens and Overseers of the said poor Parish, for the said purposes, as the said Justices shall think fit, according to the intent of this Law. And if the said Hundred shall not to be thought to the said Justices able, and fit to relieve the said several Parishes not able to provide for themselves as aforesaid, Then the Justices of Peace at their general quarter Sessions, or the greater number of them, shall rate and assess, as aforesaid, any other of other Parishes, or out of any Parish within the said County for the purposes aforesaid, as in their direction shall seem fit. And that it shall be lawful as well for the present as subsequent Churchwardens and Overseers, or any of them, by warrant from any such Justices of

Source: "An Act for the Relief of the Poor" (1601) https://www.sochealth.co.uk/national-health-service/health-law/poor-law-1601/ (consulted May 23, 2020).

peace as is aforesaid, to levy as well the said sums of money and all arrearages of everyone that shall refuse to contribute according as they shall be assessed, by distress and sale of the offenders goods, as the sums of money, or stock which shall be behind upon any account to be made as aforesaid, rendering to the parties the overplus, and in defect of such distress, it shall be lawful for any two Justices of the Peace, to commit him or them to the common Gaol of the County, there to remain without bail or mainprize, until payment of the said sum, arrearages and stock. . . .

[The overseers shall] erect, build and set up in fit and convenient places of habitation . . . to be taxed rated and gathered, in manner before expressed, convenient houses of dwelling for the said impotent poor. . . .

And be it further enacted, That the Father and grandfather, and the Mother and Grandmother, and the children of every poor, old, blind, lame, and impotent person, or other poor person, not able to work, being of a sufficient ability, shall at their own charges relieve and maintain every such poor person in that

manner, and according to that rate, as by the Justices of peace of that County where such sufficient persons dwell, or the greater number of them, at their general quarter Sessions shall be assessed, upon pain that every one [of] them shall forfeit twenty shillings for every month which they shall fail therein. . . .

And be it further enacted by the authority aforesaid, that the Justices of peace of every County or place corporate, or the more part of them in their general Sessions to be holden next after the feast of Easter next, and so yearly as often as they shall think meet, shall rate every parish to such a weekly sum of money as they shall think convenient, so as no parish be rated above the sum of five pence, nor under the sum of a halfpenny, weekly to be paid, and so as the total sum of the taxation of the parishes in every County, amount not above the rate of two pence for every parish within the said County. Which sums so taxed, shall be yearly assessed by the agreement of the parishioners within themselves, or in default thereof, by the Churchwardens and petty Constables of the same parish. . . .

QUESTIONS

- Which of the stipulations most stands out to you? Why?
- What was England's view of the poor at the time, as illustrated by the excerpt?

16.7 CAHIER OF THE THIRD ESTATE OF DOURDAN (1789)

In 1789, Dourdan, France had a population of 7,800. Its inhabitants were called together in March 1789 to draw up lists of grievances and recommendations for reform as well as to elect deputies to the Estates-General, France's legislature which had not met since 1614. The people of this small city took their duties seriously. Today, located in the department of Essonne just south of Paris, this list expressed the views of the common people related to tax collection and equality more generally.

2. That all the orders, already united by duty and a common desire to contribute equally to the needs of the State, also deliberate in common concerning its needs. . . .

6. That, since the maintenance of the commonwealth necessitates an effective revenue, all taxes established since 1614, the year of the last meeting of the Estates General, be confirmed provisionally by His Majesty on the request of the Estates General, and the collection thereof ordered during a limited period of time, not to exceed one year, despite the fact that, owing to lack of consent of the nation, such taxes may be regarded as illegal. . . .

8. That the taxes on land and on all real or nominal property, the domains of the Crown, and other branches of revenue deriving from establishments useful to the public, such as postal and messenger service, etc., be preferably assigned to the aforementioned primarily necessary charges.

9. That the national debt be verified; that the payment of arrears of said debt be assured by such indirect taxes as may not be injurious to the husbandry, industry, commerce, liberty, or tranquility of the citizens. . . .

12. That every tax, direct or indirect, be granted only for a limited time, and that every collection beyond such term be regarded as peculation, and punished as such. . . .

15. That every personal tax be abolished; that thus the *capitation* [head tax] and the *taille* [land tax] and its accessories be merged with the *vingtièmes* [5% on income] in a tax on land and real or nominal property.

16. that such tax be borne equally, without distinction, by all classes of citizens and by all kinds of property, even feudal and contingent rights.

17. that the tax substituted for the *corvée* [labor service on public works] be borne by all classes of citizens equally and without distinction. That said tax, at present beyond the capacity of those who pay it and the needs to which it is destined be reduced by at least one-half. . . .

Finances

1. That if the Estates General considers it necessary to preserve the fees of *aides* [indirect taxes on consumption], such fees be made uniform throughout the entire kingdom . . . that the odious tax of *trop-bu* [a tax

Source: John H. Stewart, ed., *A Documentary Survey of the French Revolution* (New York: Macmillan, 1951), 76–84.

on wine-growers who exceeded what could be consumed for health] especially, a source of constant annoyance in rural districts, be abolished forever.

2. That the tax of the *gabelle* [on salt] be eliminated if possible, or that it be regulated among the several provinces of the kingdom. . . .

3. That the taxes on hides, which have totally destroyed that branch of commerce and caused it to go abroad, be suppressed forever.

Commerce

6. That all toll rights and other similar ones be suppressed throughout the interior of the kingdom, that customhouses be moved back to the frontiers, and that rights of *traite* [internal and external customs duties] be entirely abolished.

QUESTIONS

- What did the citizens most value, in terms of tax policy?
- What elements of modern policies appear in this document?

16.8 GRAHAM GORI, "14 KILLED IN BOLIVIAN RIOTS" (2003)

This account of riots in La Paz, Bolivia, written by Graham Gori of the Associated Press, appeared on February 13, 2003. It depicts the uncertainty caused by proposed changes in the income tax. Thirty-four people died in these protests (not 14, as first reported), setting the stage for more widespread resistance to government mandates. They were headed by Indigenous Bolivians and ultimately forced President Sanchez de Lozada to resign and flee the country for the United States, where he was later put on trial and convicted of committing genocide (although a judge later threw out the verdict). Tax reform lit the flame that ultimately consumed his presidency.

At least 14 people were killed in the Bolivian capital La Paz overnight as anti-government tax protests turned into riots.

The violence began when 7,000 striking police officers and civilian protesters clashed with government troops over a proposal by the Bolivian president, Gonzalo Sanchez de Lozada, to raise taxes on the poor.

Rioters set seven buildings on fire, and troops used rubber bullets and tear gas in response. The fighting subsided after five hours, but sporadic gunfire continued through the night.

Officials said that 14 people had been killed, with at least 100 others injured.

Mr Sanchez de Lozada escaped from the besieged presidential palace in an ambulance. He later gave a televised speech, in which he suspended the tax increase and ordered the withdrawal of government troops. . . . But with no police force, the president's call for peace had little effect as the city descended into chaos.

Police officers dressed in green fatigues seized the foreign ministry, firing tear gas in support of demonstrators who laid siege to the presidential palace. . . .

Fires raged in government buildings as firefighters abandoned their posts and joined the police in the protests. The buildings were still smoldering well after dark. . . .

Bolivia, a country well known for its violent repression of mass demonstrations, has not seen such a bloody incident since the country elected its first democratic government in 1982.

"The big difference is that the government always had the police to defend the constitution," said Carlos Toranzo, a political analyst in La Paz. "This time, the police left the fate of the nation in the hands of the looters."

Other analysts said that the violence was the result of tension built up over a decade of economic reforms. The reforms have left Bolivia as the poorest country in South America.

"The government should have known better than to squeeze more money from the poor like this," said Oswaldo Reyes, a 70-year-old who went to hospital to give blood.

Source: https://www.theguardian.com/world/2003/feb/13/1#maincontent (consulted May 27, 2020).

Street protests began on Monday after Mr Sanchez de Lozada, struggling to lift the country out of a five-year recession, approved tax hikes.

Unions, businesses and others came out against the increases, but the police revolt appeared to spark the violent street clashes with government troops.

Officers in the capital are paid the equivalent of about 880 bolivianos (£150) a month, a salary that would have been eroded by proposed income tax increases ranging from 7% to 13%. They have demanded a 40% pay rise.

QUESTIONS

- Why did the riots emerge?
- After reading the article, do you think the riots were justified? Why or why not?

16.9 THOMAS PIKETTY, *CAPITAL IN THE TWENTY-FIRST CENTURY* (2014)

French academic Thomas Piketty's dense economics treatise, based on fifteen years of statistical investigation, was a surprise bestseller. In addition to demonstrating the similarities of economic development and taxation policies despite significant national differences, Piketty illustrated the effects of financial globalization. He made a strong case for progressive taxation as part of the social compact of modern states and demonstrates conclusively that its decline leads directly to increasing income inequality. He detailed the trend in international competition in taxation by which those with significant capital escape taxes on labor, a phenomenon he described as "a race to the bottom."

[T]axes consumed less than 10 percent of national income in all four countries [France, Sweden, the United Kingdom, and the United States] during the nineteenth century and up to World War I. . . . Between 1920 and 1980, the share of national income that the wealthy countries chose to devote to social spending increased considerably. In just half a century, the share of taxes in national income increased by a factory of at least 3 or 4 (and in the Nordic countries more than 5). Between 1980 and 2010, however, the share stabilized everywhere. This stabilization took place at different levels in each country, however: just over 30 percent of national income in the United States, around 40 percent in Britain, and between 45 and 55 percent on the European continent. . . . In other words, all the rich countries, without exception, went in the twentieth century from an equilibrium in which less than a tenth of their national income was consumed by taxes to a new equilibrium in which the figure rose to between a third and half. . . .

[M]odern redistribution does not consist in transferring income [through taxation] from the rich to the poor, at least not in so explicit a way. It consists rather in financing public services and replacement incomes that are more equal for everyone, especially in the areas of health, education, and pensions. . . . Modern redistribution is built around a logic of rights and a principle of equal access to a certain number of goods deemed to be fundamental. . . .

The major twentieth-century innovation in taxation was the creation of and development of the progressive income tax. This institution, which played a key role in the reduction of inequality in the last century, is today serious threatened by international tax competition. . . . The same is true of the progressive tax on inheritances, which was the second major fiscal innovation of the twentieth century and has also been challenged in recent decades. . . .

It would be wrong, however, to conclude that progressive taxation plays only a limited role in modern redistribution. First, even if taxation overall is fairly close to proportional for the majority of the population, the fact that the highest incomes and largest fortunes are taxed at significantly higher (or lower) rates can have a

Source: Thomas Piketty, *Capital in the Twenty-First Century*, trans. Arthur Goldhammer (Cambridge, MA: The Belknap Press of Harvard University Press, 2014 [2013]), 475–76, 479, 493, 495–96.

strong influence on the structure of inequality. In particular, the evidence suggests that progressive taxation of very high incomes and very large estates partly explains why the concentration of wealth never regained its astronomic Belle Époque levels after the shocks of 1914–1945. Conversely, the spectacular decrease in the progressivity of the income tax in the United States and Britain since 1980, even though both countries had been among the leaders in progressive taxation after World War II, probably explains much of the increase in the very highest earned incomes. At the same time, the recent rise of tax competition in a world of free-flowing capital has led many governments to exempt capital income from the progressive income tax. . . . The result is an endless race to the bottom, leading, for example, to cuts in corporate tax rates and the exemption of interest, dividends, and other financial revenues from the taxes to which labor incomes are subject.

QUESTIONS

- What did Piketty advocate, specifically?
- Is Piketty's argument convincing? Why or why not?

17

THE AGE OF THE SUPERPOWERS

Political Change, 1945–2001

17.1 A NEWSPAPER ACCOUNT OF THE NIGHT OF THE BARRICADES (MAY 12–13, 1968)

This account of events in Paris in the mainstream newspaper *Le Monde* suggests the depth of commitment of the student movement, their leftist ideals, and the provocations on both sides before the violence started early in the morning of May 13th. It is sympathetic to the students yet decidedly factual in tone.

Late Saturday morning M. Maurice Grimaud, police prefect, provided a balance sheet of the tragic night in the Latin Quarter: 367 injured were counted in the hospitals, 251 of whom were members of the forces of order, and 102 students. Of the 367 injured 54 were hospitalized, among whom four students and 18 policemen were in serious condition.

As for arrests, the number has reached 461, of whom 60 were foreigners. The police prefect adds that 63 of the arrested will be brought before judges: 26 students, 3 high-schoolers, and the rest—34 individuals—were not students. . . .

7:30 pm. a cortege estimated to be more than 10,000 strong forms.

8:00 pm. Shoulder to shoulder, students, teachers, high-schoolers take the Rue Monge in order to reach the Boulevard Saint-Germain. Other young people mix in with the cortege that is estimated at this point to be more that 20,000 people strong. The marshals of the UNEF [student union] closely guard the flanks of the demonstrators and form a barrier when the mass passes before the helmeted and shield bearing [police] detachments. In this way any incidents are avoided. . . .

8:40 pm. The leaders of the demonstration . . . meet to make arrangements for after the demonstration. Quite quickly orders are given, among them that "the Latin Quarter must be occupied at whatever the cost." . . . Even so, from this moment small groups tear off the fences around trees and traffic signs and use them to rip up the paving stones. This initiative leads to occasionally violent discussions with demonstrators who want to ensure the demonstration a peaceful aspect. The argument most often used by those who were to become the partisans of the construction of barricades is that these are only defensive measures aimed at parrying any surprise attack.

9:15 pm, Rue Le Goff, when the first barricades goes up: a few cars, publicity panels, fences around trees, paving stones. The barrier, which quickly rose up, will set the example. The young people who "go to the front lines," taking position across from the police positioned around the Pantheon and the Sorbonne. . . .

10:05 pm. The Rector of the Sorbonne makes it known that he is ready to receive the students' representatives. . . . Daniel Cohn-Bendit, leader of the March 22 Movement, standing atop a barricade, calls for calm and *sang froid*. He issues the following watchword: "occupation of the Latin Quarter, but without attacking the police."

As the barricades multiply almost everywhere, though within a limited perimeter, the security forces receive reinforcements from units that had until then been positioned outside the Latin Quarter and close

Source: *Le Monde*, (May 12-13, 1968), trans. Mitchell Abidor (2008), https://www.marxists.org/history/france/may-1968/night-barricades.htm (consulted June 6, 2019).

down the area, which with each passing minute takes on an insurrectional air.

This first operation by the forces of order creates a certain disquiet among many students, who begin to retreat. Others, on the contrary, build more barricades, which sprout up in even greater number and which will end by giving the image of a fortified camp.

Sixty barricades will be put up in this way and be continually fortified. Many of them were higher than two meters tall.

A veritable frenzy takes hold of the demonstrators in their hunt for materials that can reinforce the barricades they are building: cars, wood beams, rolls of wire, breeze blocks, scaffolding. Construction sites are pillaged. Helmets are taken, work vests; bulldozers are started up. There are soon anthills piling up, built of all that can be dragged along.

Between 11:00 and midnight the demonstration has taken on a strength and a dimension that some had sought to give it since Monday. There's a sort of laborious, almost meticulous exaltation. A contagious enthusiasm, almost a joy. . . .

1:35 am. At the same time, behind the barricades, the several thousand demonstrators who remained were joined by a few hundred young people from the *Federation des étudiants révolutionnaires* (Federation of revolutionary students) who, red flags at the lead, took up position. . . . Those living along the river tossed food to them from their windows; they were brought drinks. Despite the depredations of all kinds, and especially the smashing and flipping over of cars, a visible sympathy seems to have taken hold between the uncompromising ones at the barricades and their spectators. The presence of older men can be noted in their ranks, who don't hesitate to give advice, to assist in the construction of barricades. For them, as for a certain number of young workers, it's a matter of demonstrating against "the bourgeois order."

1:45 am. Cohn-Bendit leaves the rectorate and declares: "We didn't engage in negotiations; we said to the Rector: "'What's happening this evening in the streets is that an entire youth is expressing itself against a certain society.'"

2:15 am after the reading of the riot act the order was given to the police to suppress the barricades and to disperse the demonstrators. 500 CRS [national security force], shields in one hand, truncheons in the other, move out on the Rue Auguste Comte and advance on the Boulevard St. Michel, pushing back the students in front of them. . . .

The demonstrators who are singing "the Internationale" and "the Marseillaise" reply by throwing stones and diverse projectiles. The forces of order, in this first phase of their action, don't seek close contact, which could be deadly, but remain at a distance, firing tear gas grenades with their rifles without let up. . . .

2:40 am. A first barricade falls on the Boulevard St Michel. In order to delay the slow but already ineluctable advance of the forces of order the students ignite their barricades with gas and set fire to tourist buses that they push into the middle of the street. In the face of the determination of the demonstrators the police will soon use offensive grenades. There are many wounded on both sides. . . .

3:00 am, and while for more than an hour the students have been chanting "De Gaulle Assassin" the police charges are multiplying and they are removing the barricades one after another after strong resistance. . . . The demonstrators only abandon their positions after being sure that they can do nothing more. And yet everything will have been tried during that night of riot: Molotov cocktails, burned cars, spreading of sand with bulldozers found at construction sites.

Despite the many fires, for about a hundred burned cars can be counted, the progress of the forces of order took place without obstacle, and the demonstrators found themselves backed into an increasingly limited space.

4:20 am . . . The last combatants take refuge in the offices of the École Normale Supérieure on the Rue d'Ulm, which will receive grenade fire. The Mouffetard quarter, the last pocket of resistance, is "cleaned up."

QUESTIONS

- Why do you think the activists were willing to go to such lengths?
- Would you have wanted to join them?

17.2 OLDŘICH ČERNÍK, RECOLLECTIONS OF THE CRISIS OF 1968 (1989)

Oldřich Černík (1921–1994) was prime minister of Czechoslovakia from April 1968 until January 1970. A longtime Communist Party (CPCz) official, Černík was in a central position to watch concern about the pace and degree of Czechoslovak reforms grow in other Warsaw Pact countries, most notably the Soviet Union. He survived the initial crackdown by distancing himself from Alexander Dubček, but as one of the chief architects of the Prague Spring, Černík was expelled from the Party in 1970. This recollection appeared in the Soviet newspaper *Izvestiya* (December 5, 1989) after the final collapse of the Communist regime in Czechoslovakia.

The process of post-January development in our country lasted only eight months. There was not a single instance during that time when the authorities had to resort to coercive methods or apply pressure against anti-socialist forces. The reason for this was simply that there were no mass protest actions or anti-socialist demonstrations in the ČSSR during that period, none at all. Yet even so, this process was interrupted and terminated by military intervention from outside. Why?

The development of events in Czechoslovakia . . . affected the interests of the fraternal communists and workers' parties of the countries in the socialist camp. The ideological legacy of the period of administrative-bureaucratic rule, an oppressive legacy of Stalinism, still prevailed in all the socialist countries in Eastern Europe. . . . The theoretical line swamped the practical construction of socialism; principles that were far removed from reality stifled new and innovative decisions; and every attempt to fashion a new program—one that was responsive to life's realities and would ease social tensions—was constantly thwarted by the concept of the leading role of the party. . . .

In the opinion of the CPSU [Soviet Communist Party] and the other parties, the CPCz and the Czechoslovak state at the time were headed by right-wing opportunist forces who through their policy of socialist reforms were seriously undermining the leading role of the CPCz and thus were fostering conditions conducive to the activity of anti-socialist forces.

QUESTIONS

- What was changing in Czechoslovakia at the time?
- What did Černík mean by "The theoretical line swamped the practical construction of socialism"?

Source: Reprinted in Jaromir Navratil, ed., *The Prague Spring: A National Security Archive Documents Reader*, trans. Mark Kramer, Joy Moss, and Ruth Tosek (Budapest: Central European University Press, 1998), 424–425.

17.3 WILLIAM HINTON, FANSHEN: AGRARIAN REVOLUTION IN CHINA (1948)

Fanshen means "to turn over." In rural China, beginning in the late 1930s and accelerating across the 1940s, the Communist Party sponsored land reforms and redistribution that constituted a revolution. This account of Changchuang ("Long Bow") village in north China was written by William Hinton, a farmer and writer who visited on behalf of the United Nations Relief and Rehabilitation Administration, based on notes taken in 1948. He remained in the region for more than five years helping to break up estates, teaching the peasants to read, instituting village councils, and protecting the equality of women. The lessons in managing the complicated process of instituting sweeping agrarian reforms and simultaneously implementing democratization learned by the Chinese Communists in places like Long Bow in 1948 were later applied all over the country.

Shansi-Hopei-Honan-Shantung Border Region Government, Proclamation to the Peasants (March 1948)

Why should the poor and hired peasants lead? The poor and hired peasants should lead because they make up from 50 to 70 percent of the population, are the most numerous, and work the hardest all year long. They plant the land, they build the buildings, they weave the cloth, but they never have enough food to eat, a roof to sleep under, or clothes to wear. Their life is the most bitter, they are oppressed and exploited and pushed around. Hence they are the most revolutionary. From birth they are a revolutionary class. Inevitably they are the leaders of the fanshen movement. This is determined by life itself. . . .

In the course of the past two years our Border Region has carried our powerful, enthusiastic land reform movement. Already over ten million people have thoroughly *fanshened* but there are still areas with a population of 20 million who have only partially *fanshened* or not *fanshened* at all. . . .

The Draft Agrarian Law is designed to correct all such mistakes. Articles One and Three call for destruction of the feudal system and the creation of a system of "land to the tiller."

What does this mean? It means that no matter who you are, whether you are a county magistrate, a commander-in-chief, or an official of whatever level, if you are a feudal exploiter, your property will be confiscated. Nothing will or can protect you. . . .

Article Six says that property will be distributed according to the number of people in the family. It is very simple—those who are politically suspect will get some, and those who are not politically suspect will get some. Those with merit will get some and those without merit will get some. Landlords will get a share and rich peasants will get a share

Source: William Hinton, *Fanshen: A Documentary of Revolution in a Chinese Village* (New York: Vintage Books, 1966), 269–271.

also. Some middle peasants will give up a little, some will get a little, most will not be touched at all. That which was not equally divided in the past is to be divided. Those who got too little in the past will get more. Those who got too much will give it up. The surplus will be used to fill the holes. Everything will be divided so that everyone will have a fair share.

QUESTIONS

- What did land reform entail?
- Do these reforms seem fair? Why or why not?

17.4 CHAI LING, INTERVIEW DURING TIANANMEN SQUARE PROTESTS (MAY 28, 1989)

Chai Ling (b. 1966) was an important student leader during the Tiananmen Square crisis in Beijing. She was a major proponent of and participant in a hunger strike that drew attention to the students' protests. Elected commander of a group called Defend Tiananmen Square, she agreed to help evacuate the students but later changed her mind, claiming that she had been pressured to agree. She was placed on a police blacklist for arrest. This interview was conducted in a hotel room by journalist Philip Cunningham on May 28, 1989, a week before the army intervened. Chai Ling left Beijing the night of June 3rd and escaped China after months in hiding. She emigrated to the United States, where she established a nonprofit organization called All Girls Allowed, aimed at protesting human rights violations related to China's one-child policy.

I think these may be my last words. My name is Chai Ling. I am twenty-three years old. My home is in Shandong Province. I entered Beijing University in 1983 and majored in psychology. I began my graduate studies at Beijing Normal University in 1987. . . .

The situation has become so dangerous. The students asked me what we were going to do next. I wanted to tell them that we were expecting bloodshed, that it would take a massacre, which would spill blood like a river through Tiananmen Square, to awaken the people. But how could I tell them this? How could I tell them that their lives would have to be sacrificed in order to win?

If we withdraw from the square, the government will kill us anyway and purge those who supported us. If we let them win, thousands would perish, and seventy years of achievement would be wasted. Who knows how long it would be before the movement could rise again? The government has so many means of repression—execution, isolation. . . .

I feel so helpless. How can I change the world? I am only one person. . . . We should not kill each other anymore! Our chances are too slim as it is.

I was extremely sad because, once again, I saw all kinds of people trying to betray us and put an end to this movement. At the start of the hunger strike there were about a thousand students participating, ruining their health. It infuriates me to think that there are people who want to ruin what these 1,000—and later several thousand—students are risking their lives for. . . .

I had a conversation with a plainclothes cop on April 25. I asked him what the sentence was for counter-revolutionary activities. He said that it used to be three to five years, but now it is seventeen. I'd be forty after seventeen years in prison. I'm really not willing to do that.

Source: "Interview at Tiananmen Square with Chai Ling," Asia for Educators, reprinted on http://afe.easia.columbia.edu/special/china_1950_chailing.htm (consulted June 7, 2019).

Yesterday I told my husband that I was no longer willing to stay in China. I realize that many students won't understand why I'm withdrawing from this movement and I will probably be criticized for this. But I hope that while I can no longer continue with this work there will be others who can. Democracy isn't the result of just one person's efforts. During the hunger strike I had said that we were not fighting so that we could die but so that we could live. I was fighting for life, because democracy cannot be accomplished by a single generation. Now I'm even more convinced of this. If I don't die, I vow to teach my child, from the day he is born, to grow up to be an honest, kind, fair, and independent Chinese. . . .

I believe that democracy is a natural desire. It should guarantee human rights and independence, and foster self-respect—all of which people are entitled to.

Unfortunately, the basic human instinct for independence has been greatly inhibited and degraded among the Chinese. Some out-of-town students even came to us, asking for food, lodging, and instructions for what to do next. I thought, they have hands, eyes, their own minds; they can take care of themselves. They are supporting a very good cause but, honestly, many of these students are irresponsible; they are accustomed to living in a feudal society in which they do not have to make decisions for themselves.

The square is our last stand. If we lose it, China will retreat into another dark age, the people will once again turn against one other, with no real feelings or communication between them. If a nation's own people don't stay and help it to grow and develop, who will? But I will not be there to protect the square because I'm different from the others: my name is on the blacklist. I don't want to die.

Before this movement, I dreamt about going abroad—to study psychology—but friends warned me not to think of America as a paradise. They said that there are a lot of overseas Chinese there and that their competitive instincts were overwhelming. I want to say to all those Chinese outside of China, those who already have freedom and democracy, and who have never had their lives endangered, to stand up and unite, to put an end to the fighting among us. There are so many kids here risking their own lives for what you have. Do what you can, break down the barriers and don't be selfish anymore. Think about our race. One billion people can't just fade away.

QUESTIONS

- Why was the Tiananmen Square movement so important in Ling's mind?
- Would you have also made Ling's decision to leave China?

17.5 THE MUSLIM BROTHERHOOD IN PALESTINE, THE COVENANT OF THE ISLAMIC RESISTANCE MOVEMENT, OR HAMAS (1988)

This Covenant was signed in August 1988 by the Muslim Brotherhood in Palestine to reject the idea of a negotiated peace with Israel as advocated by the Palestinian Liberation Organization. The following quote, used as a heading in the document, set the tone: "Israel will exist and will continue to exist until Islam will obliterate it, just as it obliterated others before it" (The Martyr, Imam Hassan al-Banna, of blessed memory)." Its radical language was closely aligned with that of Iran and groups referred to as "fundamentalist" that proclaimed a *jihad* to defend Islam against any and all threats. The reference to *The Protocols of the Elders of Zion*, invented by the Russian secret police, shows some of the links to earlier anti-Semitic thinking. In the 1980s and 1990s, a number of young people affiliated with Hamas acted as suicide bombers to press the attack on Israel.

Art. 8. Allah is its target, the Prophet is its model, the Koran its constitution: Jihad is its path and death for the sake of Allah is the loftiest of its wishes.

Art. 15. The day that enemies usurp part of Moslem land, Jihad becomes the individual duty of every Moslem. In face of the Jews' usurpation of Palestine, it is compulsory that the banner of Jihad be raised. To do this requires the diffusion of Islamic consciousness among the masses, both on the regional, Arab and Islamic levels. It is necessary to instill the spirit of Jihad in the heart of the nation so that they would confront the enemies and join the ranks of the fighters. . . .

Art. 16. It is necessary to follow Islamic orientation in educating the Islamic generations in our region by teaching the religious duties, comprehensive study of the Koran, the study of the Prophet's Sunna (his sayings and doings), and learning about Islamic history and heritage from their authentic sources. This should be done by specialised and learned people, using a curriculum that would healthily form the thoughts and faith of the Moslem student. Side by side with this, a comprehensive study of the enemy, his human and financial capabilities, learning about his points of weakness and strength, and getting to know the forces supporting and helping him, should also be included. Also, it is important to be acquainted with the current events, to follow what is new and to study the analysis and commentaries made of these events. Planning for the present and future, studying every trend appearing, is a must so that the fighting Moslem would live knowing his aim, objective and his way in the midst of what is going on around him.

Art. 17. The Moslem woman has a role no less important than that of the Moslem man in the battle of liberation. She is the maker of men. Her role in guiding and educating the new generations is great. The enemies have realised the importance of her role. They consider that if they are able to direct and bring her up they way they wish, far from Islam, they would have won the battle. That is why you find them giving these

Source: "The Convenant of the Islamic Resistance Movement" (August 18, 1988), https://avalon.law.yale.edu/20th_century/hamas.asp (consulted June 10, 2019).

attempts constant attention through information campaigns, films, and the school curriculum, using for that purpose their lackeys who are infiltrated through Zionist organizations under various names and shapes. . . .

Art. 28 . . . Israel, Judaism and Jews challenge Islam and the Moslem people. "May the cowards never sleep."

Art. 31. The Islamic Resistance Movement is a humanistic movement. It takes care of human rights and is guided by Islamic tolerance when dealing with the followers of other religions. It does not antagonize anyone of them except if it is antagonized by it or stands in its way to hamper its moves and waste its efforts.

Under the wing of Islam, it is possible for the followers of the three religions—Islam, Christianity and Judaism—to coexist in peace and quiet with each other. Peace and quiet would not be possible except under the wing of Islam. Past and present history are the best witness to that. . . .

Art. 32. World Zionism, together with imperialistic powers, try through a studied plan and an intelligent strategy to remove one Arab state after another from the circle of struggle against Zionism, in order to have it finally face the Palestinian people only. Egypt was, to a great extent, removed from the circle of the struggle, through the treacherous Camp David Agreement. They are trying to draw other Arab countries into similar agreements and to bring them outside the circle of struggle.

The Islamic Resistance Movement calls on Arab and Islamic nations to take up the line of serious and persevering action to prevent the success of this horrendous plan, to warn the people of the danger emanating from leaving the circle of struggle against Zionism. Today it is Palestine, tomorrow it will be one country or another. The Zionist plan is limitless. After Palestine, the Zionists aspire to expand from the Nile to the Euphrates. When they will have digested the region they overtook, they will aspire to further expansion, and so on. Their plan is embodied in the "Protocols of the Elders of Zion", and their present conduct is the best proof of what we are saying.

Art. 34 . . . This is the only way to liberate Palestine. There is no doubt about the testimony of history. It is one of the laws of the universe and one of the rules of existence. Nothing can overcome iron except iron. Their false futile creed can only be defeated by the righteous Islamic creed. A creed could not be fought except by a creed, and in the last analysis, victory is for the just, for justice is certainly victorious.

QUESTIONS

- Which of the articles most stands out? Why?
- How did this document support suicide bombings?

17.6 THE HISTORIC PROGRAM OF THE FSLN (SANDINISTA NATIONAL LIBERATION FRONT) OF NICARAGUA (1969)

The Program of the Sandinistas was first proclaimed in 1969 as part of the resistance to the U.S.-backed dictatorship in Nicaragua. It owed much to Che Guevara and to Maoism. The Program was reissued in 1981 as the Sandinistas became the leading force in the Nicaraguan government. Most of the inequities identified in the late 1960s were still relevant twelve years later. In 1981, the United States was already working to isolate and undermine the country while funding the "Contras" based in El Salvador and Honduras to overthrow the Sandinista government. U.S. scholar Will Reissner translated the document.

The Sandinista National Liberation Front (FSLN) arose out of the Nicaraguan people's need to have a "vanguard organization capable of taking political power through direct struggle against its enemies and establishing a social system that wipes out the exploitation and poverty that our people have been subjected to in past history."

The FSLN is a politico-military organization, whose strategic objective is to take political power by destroying the military and bureaucratic apparatus of the dictatorship and to establish a revolutionary government based on the worker-peasant alliance and the convergence of all the patriotic anti-imperialist and anti-oligarchic forces in the country.

The people of Nicaragua suffer under subjugation to a reactionary and fascist clique imposed by Yankee imperialism in 1932, the year Anastasio Somoza García was named commander in chief of the so-called National Guard (GN).

The Somozist clique has reduced Nicaragua to the status of a neocolony exploited by the Yankee monopolies and the country's oligarchic groups.

The present regime is politically unpopular and juridically illegal. The recognition and aid it gets from the North Americans is irrefutable proof of foreign interference in the affairs of Nicaragua.

The FSLN has serious and with great responsibility analyzed the national reality and has resolved to confront the dictatorship with arms in hand. We have concluded that the triumph of the Sandinista people's revolution and the overthrow of the regime that is an enemy of the people will take place through the development of a hard-fought and prolonged people's war. . . .

I.A. It will severely punish the gangsters who are guilty of persecuting, informing on, abusing, torturing, or murdering revolutionaries and the people. . . .

I.AA. It will expropriate the landed estates, factories, companies, buildings, means of transportation,

Source: Peter Rosset and John Vandermeer, eds., *Nicaragua: Unfinished Revolution—The New Nicaragua Reader* (New York: Grove Press, 1986), 181–89, 181–82, 184, 186, 188.

and other wealth usurped by the Somoza family and accumulated through the misappropriation and plunder of the nation's wealth.

I.BB. It will expropriate the landed estates, factories, companies, buildings, means of transportation, and other wealth usurped by the politicians and military officers, and all other accomplices, who have taken advantage of the present regime's administrative corruption.

I.CC. It will nationalize the wealth of all the foreign companies that exploit the mineral, forest, maritime, and other kinds of resources.

III.A. It will push forward a massive campaign to immediately wipe out "illiteracy."

III.B. It will develop the national culture and will root out the neocolonial penetration in our culture. . . .

III.I.1. It will rescue the university from the domination of the exploiting classes, so it can serve the real creators and shapers of our culture: the people. University instruction must be oriented around man, around the people. The university must stop being a breeding ground for bureaucratic egotists.

VI.A. It will end the unjust exploitation the Atlantic Coast has suffered throughout history by the foreign monopolies, especially Yankee imperialism. . . .

VII. The Sandinista people's revolution will abolish the odious discrimination that women have been subjected to compared to men; it will establish economic, political, and cultural equality between woman and man. . . .

XI.A. It will actively support the struggle of the peoples of Asia, Africa, and Latin America against the new and old colonialism and against the common enemy: Yankee imperialism. . . .

QUESTIONS

- How would the "Program" have appealed to Nicaraguans?
- What was the document's narrative of Central American history? What other events can you think of that would support such a narrative?

17.7 KWAME NKRUMAH, *NEO-COLONIALISM: THE LAST STAGE OF IMPERIALISM* (1965)

Benefiting from U.S. and British higher education and his own experiences as a political organizer of agricultural collectives, Kwame Nkrumah (1909–1972) led Gold Coast (now Ghana) to independence in 1957. He soon emerged as a major political thinker. Nkrumah was a vital supporter of Pan-Africanism, but his critique of the international system in this 1965 work both echoed and modernized Vladimir Ilyich Lenin's *Imperialism: The Highest Stage of Capitalism* (1916). Nkrumah's examples of the process of neo-colonialism focused on Africa but applied globally.

The essence of neo-colonialism is that the State which is subject to it is, in theory, independent and has all the outward trappings of international sovereignty. In reality its economic system and thus its political policy is directed from outside.

The methods and form of this direction can take various shapes. For example, in an extreme case the troops of the imperial power may garrison the territory of the neo-colonial State and control the government of it. More often, however, neo-colonialist control is exercised through economic or monetary means. The neo-colonial State may be obliged to take the manufactured products of the imperialist power to the exclusion of competing products from elsewhere. Control over government policy in the neo-colonial State may be secured by payments towards the cost of running the State, by the provision of civil servants in positions where they can dictate policy, and by monetary control over foreign exchange through the imposition of a banking system controlled by the imperial power.

Where neo-colonialism exists the power exercising control is often the State which formerly ruled the territory in question, but this is not necessarily so. For example, in the case of South Vietnam the former imperial power was France, but neo-colonial control of the State has now gone to the United States. It is possible that neo-colonial control may be exercised by a consortium of financial interests which are not specifically identifiable with any particular State. The control of the Congo by great international financial concerns is a case in point.

The result of neo-colonialism is that foreign capital is used for the exploitation rather than for the development of the less developed parts of the world. Investment under neo-colonialism increases rather than decreases the gap between the rich and the poor countries of the world.

The struggle against neo-colonialism is not aimed at excluding the capital of the developed world from operating in less developed countries. It is aimed at preventing the financial power of the developed countries being used in such a way as to impoverish the less developed.

Non-alignment, as practised by Ghana and many other countries, is based on co-operation with all States whether they be capitalist, socialist or have a

Source: Kwame Nkrumah, *Neo-Colonialism, The Last Stage of Imperialism* (London: Thomas Nelson & Sons, 1965), https://www.marxists.org/subject/africa/nkrumah/neo-colonialism/ (consulted June 24, 2019).

mixed economy. Such a policy, therefore, involves foreign investment from capitalist countries, but it must be invested in accordance with a national plan drawn up by the government of the non-aligned State with its own interests in mind. The issue is not what return the foreign investor receives on his investments. He may, in fact, do better for himself if he invests in a non-aligned country than if he invests in a neo-colonial one. The question is one of power. A State in the grip of neo-colonialism is not master of its own destiny. It is this factor which makes neo-colonialism such a serious threat to world peace. The growth of nuclear weapons has made out of date the old-fashioned balance of power which rested upon the ultimate sanction of a major war. Certainty of mutual mass destruction effectively prevents either of the great power blocs from threatening the other with the possibility of a world-wide war, and military conflict has thus become confined to 'limited wars'. For these neo-colonialism is the breeding ground.

Such wars can, of course, take place in countries which are not neo-colonialist controlled. Indeed their object may be to establish in a small but independent country a neo-colonialist regime. The evil of neo-colonialism is that it prevents the formation of those large units which would make impossible 'limited war'. To give one example: if Africa was united, no major power bloc would attempt to subdue it by limited war because from the very nature of limited war, what can be achieved by it is itself limited. . . .

QUESTIONS

- What did Nkrumah mean by "neo-colonialism"? What made it "neo"?
- What contemporary events seem to fit Nkrumah's definition?

17.8 ALICE DESCRIBES THE RWANDAN GENOCIDE (2009)

Alice's story was gathered, transcribed, and translated by the United Nations' Survivors Fund as a means of preserving the memory of the event and of ensuring that survivors' voices were heard. With only a tiny fraction of the perpetrators facing punishment and most punishments constituting a slap on the wrist, such measures helped promote reconciliation. The Hutu paramilitary organization *Interahamwe*, "those who work together," were the most militant perpetrators. Their use of sexual violence led to unwanted pregnancies and the spread of sexually transmitted diseases, especially HIV. Survivors faced the consequences for the rest of their lives.

When genocide started, I was in South West Rwanda. I had just moved to the area, and hardly knew anyone. The place was peaceful until the 11th April when the killing of Tutsis began.

Groups of *interahamwe* were searching for Tutsis to kill. They collected all those they labelled Tutsis in one place. They then separated the men from the women. Hundreds of *interahamwe* surrounded us, all armed with machetes, guns and clubs. They then proceeded to hack all the men to death.

Day after day more people were brought to the site. The head of the *interahamwe* would select people to kill, and women and girls to rape. I cannot remember how many times I was taken, raped, then returned to be united with my son. Nor can I remember how many times I wished I could be killed with my child instead of being put through the daily torture of gang rapes and violence. I will never forget the pain and fear on the faces of the children. There was no one to save

them. They cried and screamed until their last breaths. It was a long painful death. They who were lucky were shot dead. I must have witnessed thousands of people killed.

I survived the ordeal after being raped every day for 60 days. But I did not escape the killer HIV virus. I tested HIV positive. My son, now in his early teens, doesn't know. I pretend that everything will be alright. I still have a few relatives who can take care of him when I die. I am currently working in a bank and earning enough to pay for my treatment. But there are many women like me who can't afford treatment, and who are waiting for their deaths.

The killers still have their families. They have parents, children and homes to go to. They get their treatment paid for. While their victims live with the legacy of genocide. Survivors have nothing to back to. We have no parents, children and homes to go to. But without justice, there will never be healing for the survivors.

QUESTIONS

- Why are such stories important to preserve?
- How should nations such as Rwanda deal with the aftermath of genocide?

Source: United Nations, SURF Survivors Fund (2009), https://www.un.org/en/preventgenocide/rwanda/assets/pdf/survivor-testimonies/62%20-%20Alice2009.pdf (consulted June 25, 2019).

17.9 UNITED NATIONS, *UNIVERSAL DECLARATION OF HUMAN RIGHTS* (1948)

The Universal Declaration of Human Rights is the most comprehensive listing of rights in international law. Passed by the United Nations General Assembly in 1948, it went into force three years later. Clearly referring to the French *Declaration of the Rights of Man and Citizen* of 1789 but far surpassing it in scale and scope, the totality of the *Universal Declaration* is unenforced in even the most developed and democratic states. Today we might want to broaden its mandate even further to include rights to sexual identity and expression. The human rights listed in this document encourage the reader to consider what actions might have inspired states across the globe to outlaw those practices.

Preamble: Whereas recognition of the inherent dignity and of the equal and inalienable rights of all members of the human family is the foundation of freedom, justice and peace in the world,

Whereas disregard and contempt for human rights have resulted in barbarous acts which have outraged the conscience of mankind, and the advent of a world in which human beings shall enjoy freedom of speech and belief and freedom from fear and want has been proclaimed as the highest aspiration of the common people,

Whereas it is essential, if man is not to be compelled to have recourse, as a last resort, to rebellion against tyranny and oppression, that human rights should be protected by the rule of law,

Whereas it is essential to promote the development of friendly relations between nations,

Whereas the peoples of the United Nations have in the Charter reaffirmed their faith in fundamental human rights, in the dignity and worth of the human person and in the equal rights of men and women and have determined to promote social progress and better standards of life in larger freedom. . . .

Article 2. Everyone is entitled to all the rights and freedoms set forth in this Declaration, without distinction of any kind, such as race, colour, sex, language, religion, political or other opinion, national or social origin, property, birth or other status. . . .

Article 3. Everyone has the right to life, liberty and security of person.

Article 4. No one shall be held in slavery or servitude; slavery and the slave trade shall be prohibited in all their forms.

Article 5. No one shall be subjected to torture or to cruel, inhuman or degrading treatment or punishment.

Article 6. Everyone has the right to recognition everywhere as a person before the law.

Article 7. All are equal before the law and are entitled without any discrimination to equal protection of the law. . . .

Article 15. (1) Everyone has the right to a nationality. (2) No one shall be arbitrarily deprived of his nationality nor denied the right to change his nationality.

Source: United Nations, *Universal Declaration of Human Rights* (1948), https://www.un.org/en/universal-declaration-human-rights/ (consulted 26 June 2019).

Article 16. (1) Men and women of full age, without any limitation due to race, nationality or religion, have the right to marry and to found a family. They are entitled to equal rights as to marriage, during marriage and at its dissolution. (2) Marriage shall be entered into only with the free and full consent of the intending spouses. (3) The family is the natural and fundamental group unit of society and is entitled to protection by society and the State. . . .

Article 18. Everyone has the right to freedom of thought, conscience and religion; this right includes freedom to change his religion or belief, and freedom, either alone or in community with others and in public or private, to manifest his religion or belief in teaching, practice, worship and observance.

Article 19. Everyone has the right to freedom of opinion and expression; this right includes freedom to hold opinions without interference and to seek, receive and impart information and ideas through any media and regardless of frontiers. . . .

Article 21. (1) Everyone has the right to take part in the government of his country, directly or through freely chosen representatives. . . . (3) The will of the people shall be the basis of the authority of government; this will shall be expressed in periodic and genuine elections which shall be by universal and equal suffrage and shall be held by secret vote or by equivalent free voting procedures. . . .

Article 23. (1) Everyone has the right to work, to free choice of employment, to just and favourable conditions of work and to protection against unemployment. (2) Everyone, without any discrimination, has the right to equal pay for equal work. (3) Everyone who works has the right to just and favourable remuneration ensuring for himself and his family an existence worthy of human dignity, and supplemented, if necessary, by other means of social protection. . . .Article 25. (1) Everyone has the right to a standard of living adequate for the health and well-being of himself and of his family, including food, clothing, housing and medical care and necessary social services, and the right to security in the event of unemployment, sickness, disability, widowhood, old age or other lack of livelihood in circumstances beyond his control. . . .

Article 26. (1) Everyone has the right to education. Education shall be free, at least in the elementary and fundamental stages. Elementary education shall be compulsory. . . . (2) Education shall be directed to the full development of the human personality and to the strengthening of respect for human rights and fundamental freedoms. It shall promote understanding, tolerance and friendship among all nations, racial or religious groups, and shall further the activities of the United Nations for the maintenance of peace. . . .Article 28. Everyone is entitled to a social and international order in which the rights and freedoms set forth in this Declaration can be fully realized. . . .

QUESTIONS

- Which of the articles is the most appealing to you?
- Is there anything that the Declaration leaves out? How might it be improved?

18

LEFT IN THE LURCH
Decolonization, 1914–Present

18.1 MUSTAFA KEMAL ATATÜRK, THE TURKISH REVOLUTION (1927)

Mustafa Kemal Atatürk (1881-1938) was a high-ranking military officer who led a Turkish National Movement that successfully defeated occupying allied forces. He then abolished the Ottoman government and formed a secular, nationalistic Turkish Republic in 1923 serving as its first president until his death. This speech recalling the beginnings of the movement was given at a convention of his People's Party in October 1927. Excerpts were translated into English by the Turkish Ministry of Education in 1967. Mustafa Kemal Atatürk's ideas on development, nationalism, and secularism became known as Kemalism.

The group of powers which included the Ottoman Empire had been defeated in the Great War. The Ottoman Army had been crushed on all fronts and an armistice had been signed with harsh conditions. The people were tired and poor. . . . The Caliph was seeking some way to save his person and his throne. The Cabinet . . . It was slavishly polite and obedient to the will of the Sultan alone and was willing to agree to anything that might keep it and the Sultan in power.

The Entente Powers did not see any need to abide by the terms of the armistice. Their warships and troops remained in Istanbul. The Vilayet of Adana was occupied by the French; Urfa, Maras and Antep by the British; Konya and Antalya by the Italians. Merzifon and Samsun were occupied by British troops. Foreign officers and officials and their special agents were very active everywhere. On 15th May, the Greek Army too had landed at Izmir with the consent of the Entente Powers. . . .

Here I must explain a very important point: the nation and the army had no suspicion at all of the Sultan Caliph's treachery. On the contrary, because of the religious and traditional ties that had been handed down for centuries, they remained loyal to the throne and its occupant. . . .

[O]nly one course of action was possible: the creation of a new and completely independent Turkish state, founded on the principle of national self-determination. . . .

The Turkish nation should live in honour and dignity. Such a condition could only be attained by complete independence. No matter how wealthy and prosperous a nation may be, if it is deprived of its independence it no longer deserves to be regarded as anything more than a slave in the eyes of the civilised world. . . . Indeed, it is unthinkable that any group of people should ever voluntarily accept the humiliation of being ruled over by a foreign master.

But the Turk is dignified and proud; he is also capable and talented. Such a nation would prefer to die rather than subject itself to a life of slavery. Therefore independence or death! . . .

Source: http://web.archive.org/web/20030202062524/http://ataturk.turkiye.org/soylev/spchtm/spchdizi.htm (Consulted 22 July 2019).

I sent circulars to all commanding officers and higher civilian officials, urging them to move forward with the formation of national organizations all over the country. The people had not been fully informed about the occupation of Izmir, Manisa and Aydin. They had not as yet reacted to this terrible blow. It was not a good thing for the people to remain silent in the face of this injustice; what was necessary, therefore, was to rouse them and spur them to action.

QUESTIONS

- What was so revolutionary about Kemal's ideas and actions?
- How might the Turkish Revolution have influenced other nations?

18.2 HO CHI MINH, "APPEAL MADE ON THE OCCASION OF THE FOUNDING OF THE INDOCHINESE COMMUNIST PARTY" (1930)

Ho Chi Minh (1890?–1969), born Nguyen Sinh Cung, studied in Paris where he joined a group of Vietnamese nationalists and became a communist. Ho visited China and the Soviet Union and worked for the Comintern. He helped merge various Communist Parties and factions in 1930 where he delivered this address on February 18, 1930. The Communist Viet Minh movement resisted both French oversight and Japanese occupation during World War II. They staged a revolution in August 1945: A Democratic Republic controlled the North. Party leaders promptly declared independence. Warfare against France, the Republic of South Vietnam, and the United States between 1946 and 1975 left the Communists as the rulers of the entire country. In this address, Ho linked communism in Indochina to the global push for decolonization. Many Vietnamese communists fought more for national liberation than Marxist-Leninist principles.

Workers, peasants, soldiers, youth, and students!
Oppressed and exploited compatriots!
Sisters and brothers! Comrades!

Imperialist contradictions were the cause of the 1914-18 World War. After this horrible slaughter, the world was divided into two camps: One is the revolutionary camp including

the oppressed colonies and the exploited working class throughout the world. The vanguard force of this camp is the Soviet Union. The other is the counterrevolutionary camp of international capitalism and imperialism whose general staff is the League of Nations.

During this World War, various nations suffered untold losses in property and human lives. The French imperialists were the hardest hit. Therefore, in order to restore the capitalist forces in France, the French imperialists have resorted to every underhand scheme to

intensify their capitalist exploitation in Indochina. They set up new factories to exploit the workers with low wages. They plundered the peasants' land to establish plantations and drive them to utter poverty. They levied many heavy taxes. They imposed public loans upon our people. In short, they reduced us to wretchedness. . . . World War II will break out. When it breaks, the French imperialists will certainly drive our people to a more horrible slaughter. . . . [I]f we give them a free hand to stifle the Vietnamese revolution, it is tantamount to giving them a free hand to wipe our race off the earth and drown our nation in the Pacific.

However the French imperialists' barbarous oppression and ruthless exploitation have awakened our compatriots, who have all realized that revolution is the only road to life, without it they will die out piecemeal. This is the reason why the Vietnamese revolutionary movement has grown even stronger with each

Source: Bernard F. Fall, ed., *Ho Chi Minh on Revolution: Selected Writings, 1920-66* (New York: New American Library, 1967), 129-30.

passing day. The workers refuse to work, the peasants demand land, the pupils strike, the traders boycott. Everywhere the masses have risen to oppose the French imperialists.

The Vietnamese revolution has made the French imperialists tremble with fear. On the one hand, they utilize the feudalists and comprador [imperialist agent] bourgeois in our country to oppress and exploit our people. On the other, they terrorize, arrest, jail, deport, and kill a great number of Vietnamese revolutionaries. If the French imperialists think that they can suppress the Vietnamese revolution by means of terrorist acts, they are utterly mistaken. Firstly, it is because the Vietnamese revolution is not isolated but enjoys the assistance of the world proletarian class in general and of the French working class in particular. Secondly, while the French imperialists are frenziedly carrying out terrorist acts, the Vietnamese Communists, formerly working separately, have now united into a single party, the Communist Party of Indochina, to lead our entire people in their revolution. . . .

From now on we must join the Party, help it and follow it in order to implement the following slogans:

1. To overthrow French imperialism, feudalism, and the reactionary Vietnamese capitalist class.
2. To make Indochina completely independent.
3. To establish a worker-peasant and soldier government.
4. To confiscate the banks and other enterprises belonging to the imperialists and put them under the control of the worker-peasant and soldier government.
5. To confiscate the whole of the plantations and property belonging to the imperialists and the Vietnamese reactionary capitalist class and distribute them to poor peasants.
6. To implement the eight-hour working day.
7. To abolish public loans and poll tax. To waive unjust taxes hitting the poor people.
8. To bring back all freedoms to the masses.
9. To carry out universal education.
10. To implement equality between man and woman.

QUESTIONS

- Briefly summarize Ho's narrative of Vietnam's history.
- Why do you think Ho's message was so appealing to the Vietnamese people?

18.3 PATRICE LUMUMBA, ON RACISM AND COLONIALISM (1960)

Patrice Lumumba (1925–1961) was educated in religious schools (both Protestant and Catholic) as well as in a state-run institution. Fired from a civil service job and jailed for a year, Lumumba helped found the National Congolese Movement in 1958 and was soon its leader. A strong supporter of Pan-African ideals who sought to keep Congo united, Lumumba inspired millions. After his party and its partners won the May 1960 election, Lumumba formed the first independent government of Congo. Belgian interference in favor of one of its proxies led Lumumba to become Prime Minister not President. Trumped up charges that Lumumba was a communist encouraged Belgium to press its allies in Katanga, a province with vast mineral wealth, to declare its independence. Belgian paratroopers and United Nations peacekeeping forces intervened after some outraged Congolese troops attacked Europeans. Lumumba's political opponents abducted him in December 1960 before killing him in January 1961 with the complicity of Belgium and the U.S.

Question [from a *France-Soir* correspondent on 22 July 1960]: Some of your political opponents accuse you of being a Communist. Could you reply to that?

Answer: This is a propagandist trick aimed at me. I am not a Communist. The colonialists have campaigned against me throughout the country because I am a revolutionary and demand the abolition of the colonial regime, which ignored our human dignity. They look upon me as a Communist because I refused to be bribed by the imperialists.

Speech at the ceremony proclaiming Congo's independence (30 June 1960)

We have known sarcasm and insults, endured blows morning, noon, and night, because we were "niggers". Who will forget that a Black was addressed in the familiar *tu*, not as a friend, but because the polite *vous* was reserved for Whites only? We have seen our lands despoiled under the terms of what was supposedly the law of the land but which only recognised the right of the strongest. We have seen that this law was quite different for a White than for a Black: accommodating for the former, cruel and inhuman for the latter. We have seen the terrible suffering of those banished to remote regions because of their political opinions or religious beliefs; exiled within their own country, their fate was truly worse than death itself. . . . And, finally, who can forget the volleys of gunfire in which so many of our brothers perished, the cells where the authorities threw those who would not submit to a rule where justice meant oppression and exploitation.

Speech at the opening of the All-African Conference at Leopoldville (25 August 1960)

We have gathered here in order that together we may defend Africa, our patrimony. In reply to the actions of the imperialist states, for whom Belgium is

Sources: *Patrice Lumumba: Fighter for Africa's Freedom* (Moscow: Progress Publishers, 1961), 40, 22 and Ludo de Witte, *The assassination of Lumumba*, trans. Ann Wright and Renée Fenby (London: Verso, 2001), 2.

only an instrument, we must unite the resistance front of the free and fighting nations of Africa. We must oppose the enemies of freedom with a coalition of free men. Our common destiny is now being decided here in the Congo.

It is, in effect, here that the last act of Africa's emancipation and rehabilitation is being played. In extending the struggle, whose primary object was to save the dignity of the African, the Congolese people have chosen independence. In doing so, they were aware that a single blow would not free them from colonial fetters, that juridical independence was only the first step, that a further long and trying effort would be required. The road we have chosen is not an easy one, but it is the road of pride and freedom of man.

We were aware that as long as the country was dependent, as long as she did not take her destiny into her own hands, the main thing would be lacking. . . .

We had to create a new system adapted to the requirements of purely African evolution, change the methods forced on us and, in particular, find ourselves and free ourselves from the mental attitudes and various complexes in which colonisation kept us for centuries.

QUESTIONS

- Why would the correspondent have asked Lumumba if he was a communist?
- How might Lumumba's ideas have appealed to people outside of the Congo?

18.4 BITTER TEA IN MOZAMBIQUE (1968)

This account was published in the October 1968 edition of *Mozambique Revolution* published by the Mozambique Liberation Front (FRELIMO in Portuguese). It suggests why this young man turned to a revolutionary organization and illustrates the type of exploitation he and his family faced. This Marxist group was founded in 1962 and fought until the Portuguese left in 1975. It successfully liberated certain parts of the country even before liberation and once in power, FRELIMO supported resistance to colonialism throughout the region, but especially in Rhodesia and South Africa.

I come from Zambezia Province and am a peasant from that Province. My name is Joachim Americo Paulo Maquival. I come from Milange and am 25 years old. All my family are peasants. We cultivate millet, cassava, beans, sugar cane, etc.

We also had to work on the government land; [that is] it isn't government land, it belongs to a company, but it was the government that made us work it. . . . The government came and arrested us in our villages and sent us to the company; that is, the company paid money to the administration or the government and then the government arrested us and gave us to the company.

I began working for the company when I was 12: they paid me 15 *escudos* a month (53 cents U.S.A.). I worked from six in the morning until twelve noon, when we stopped for two hours, then again from two until six in the evening. The whole family worked for the company, my brothers, my father—my father is still there—my father earned and still earns 150 *escudos* a month ($5.30); he [works] from morning to evening. He has to pay 195 *escudos* ($7.00) yearly tax to the government. We didn't want to work for the company but . . . the government sent police to the villages and they arrested those who refused. . . . If they ran away, the police sent out photographs of them and a hunt was started. When they caught them they beat them and put them in prison, and when they came out of prison, they had to go back and work for the company, but without pay; they said that as they had run away they didn't need the money.

Thus, in our fields only our poor mothers were left who could not do much. All we had to eat was the little that our mothers were able to grow. We had neither sugar nor tea. We had to work growing tea, but we didn't know what it tasted like. Tea didn't come into our homes.

The Portuguese wage earners eared well. At the end of a month they would buy a new car perhaps, while we couldn't even buy tea and at the end of the year we didn't have enough to buy a bicycle.

Later, when I was 15, I went to a mission school and I managed to get my certificate. It was a Catholic Mission. We had to work there; we had to work in the priests' fields. The government gave the missions money for our education, but we didn't know and we worked in the fields because they said it was necessary to pay the missions.

In 1964 I joined FRELIMO because our people were exploited. It still did not [really] know . . . what to

Source: *Through African Eyes: Cultures in Change*, vol. V, *The Rise of Nationalism: Freedom Regained*, ed. Leon E. Clark (New York: Praeger, 1970), 114-17.

do about it. The people didn't know what to do. We had heard that our neighbor, Malawi, had been liberated and would come and liberate us, but we soon learned that it was we who would have to liberate ourselves. The party told us that we and no one else are responsible for ourselves. . . .

The colonialists try to deceive the world, to hide the truth; they say that our people are divided into hostile tribes, but we all face the same enemy: Portuguese colonialism.

I want to repeat: the Portuguese are great liars. For example, they say that we are terrorists. That is false; it is they who are terrorists and bandits.

For example, in our units and on missions, we have often come across unarmed Portuguese civilians. We didn't harm them . . . our struggle, our war, is not against the Portuguese people; we are struggle against the Portuguese government. . . . FRELIMO is the

enemy of the enemies of the people. We know that it is not all the people of Portugal who exploit us, but only a minority [which] is also exploiting the Portuguese people themselves. . . .

But the Portuguese soldiers are terrorists. They did do not respect our people; they want to injure them, to eat them, and now to kill them. I have often seen this. . . . They arrested an old man called Moussa, responsible for the organization of the local party branch. They beat him, tied him with ropes, and took to the post at Catur. There they beat him with rifle butts and then hung him head down over a fire. . . .

The war has changed the people's situation. Where war has already broken out the people are no longer beaten, there are no longer taxes which exploit the people, the people are not humiliated. There are hardships but this is the price of victory. We are glad to fight.

QUESTIONS

- Why did the author join FRELIMO?
- Do you think his decision was justified? Why or why not?

18.5 ZOHRA DRIF, THE BATTLE OF ALGIERS (1965)

The Algerian National Liberation Front (FLN or ALN) was created in 1954. The 1956 incident depicted here reflected a shift in tactics to urban terrorism known as the "Battle of Algiers" that was prompted by fierce French repression. Algeria won its indepence in 1962. In 1956, Zohra Dirf (b. 1934) was a law student determined to fight for Algerian independence. Along with Samia Lakhdari and Djamila Bouhired, Dirf was able to blend in with people of European descent and enter areas that would have been restricted to women dressed as observant Muslims. This incident, portrayed in the classic film *The Battle of Algiers* by Gillo Pontecorvo (1965), suggests the vital role played by women in the FLN's campaign. The bomb she left in the Milk Bar (an ice-cream parlor) killed three and wounded dozens. After independence, Drif had an illustrious career and served as Vice-President of Algeria's Senate. In 1984, amidst a lengthy and debilitating civil conflict between Islamists and secularists, Algerian women lost some of their political rights at the hands of the FLN-led government.

In August 1956, Samia and I, assuming full responsibility, chose to become "volunteers for death" to recover and free our mother, Algeria—who had been taken by force, raped, and kidnapped for 126 years—or so die. . . .

As for the civilians who perished during the war of national liberation, if they are Algerian, I would propose that they go to the ALN fighters and ask them, "Why did we die?" I know that the ALN will reply, "You are dead because your lives were part of the price we had to pay for our country to be free and independent."

And if they are French, I would propose that they go see the French authorities and ask, "Why did we die?" I do not know what the French authorities would say, but I would propose to them the one real truth there is: "You died because you were among the hundreds of thousands of Europeans that we used to subjugate and occupy a foreign country, Algeria, so that we could make it our settler colony." . . .

Samia and I had gone about our usual early-morning routine, haunted by the thought that this would either be the last day of our lives or the one that would determine all that would follow in our struggle and in our existence. We were well aware that we had as much chance of failure as we did success. Moreover, failure could take many forms, the worst one being our arrest and the torture that would surely follow.

We were to plant each bomb, ensure that it was not discovered before exploding, then make sure not to be arrested. On the morning of September 30, 1956 . . . we consecrated ourselves to preparing our chic "volunteers for death" outfits. I must say that mine was frankly quite pretty, an elegant summer dress. . . . When trying it all on we had confirmed that, with our new haircuts and makeup, we would blend in perfectly among the European *jeunesse dorée* [gilded youth]—even the most well-to-do among them. At noon we had lunch with Samia's parents, admiring their calm and serenity as our guts writhed with anxiety at the

Source: Zhora Drif, *Inside the Battle of Algiers: Memoir of a Woman Freedom Fighter*, trans. Andrew Farrand (Charlottesville, VA: Just World Books, 2017 [2013]), 106, 113–16.

thought that maybe by the day's end they would learn that one of us had been killed or arrested. . . . At one-thirty, we donned our outfits. Aware that we could not go out in the neighborhood dressed this way, we slipped long, loose, ordinary blouses over our fashionable dresses. . . .

Then Si Rachid told us that the bombs were activated and stowed in the beach bags. Their timers were set, taking into account the time necessary for the journey to the target, our settling in and ordering, consuming, and paying the bill. Si Rachid reminded us that my bomb was set for 6:25, Samia's for 6:30, and finally Djamila's for 6:35. He insisted that it was absolutely necessary to leave the premises at least eight to ten minutes before the explosion and not to hang

around the target. He concluded by reassuring us of his complete confidence in the three of us, and wished us good luck.

I jumped when I heard Si Rachid say, "It's time, *khtou* (sister)!" Oh! This magic word, *khtou*! This word, full to the brim with such human solidarity and such tender brotherhood, whipped me up, invigorated me, and galvanized me all at once. Then, spontaneously, I turned back to my new *kho* [brother], kissed him on the cheek, and said, "May Allah be with us!" I took my bomb, opened the door, and ran down the stairs, the beach bag slung behind my right shoulder like all the young girls did at the time. The word *khtou* was still dancing in my head and I felt like I was flying, buoyed by all the *khos* and *khtous* of the earth.

QUESTIONS

- Why were women valued as "volunteers for death"?
- Why was the narrator so exhilarated at the end of the excerpt?

18.6 MOHAMMED REMEMBERS PARTITION IN THE PUNJAB (1947)

This account stems from an interview conducted by researchers at the United Kingdom's National Archives as part of an exhibition on partition. Mohammed was born in 1939 and lived in Sadarpura, Punjab. This Muslim family spent about 10 weeks in a refugee camp before they crossed into Pakistan where they lived until 1969 when they moved to the U.K.. Mohammed depicted the uncertainties and communal divergences that emerged as well as the horrors of dramatic population transfer and the toxic effects of government propaganda.

It was a mixed village; we never realised that somebody was Hindu or Sikh or Muslim. In marriages, the whole village used to join in. If somebody died, the whole village would mourn. Whether it was Hindus or Sikhs, it would not make a difference.

All of a sudden, in the space of a year or so this madness came. I remember people saying slogans; *"Pakistan ka matlab kiya"*, ("What's the meaning of Pakistan?") *"La ilaha il Allah"* ("there is only one God"). People were debating whether to vote for Congress or for the Muslim League. At the time people did not understand what that would mean. There was a lot of propaganda and hate spreading against communities and religions.

India was divided. Nobody knows exactly how many people died, but it was in the millions. Nobody was brought to justice. It was not the people who did it. It was the politicians who did it.

People left their homes because they were afraid for their lives and they were driven into the camps. We were in a camp at Seleempur for two and a half months waiting to move to Pakistan. We never had any problem with our food or our animals' food because it was being brought by people who were not Muslims. They were Sikhs and Hindus—my father's friends, who looked after us while we were in camp. I have seen the children; I have seen the elders living on grass. That's terrible—children suffering and refusing to eat that stuff. But you have to live on something. They were terrible times.

The time came for that camp to move to Pakistan. We were told by the army that was guarding us that this was a temporary arrangement because nobody wanted to go. We moved 12-15 miles a day and then camped again for the night. People were so weak by staying in camp when they didn't have much food as well. . . . It was difficult for them to move and walk.

Amongst us, there were certain people who had lost most of their family, who were murdered. I remember one woman who had two small babies with her. After moving the third time, some 45 miles, her feet were swollen and she had no proper shoes on either but she had two babies to carry. After the third day, she could not carry the babies. One day she left one baby on the roadside because she could only carry one. This happened to many other women and

Source: http://www.nationalarchives.gov.uk/panjab1947/mohammed.htm (Consulted August 7, 2019).

children because they could not walk and their parents were not strong enough to carry them. If you were slow, you were more likely to be killed.

We settled in a village. Eventually, the government allotted us some land which was vacated by Hindus and Sikhs. That happened in 1947. My father died in 1958. He was still waiting to move back to his own house. He said: "this cannot happen that somebody can take away my property, my house, my land, everything".

I was brought up hating Hindus and Sikhs until I was educated and went to the civil service. I was put in charge of India-Pakistan trade, representing Pakistan. The first time I went to Amritsar, it was a completely new world. It was amazing. People greeted me in such a way; Hindus, Sikhs. People wanted to take me to their houses and eat there, spend time with their families. The first day I was completely taken aback. What I was taught in Pakistan had no reality. Hindus, Sikhs loved to see people from Pakistan. I did not see a sign of hate. I have seen similar positions over here. There is no difference between Hindus and Sikhs and Muslims . . . especially Panjabi people together.

QUESTIONS

- Does this process seem orderly?
- Why did religious categories assume so much importance after partition? Was it a natural occurrence?

18.7 JOMO KENYATTA, "THE FABLE OF THE ELEPHANT" (1938)

Born Kamau in Kenya, Kenyatta (1894?-1978) converted to Christianity and became a minor government official before becoming involved in a Kikuyu student association. Sent to the United Kingdom as an emissary, he remained there from 1931 to 1946 getting a doctorate in anthropology and becoming a public intellectual. This excerpt of *Facing Mount Kenya* was published in 1938 when he changed his name to Jomo. In 1952, he and almost 100 other Kikuyu leaders was jailed for alleged participation in the Mau Mau Rebellion. Freed in 1961, he headed the Kenyan African National Union which won the 1963 elections ahead of independence the following year. Kenyatta served as president until his death. This fable illustrated the frustration with British attitudes and government policies and suggested how to stop that exploitation.

An elephant made friendship with a man. Driven by a heavy thunderstorm, the elephant sought shelter in the man's hut that was on the edge of the forest. The elephant was allowed partial admission, but eventually he evicted the man from his hut and took full possession of the hut, saying: "My dear good friend, your skin is harder than mine, and there is not enough room for both of us. you can afford to remain in the rain while I am protecting my delicate skin from the hailstorm."

The man, seeing what his friend had done to him, started to grumble . . . . The lion came along roaring, and said in a loud voice: "Don't you all know that I am the King of the Jungle!" . . . The lion, who wanted to have" peace and tranquility" in his kingdom, replied in a noble voice, saying: "I command my ministers to appoint a Commission of Enquiry to go thoroughly into this matter and report accordingly." . . .

The elephant, obeying the command of his master, got busy with other ministers to appoint the Commission of Enquiry. The following elders of the jungle were appointed to sit in the Commission: (I) Mr. Rhinoceros; (2) Mr. Buffalo; (3) Mr. Alligator; (4) The Rt. Hon. Mr. Fox to act as chairman; and (5) Mr. Leopard to act as Secretary to the Commission. On seeing the personnel, the man protested and asked if it was not necessary to include in this Commission a member from his side. But he was told that it was impossible, since no one from his side was well enough educated to understand the intricacy of jungle law. Further, that there was nothing to fear, for the members of the Commission were all men of repute for their impartiality in justice, and as they were gentlemen chosen by God to look after the interests of races less adequately endowed with teeth and claws, he might rest assured that they would investigate the matter with the greatest care and report impartially.

The Commission sat to take the evidence. The Rt. Hon. Mr. Elephant was first called. . . . and in an authoritative voice said: "Gentlemen of the Jungle,

Source: Jomo Kenyatta, *Facing Mount Kenya: The Tribal Life of the Gikuyu* (London: Mercury Books, 1961 [1938]), 47-52.

there is no need for me to waste your valuable time in relating a story which I am sure you all know. I have always regarded it as my duty to protect the interests of my friends, and this appears to have caused the misunderstanding between myself and my friend here. He invited me to save his hut from being blown away by a hurricane. As the hurricane had gained access owing to the unoccupied space in the hut, I considered it necessary, in my friend's own interests, to turn the undeveloped space to a more economic use by sitting in it myself; a duty which any of you would undoubtedly have performed with equal readiness in similar circumstances."

After hearing the Rt. Han. Mr. Elephant's conclusive evidence, the Commission called Mr. Hyena and other elders of the jungle, who all supported what Mr. Elephant had said. They then called the man, who began to give his own account of the dispute. But the Commission cut him short, saying: "My good man, please confine yourself to relevant issues. We have already heard the circumstances from various unbiased sources; all we wish you to tell us is whether the undeveloped space in your hut was occupied by anyone else before Mr. Elephant assumed his position?"

The man began to say: "No, but--" But at this point the Commission declared that they had heard sufficient evidence from both sides and retired to consider their decision. After enjoying a delicious meal at the expense of the Rt. Hon. Mr. Elephant, they reached their verdict, called the man, and declared as follows: "In our opinion this dispute has arisen through a regrettable misunderstanding due to the backwardness of your ideas. We consider that Mr. Elephant has fulfilled his sacred duty of protecting your interests. As it is clearly for your good that the space should be put to its most economic use, and as you yourself have not yet reached the stage of expansion which would enable you to fill it, we consider it necessary to arrange a compromise to suit both parties. Mr. Elephant shall continue his occupation of your hut, but we give you permission to look for a site where you can build another hut more suited to your needs, and we will see that you are well protected." The man, having no alternative, and fearing that his refusal might expose him to the teeth and claws of members of the Commission, did as they suggested. But no sooner had he built another hut than Mr. Rhinoceros charged in with his horn lowered and ordered the man to quit. A Royal Commission was again appointed to look into the matter, and the same finding was given. This procedure was repeated until Mr. Buffalo, Mr. Leopard, Mr. Hyena and the rest were all accommodated with new huts. Then the man decided that he must adopt an effective method of protection, since Commissions of Enquiry did not seem to be of any use to him. He sat down and said: "*Ng' enda thi ndeagaga motegi,*" which literally means" there is nothing that treads on the earth that cannot be trapped," or in other words, you can fool people for a time, but not forever.

Early one morning, when the huts already occupied by the jungle lords were all beginning to decay and fall to pieces, he went out and built a bigger and better hut a little distance away. No sooner had Mr. Rhinoceros seen it than he came rushing in, only to find that Mr. Elephant was already inside, sound asleep. Mr. Leopard next came in at the window, Mr. Lion, Mr. Fox, and Mr. Buffalo entered the doors, while Mr. Hyena howled for a place in the shade and Mr. Alligator basked on the roof. Presently they all began disputing about their rights of penetration, and from disputing they came to fighting, and while they were all embroiled together the man set the hut on fire and burnt it to the ground, jungle lords and all. Then he went home, saying: "Peace is costly, but it's worth the expense," and lived happily ever after.

QUESTIONS

- What is the message of the fable?
- What did Kenyatta mean by ""Peace is costly, but it's worth the expense"?

19

ANXIETIES AND OPPORTUNITIES IN THE TWENTY-FIRST CENTURY

19.1 BRENTON HARRISON TARRANT, "THE GREAT REPLACEMENT" (2019)

This hate-filled, profoundly racist, neo-Nazi manifesto was purportedly written by Australian Brenton Harrison Tarrant (b. 1991). It was distributed just before Tarrant committed terrorist attacks during Friday prayers against two mosques in Christchurch, New Zealand, on March 15, 2019, murdering 51 and injuring 40. He livestreamed the attack on Al Noor mosque on Facebook. That video and this text have been banned in both Australia and New Zealand. Tarrant was closely affiliated with white supremacists around the world as a part of the "alt-right," which rejects mainstream politics and uses social media to disseminate hate speech and criticize racial, religious, and gender equality. His warped view of historical reality and radical action reveals a deep desperation. He is serving life imprisonment without possibility of parole.

This is WHITE GENOCIDE.

To return to replacement fertility levels is priority number one. But it is no simple task. There are myriad reasons behind the decline in fertility rates and the destruction of the traditional family unit.

We must inevitably correct the disaster of hedonistic, nihilistic individualism. But it will take some time, time we do not have due to the crisis of mass immigration.

Due to mass immigration we lack the time scale required to enact the civilizational paradigm shift we need to undertake to return to health and prosperity.

Mass immigration will disenfranchise us, subvert our nations, destroy our communities, destroy our ethnic binds, destroy our cultures, destroy our peoples.

Long before low fertility levels ever could. Thus, before we deal with the fertility rates, we must deal with both the invaders within our lands and the invaders that seek to enter our lands.

We must crush immigration and deport those invaders already living on our soil. It is not just a matter of our prosperity, but the very survival of our people. . . .

Why did you carry out the attack?

To most of all show the invaders that our lands will never be their lands, our homelands are our own and that, as long as a white man still lives, they will NEVER conquer our lands and they will never replace our people.

To take revenge on the invaders for the hundreds of thousands of deaths caused by foreign invaders in European lands throughout history.

To take revenge for the enslavement of millions of Europeans taken from their lands by the Islamic slavers.

To take revenge for the thousands of European lives lost to terror attacks throughout European lands. . . .

To take revenge for Ebba Akerlund [an eleven-year-old Swedish girl killed in a 2017 terrorist attack by Islamicists].

To directly reduce immigration rates to European lands by intimidating and physically removing the invaders themselves.

Source: Brenton Harrison Tarrant, "The Great Replacement" (2019), reproduced at https://www.google.com/url?sa=t&rct=j&q=&esrc=s&source=web&cd=&ved=2ahUKEwi1hay805zuAhUQF1kFHV2FAb0QFjAAegQIARAC&url=https%3A%2F%2Fwww.ilfoglio.it%2FuserUpload%2FThe_Great_Replacementconvertito.pdf&usg=AOvVaw29Bj2u_tNIhE-gsr3d_qqb (consulted January 14, 2021).

To agitate the political enemies of my people into action, to cause them to overextend their own hand and experience the eventual and inevitable backlash as a result.

To incite violence, retaliation and further divide between the European people and the invaders currently occupying European soil.

To avenge those European men and women lost in the constant and never ending wars of European history who died for their lands, died for their people only to have their lands given away to any foreign scum that bother to show up.

QUESTIONS

- What is "The Great Replacement"?
- Why do think that this ideology found significant support in the modern world?

19.2 PEW RESEARCH CENTER, PUBLIC OPINION ON CLIMATE CHANGE (2015)

The two charts below depict data gathered by the Pew Research Center from a public opinion survey of 40 countries. More than half of those surveyed believe that global climate change is a serious problem, although the variation by region is great. Led by Brazil, Latin America, Africa, and Europe are most concerned regions. This concern is perhaps driven by drought, desertification, deforestation, and extreme weather. When examining these charts, consider potential gaps between public opinion, the policies of international organizations, and national interest.

FIGURE 19.1   Concerns about global climate change.

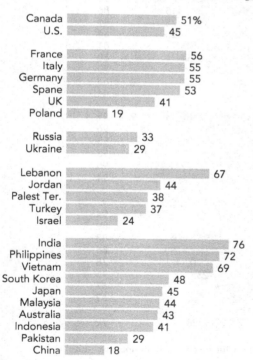

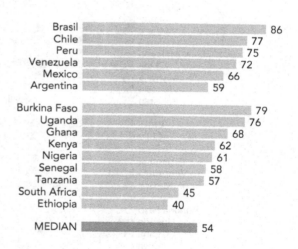

Source: Spring 2015 Global Attitudes survey. Q32. Pew Research Center.

FIGURE 19.2 Global climate change is harming/will harm people around the world. . .

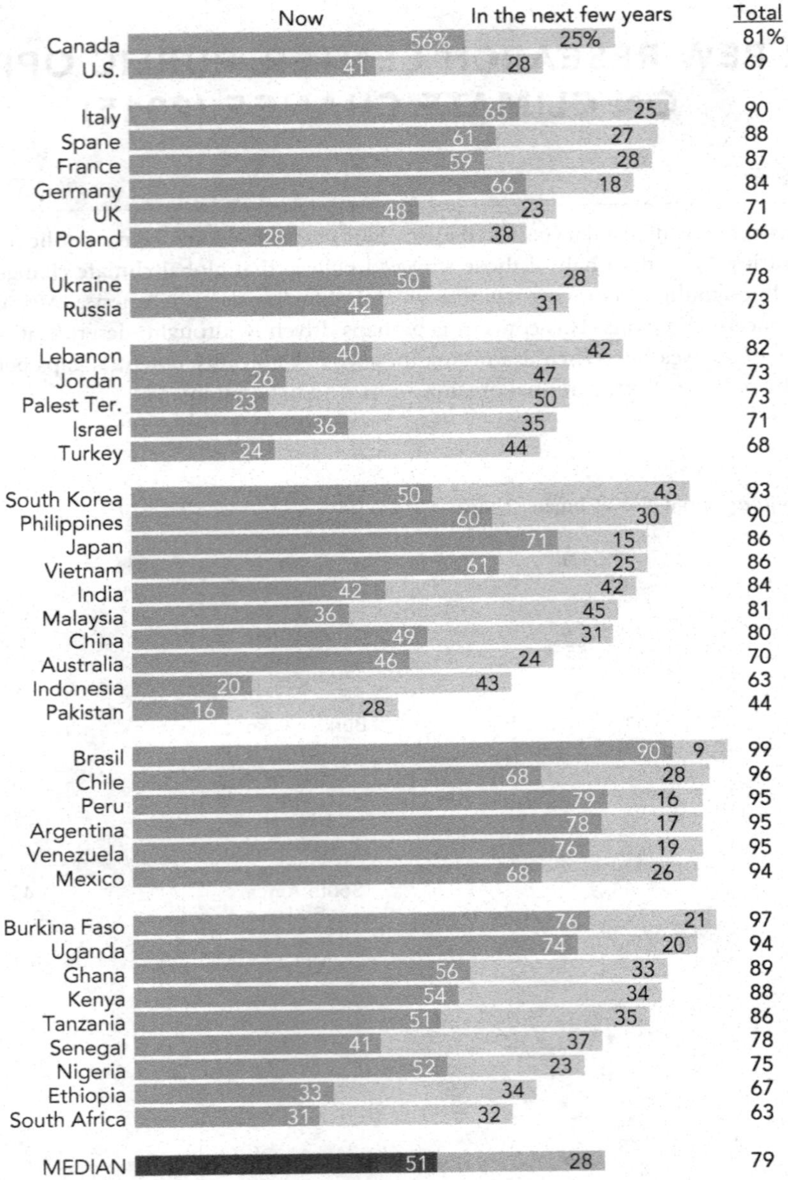

	Now	In the next few years	Total
Canada	56%	25%	81%
U.S.	41	28	69
Italy	65	25	90
Spane	61	27	88
France	59	28	87
Germany	66	18	84
UK	48	23	71
Poland	28	38	66
Ukraine	50	28	78
Russia	42	31	73
Lebanon	40	42	82
Jordan	26	47	73
Palest Ter.	23	50	73
Israel	36	35	71
Turkey	24	44	68
South Korea	50	43	93
Philippines	60	30	90
Japan	71	15	86
Vietnam	61	25	86
India	42	42	84
Malaysia	36	45	81
China	49	31	80
Australia	46	24	70
Indonesia	20	43	63
Pakistan	16	28	44
Brasil	90	9	99
Chile	68	28	96
Peru	79	16	95
Argentina	78	17	95
Venezuela	76	19	95
Mexico	68	26	94
Burkina Faso	76	21	97
Uganda	74	20	94
Ghana	56	33	89
Kenya	54	34	88
Tanzania	51	35	86
Senegal	41	37	78
Nigeria	52	23	75
Ethiopia	33	34	67
South Africa	31	32	63
MEDIAN	51	28	79

Note: Data for "Not for many years," "*Never" and volunteered category "Climate change does not exist" not shown.
Source: Spring 2015 Global Attitudes survey. Q41. Pew Research Center.

QUESTIONS

- Which statistic most surprises you? Why?
- How can you explain the large regional gaps in terms of the "immediacy of climate change"?

19.3 DONGCHEN ZHOU, "CARING FOR COVID-19 PATIENTS IN WUHAN" (2020)

This account was published by a major pharmaceutical company to highlight its products. The account of Dr. Dongchen Zhou, as told to Rebecca Kanthor, depicted the uncertainties of personal protective gear and the difficulties of preventing infection during the first months of the pandemic in the initial epicenter of Wuhan, China.

I was part of the fourth group of doctors from across China to be sent to Wuhan to help with relief efforts. On the plane, some of us were excited, some were nervous. I felt calm because, 17 years ago, I had done my internship during the SARS epidemic, so I had experience in this kind of situation. . . .

We were sent to Wuhan Union Hospital Oncology Center. There were 13 wards and 1,000 patients there. We worked with the same patients each day, but in rotating shifts. One day you'd be on the day shift, and the next you'd be on the afternoon shift, and the next day you'd be on the overnight shift. At the end of the day, we'd return to the hotel, pick up our meals and take them back to our rooms to eat alone. It was quite lonely, so I'd call my kids every night and do a short video chat with them.

In the ward, protective equipment and clothing was in short supply at first. We had brought some of our own and our hospitals sent us with some as well, but it just wasn't enough. When we ran out of hospital scrubs, we started wearing patient hospital clothes instead. . . .

It takes a really long time to prepare yourself for working on the ward. In the beginning it took us an hour to put on all the gear—gloves, goggles, masks, protective clothing. At each step, we had to make sure there were no exposed areas. And once inside the ward, we had to inspect each other's protective equipment every 30 minutes.

During our eight-hour shift we couldn't eat or drink. And when we were in the patient ward, we couldn't use the bathroom because leaving the ward takes a very long time, and removing all the protective clothing safely takes almost as much time as it takes to put on.

Every single step has to be taken carefully because it is so dangerous—your protective clothes have the virus on them and you can easily be infected. Or the person next to you taking off their protective equipment could infect you. So you have to take off each piece of protective gear under supervision.

Even when I was talking with my colleagues, I had to always wear a mask. I worked in Wuhan for about a month alongside many colleagues whose faces I never saw.

In the beginning there were 60 patients on our ward, some as young as 20 and others as old as 80.

Each day we would assess their condition, see if any changes were needed to their treatment plan, and order any further treatment. For those in very serious

Source: Rebecca Kanthor, "'I Was on the Front Lines of the COVID-19 Outbreak in Wuhan': A Doctor Shares His Story" (March 27, 2020), https://www.jnj.com/personal-stories/meet-doctor-helping-treat-coronavirus-outbreak-in-wuhan (consulted January 21, 2021).

condition, we needed to conduct many tests and take measures to help them. . . .

The patients were often in poor mental health because they'd been isolated for so long. They struggled with stress, anxiety and depression. We talked with them and tried to ease their anxiety, tailoring our approach to each patient because everyone was handling the experience differently. Each of us had our own way. . . . We'd also give them fruit and other foods to try and cheer them up.

I never asked the patients about their families because some of them had lost family members to the virus already. But if they talked about their family members, we tried to get in touch with them and help them connect.

A few days ago [March 2020], our hospital ward was finally closed and all of the patients were discharged to go home. We didn't lose a single patient, and none of my colleagues were infected. I've now been moved to another hospital in Wuhan to continue working. I don't know when I'll be going back to Hangzhou to be with my family.

QUESTIONS

- How does Zhou portray the early days of the pandemic in Wuhan?
- What are your own memories of the first days of the pandemic? Are they similar to or different from Zhou's?

19.4 RELIGIOUS DISCRIMINATION IN TUNISIA (2016)

Many unabashedly secular governments in the Muslim world, like that of Tunisia, sought to limit the role of Islam. As a powerful symbol of faith, the hijab, or woman's headscarf, was a particular object of regulation. In 1981, Tunisia issued Circular 108, which banned the hijab in schools and offices. Harassment accelerated after Zine el-Abidine Ben Ali (r. 1989–2011) seized power. Anger at this kind of religious discrimination helped motivate the crowds that pushed Ben Ali from power in 2011, but the ban remained in place under the new regime. The author, "Ines," provided this testimony to the Truth and Dignity Commission in 2016.

I was 19 when I decided to wear the hijab. I was advanced in high school and graduated with good grades. When they prevented me from entering college, my mother came to me and said, "You can take it off to continue your studies." But she didn't force me to take it off. When I decided to keep it, she accepted my choice. I didn't expect what happened to me. I didn't see all of that happening to me only because of covering my head, to be barred from continuing my education. I did not know about Circular 108. I never understood the problem with covering my hair—until now.

I went to Institut Supérieur de Gestion (ISG) in October 2002 in Sousse. At that time, there were only two other girls covering their heads in the college. In the beginning, there were no problems, but . . . [t]he college director decided to begin a crackdown on veiled students. A week after I wore the hijab, many students wore it. And they started to notice that our numbers increased, coinciding with November 7th.

The director decided to prevent us from entering and forced us to take off the hijab even before we arrived to the college. She said, "I want you to take it off while you are at the street. I don't want to see it." The harassment began. . . . I left [home] at 5 am to arrive very early, before the guards. We were going early and locking ourselves in the bathrooms and didn't make a sound.

But then they noticed what we were doing, and the director requested a smith to build a high fence with only one small door. She stationed a woman there whose job was only to take off our hijabs. We had to leave our hijab with her to enter, because some girls would take their hijab off at the gate and put it on later. This made me miss a lot of classes, and thus, I was prevented from taking three exams. Even with missing all these classes, my scores were good.

I did not continue my studies after the first year. I tried to wear a hat over my hijab. I tried different types of hijab just to cover my hair. And the director told me, "No, I want to see your hair." Since I was 12, I was dreaming about ISGS and wanted to become a computer scientist. Some days, I just went and stood in front of the gate, but they didn't let me enter. One day, she saw me, and she pulled me and I fell down on the floor. She was yelling at me: "What backwardness!

Source: International Center for Transitional Justice, "'It Was a Way to Destroy Our Lives:' Tunisian Women Speak Out on Religious Discrimination" (June 14, 2016), https://www.ictj.org/news/tunisia-women-speak-out-religious-discrimination-TDC (consulted January 8, 2021).

What a backwardness!" Then she dragged me to her office and asked for my student ID. She was yelling. Still, I went to the college every day, and stood seeing how other students entered but not me. Then, I could not take it anymore. I got depressed and fell sick all the summer. Next year, I asked to take a year off for health reasons. The college doctor agreed, and I filled [out] the paper, but she did not approve it.

Even today, when I pass by the college, I feel suffocated. I was deprived of my right. Why? Only because I covered my hair? I have no political connections. I didn't know about political Islam. I told them so. It's a serious violation, to take away your right to education. 14 years later, and the story still makes me cry. My friends who went to college with me are now professors. In Tunisia, it's very important to go to college, even for girls. Once I was telling my mother in law that my sister is working on her PH.D. and she told me "and you have a high school and a zero!"

QUESTIONS

- Why did Ben Ali decide to fight to keep her hijab?
- Why were authorities so intent on banning the hijab?

19.5 EVO MORALES, "FROM COCA TO CONGRESS" (2002)

Bolivian Juan Evo Morales Ayma (in office 2006–2019) was the first Indigenous president of Bolivia. His Movement for Socialism Party (MAS) fought the role of multinational corporations and the U.S.-backed war on drugs in the name of Indigenous peoples whose only cash crop was coca, the raw material for cocaine as well as other drugs and medicines. His populist rhetoric successfully mobilized the Indigenous population to support his party's nationalist economic and political policies.

Morales: "After long experiences of broken promises in the countryside we had come to the conclusion that what we needed was a way to change the whole political system. As long as we carried on voting for the mainstream parties, we knew we were going to keep seeing massacres, militarization and bad economic policies. . . .

The Ecologist: Why do you think the movement grew so fast?
Morales: "I think above all because we represent honesty and not corruption. . . ."Nobody can say that we have sold out, that we have received money and I have received so many offers. The ex-president, Jaime Paz Zamora, offered me the vice-presidency of the republic. Other parties wanted to make me senator. But I have always tried to stay at the service of the social movements. . . ."

The Ecologist: Why is this happening in Bolivia now?
Morales: "I think that every millennium brings its change, and that this is the millennium of the united nations of Indigenous people. Why now? Ever since I was a child we have had different Indigenous movements in Bolivia, but they always ended up divided or co-opted by the government. This movement is different, both because it is massive and able to incorporate a whole diversity of figures and social organisations, and because we have our feet firmly on the ground. . . ."

The Ecologist: What are the main planks of MAS's [Movement to Socialism] politics?
Morales: "More than anything, the struggle for dignity and sovereignty. And not just in terms of territory, but sovereignty in terms of food production, in terms of the decisions that the people make. We believe that the Indigenous people, the Quechua and Aymara, are the absolute owners of the land."

The Ecologist: What does the US want to achieve in Bolivia?
Morales: "The US is seeking hegemony on a world scale and has always sought to dominate Latin America. The "war against drugs" is just a pretext for the US to control our countries. The war against drugs is false. The origin of the narcotics trade is the US itself, which constitutes the principal market for cocaine. Why don't they eradicate the demand? If it weren't for the money that the US drug trade moves not a single leaf of coca would go towards the drug trade. And it's not just

Source: Evo Morales, "From Coca to Congress," Interview with *The Ecologist* (November 11, 2002) posted on ZNET, https://web.archive.org/web/20160105223036/https://zcomm.org/znetarticle/from-coca-to-congress-by-evo-morales/ (consulted January 10, 2021).

consumption. According to the UN, 50 per cent of drug money is laundered in the US. You can only stop that by getting rid of banking secrecy laws. "I think the main interest in the war against drugs is penalising social protest. In the 1960s they accused the Bolivian miners of being communists in order to persecute them. Then they accused poor people of being 'narcos' in the 1980s and 1990s, and now after September 11 they are calling us terrorists. These are forms of criminalizing protest." . . .

The Ecologist: What is life like for a typical family in Chapare?
Morales: " . . . Given the complete lack of markets for non-coca agricultural goods, though, it's hard to say to a peasant that they should not produce any coca. For the Indigenous movement, having land means having work, but the problem is that there is no market. Poor people in the cities cannot buy, and we cannot sell. . . . That's where the coca comes in. Some can be sold in the legal market, and some is sold illegally. Paradoxically, with the eradication campaigns the price has gone up in the legal market making it more difficult for people to buy. But the price has also gone up in the illegal market, making it more attractive to grow. . . . "

The Ecologist: How will you achieve this?
Morales: "On a political level it's about refounding Bolivia on a new basis. On an economic level it's about stopping and reversing privatization. We want to get our companies and natural resources back, because we can't allow them to be concentrated in the hands of a few transnational corporations. On a social level we have to end corruption and repression, for example, the state financing of mercenaries. That money must be used for social costs, such as education and health. On the level of justice it's important to replace the system of injustice with one of justice. Today they call what can be bought justice. Rights depend on money. This has to end."

QUESTIONS

- What would have been especially appealing about Morales' message?
- Do you agree with his argument about the U.S.-led War on Drugs? Why or why not?

19.6 PREAMBLE OF THE PLATFORM OF THE U.S. REPUBLICAN PARTY (2016, 2020)

Signed by Senator John Barrasso of Wyoming, Governor Mary Fallin of Oklahoma, and Representative Virginia Foxx of North Carolina on behalf of the platform committee, the preamble integrated populist themes with traditional Republican Party stances. The document reflected many of the views of Republican candidate Donald J. Trump, a real estate developer and media personality with no previous political experience, on how to "Make America Great Again." The Platform was not revised for the 2020 election. Trump lost the popular vote in 2016 and was decisively defeated in 2020, but won the first election thanks to the structure of the Electoral College.

With this platform, we the Republican Party reaffirm the principles that unite us in a common purpose.

We believe in American exceptionalism.

We believe the United States of America is unlike any other nation on earth. . . .

We believe America is exceptional because of our historic role—first as refuge, then as defender, and now as exemplar of liberty for the world to see.

We affirm—as did the Declaration of Independence: that all are created equal, endowed by their Creator with inalienable rights of life, liberty, and the pursuit of happiness.

We believe in the Constitution as our founding document.

We believe the Constitution was written not as a flexible document, but as our enduring covenant.

We believe our constitutional system—limited government, separation of powers, federalism, and the rights of the people—must be preserved uncompromised for future generations.

We believe political freedom and economic freedom are indivisible.

When political freedom and economic freedom are separated—both are in peril; when united, they are invincible.

We believe that people are the ultimate resource—and that the people, not the government, are the best stewards of our country's God-given natural resources. . . .

This platform lays out—in clear language—the path to making America great and united again.

For the past 8 years America has been led in the wrong direction.

Our economy has become unnecessarily weak with stagnant wages. People living paycheck to paycheck are struggling, sacrificing, and suffering.

Americans have earned and deserve a strong and healthy economy. . . .

The President and the Democratic party have abandoned their promise of being accountable to the American people. . . .

We, as Republicans and Americans, cannot allow this to continue. That is why the many sections of this platform affirm our trust in the people, our faith in

Source: https://ballotpedia.org/The_Republican_Platform_and_RNC_Platform_Committee,_2016 (consulted January 11, 2021).

their judgment, and our determination to help them take back their country.

This means removing the power from unelected, unaccountable government.

And this means returning to the people and the states the control that belongs to them. It is the control and the power to make their own decisions about what's best for themselves and their families and communities.

QUESTIONS

- Which lines most stand out to you? Why?
- Why do you think this rhetoric was so appealing to some Americans?

19.7 UNITED NATIONS PROPOSALS TO REDUCE INEQUALITY WITHIN AND AMONG COUNTRIES (2014)

In 2014, the United Nations' Open Working Group proposed a set of seventeen goals and targets to guide economic development after 2015. Each set detailed policies that governments and international institutions were to implement according to local conditions. Goal 10 concerns reducing inequality. Consider how likely these proposals are to be implemented and how effective they are likely to be.

Goal 10. Reduce inequality within and among countries

10.1 by 2030 progressively achieve and sustain income growth of the bottom 40% of the population at a rate higher than the national average;

10.2 by 2030 empower and promote the social, economic and political inclusion of all irrespective of age, sex, disability, race, ethnicity, origin, religion or economic or other status;

10.3 ensure equal opportunity and reduce inequalities of outcome, including through eliminating discriminatory laws, policies and practices and promoting appropriate legislation, policies and actions in this regard;

10.4 adopt policies especially fiscal, wage, and social protection policies and progressively achieve greater equality;

10.5 improve regulation and monitoring of global financial markets and institutions and strengthen implementation of such regulations;

10.6 ensure enhanced representation and voice of developing countries in decision making in global international economic and financial institutions in order to deliver more effective, credible, accountable and legitimate institutions;

10.7 facilitate orderly, safe, regular and responsible migration and mobility of people, including through implementation of planned and well-managed migration policies;

10.a implement the principle of special and differential treatment for developing countries, in particular least developed countries, in accordance with WTO [World Trade Organization] agreements;

10.b encourage ODA [Office of Development Assistance] and financial flows, including foreign direct investment, to states where the need is greatest, in particular LDCs [Least Developed Countries], African countries, SIDS [Small Island Developing States], and LLDCs [Land-Locked Developing Countries], in accordance with their national plans and programmes;

10.c by 2030, reduce to less than 3% the transaction costs of migrant remittances [money sent from abroad] and eliminate remittance corridors with costs higher than 5%.

QUESTIONS

- Which of these proposals is the most important?
- Do the proposals seem realistic to you? How might the UN implement them?

Source: United Nations' Open Working Group, *Proposals for Sustainable Development Goals* (2014), https://sustainabledevelopment .un.org/focussdgs.html (consulted January 13, 2021).

CREDITS

Source 2.8 Used with permission of Columbia University Press, from George E. Dutton, Jayne S. Werner, and John K. Whitmore, eds., Sources of Vietnamese Tradition, 2012; permission conveyed through Copyright Clearance Center, Inc.

CHAPTER 3

Source 3.1 Used with permission of University of Chicago Press, from Dora L. Costa and Naomi R. Lamoreaux eds., Understanding Long-Run Economic Growth: Geography, Institutions, and the Knowledge Economy; permission conveyed through Copyright Clearance Center, Inc.

Source 3.2 Reprinted in Edward A. Van Dyck, Report upon the Capitulations of the Ottoman Empire since the Year 1150, part 1 (Washington D.C.: Government Printing Office, 1881), 91–92.

Source 3.3 Voyages of Samuel de Champlain, 1604–1618, ed. W. L. Grant (New York: Charles Scribner's Sons, 1907), 49–50, 151–52.

Source 3.4 Quoted in Beyond the Codices: The Nahua View of View of Colonial Mexico, trans. and ed. Arthur J. O. Anderson, Frances Berdan, and James Lockhart (Berkeley: University of California Press, 1976), 181, 183, 185, 187, 189.

Source 3.5 Toolbox Library: Primary Resources in U.S. History and Literature National Humanities Center Copyright © National Humanities Center. All rights reserved. nationalhumanitiescenter.org

Source 3.6 Used with permission of Rowman & Littlefield Publishing Group, from Colonial Spanish America: A Documentary History, Kenneth Mills and William B. Taylor, eds., 1998; permission conveyed through Copyright Clearance Center, Inc.

Source 3.7 By permission of Oxford University Press.

CHAPTER 4

Source 4.1 Used with permission of Columbia University Press, from Ryusaku Tsunoda, Wm Theorore de Bary, and Donald Keene, eds., Sources of Japanese Tradition, 1958; permission conveyed through Copyright Clearance Center, Inc.

Source 4.3 Reproduced with permission of Cambridge University Press through PLSclear.

Source 4.4 Reprinted by permission of Hackett Publishing Company, Inc. All rights reserved.

Source 4.5 Hans J. Hillerbrand, ed., The Reformation (New York: Harper & Row, 1964), 89–91, 94, 99–100. Source of original German text: Detlef Ploese and Guenther Vogler, eds., Buch der Reformation. Eine Auswahl zeitgenössischer Zeugnisse (1476–1555) (Berlin: Union Verlag, 1989), 245–53. Reprinted on: http://germanhistorydocs.ghi-dc.org/pdf/eng/Doc.64-ENG-Luther_Charles.pdf

Source 4.6 Adapted from Eugen Weber, ed., The Western Tradition, vol. 2, From the Renaissance to the Present, 5th ed. (Lexington, MA: D.C. Heath and Co, 1995), 86–87.

Source 4.7 Used with permission of University of Oklahoma Press, from Adrián Recinos and Delia Goetz, ed. and trans., The Annals of the Cakchiquels: translated from the Cakchiquel Maya, 1953; permission conveyed through Copyright Clearance Center, Inc.

CHAPTER 5

Source 5.1 Chinua Achebe, Things Fall Apart (New York: Anchor Books, 1994 [1959]), 85–89.

Source 5.2 Wm. Theodore de Bary and Richard Lufrano, eds., Sources of Chinese

Tradition: From 1600 Through the Twentieth Century, 2nd ed., vol. 2 (New York: Columbia University Press, 2000), 71–72.

Source 5.3 Reproduced with permission of Cambridge University Press through PLSclear.

Source 5.6 Reproduced with permission of Oxford University Press through PLSclear.

Source 5.7 Shen Fu, Six Records of a Floating Life, trans. Leonard Pratt and Chiang Su-hui (London: Penguin Books, 1983), 25–26, 40, 45–46, 50–51.

Source 5.8 Reproduced with permission of the Licensor through PLSclear; Elisabeth Burgos-Debray, ed., I, Rigoberta Menchú: An Indian Woman in Guatemala, trans. Ann Wright.

Source 5.9 Excerpt(s) from BATTLE HYMN OF THE TIGER MOTHER by Amy Chua, copyright © 2011 by Amy Chua. Used by permission of Penguin Press, an imprint of Penguin Publishing Group, a division of Penguin Random House LLC. All rights reserved.

CHAPTER 6

Source 6.1 From CHINESE CIVILIZATION: A Sourcebook, 2nd Edition by Patricia Buckley Ebrey. Copyright © 1981 by The Free Press. Copyright © 1993 by Patricia Buckley Ebrey. Reprinted with the permission of The Free Press, a division of Simon & Schuster, Inc. All rights reserved.

Source 6.2 © The Hakluyt Society

Source 6.5 *The General Agreement on Tariffs and Trade* (1948), 53–54, on https://www.wto.org/english/docs_e/legal_e/gatt47_e.pdf (consulted March 13, 2020).

CHAPTER 7

Source 7.2 Used with permission of Columbia University Press, from Sources of Korean Tradition, ed. Yŏng-ho Ch'oe, Peter H.

Lee, and Wm. Theodore de Bary, 2 vols; permission conveyed through Copyright Clearance Center, Inc.

Source 7.3 Reproduced with permission of Cambridge University Press through PLSclear.

Source 7.5 Reproduced with permission of Oxford University Press through PLSclear.

Source 7.6 Translation copyright © 1994 by W. Nick Hill. First U.S. edition published by Pantheon Books, 1968. Revised edition published by Curbstone Press, 2004. New revised edition published by Curbstone/Northwestern University Press, 2016. All rights reserved.

CHAPTER 9

Source 9.5 Mikiso Hane, Peasants, Rebels, and Outcasts: The Underside of Modern Japan, 2nd ed. (Lanham, MD: Rowman and Littlefield, 2016 [1982]), 186–87; Poem: Patricia E. Tsurumi, Factory Girls: Women in the Thread Mills of Meiji Japan (Princeton, NJ: Princeton University Press, 1990), 98.

CHAPTER 10

Source 10.2 Garcilaso de la Vega, Royal Commentaries of the Incas and General History of Peru, part 2, trans. Harold V. Livermore (Austin: University of Texas Press, 1966).

Source 10.6 Simon Partner, Toshié: A Story of Village Life in Twentieth-Century Japan (Berkeley: University of California Press, 2004). Reprinted with permission.

CHAPTER 11

Source 11.2 The materials listed above appeared originally in The French Revolution and Human Rights: A Brief Documentary History, translated, edited, and with an introduction by Lynn Hunt (Boston/New York Bedford/St.

Martin's, 1996), 124–129 reproduced on http://chnm.gmu.edu/revolution/d/293/

Source 11.6 Laurent DuBois and John D. Garrigus, eds. Slave Revolution in the Caribbean, 1789–1804: A Brief History with Documents (New York: Bedford/St. Martin's, 2006), 66–67.

Source 11.9 George E. Dutton, Jayne S. Werner, and John K. Whitmore, eds., Sources of Vietnamese Tradition (New York: Columbia University Press, 2012), 218–19.

CHAPTER 12

Source 12.6 Quoted in William H. Worger, Nancy L. Clark, and Edward A. Alpers, eds., Africa and the West: A Documentary History, vol. 1, From the Slave Trade to Conquest, 1441–1905, 2nd ed. (New York: Oxford University Press, 2010), 266–67.

CHAPTER 13

Source 13.3 Salomé Ureña de Henriquez, "16th of August," trans. Eric Paul Roorda, in The Dominican Republic Reader: History, Culture, Politics, ed. Eric Paul Roorda, Lauren Derby, and Raymundo Gonzálo (Durham, NC: Duke University Press, 2014), 228–30.

Source 13.5 José Martí, "Our America," in The Cuba Reader: History, Culture, Politics, ed. Aviva Chomsky, Barry Carr, and Pamela Marie Smorkaloff (Durham, NC: Duke University Press, 2003), 122–27.

CHAPTER 14

Source 14.6 Mariano Casanova, "Pastoral Letter" in The Chile Reader: History, Culture, Politics, ed. Elizabeth Quay Hutchison, Thomas Miller Klubock, Nara B. Milanich, and Peter Winn (Durham, NC: Duke University Press, 2014), 228–9.

CHAPTER 15

Source 15.2 Behind the Urals: An American Worker in Russia's City of Steel. John Scott, Copyright © 1973, Bloomington, Indiana University Press. Reprinted with permission of Indiana University Press.

Source 15.3 William Theodore de Bary and Richard Lufrano, eds., Sources of Chinese Tradition: From 1600 through the Twentieth Century, 2nd ed., vol. 2 (New York: Columbia University Press, 2000), 455–456.

Source 15.5 Copyright © 1992 Harper's Magazine. All Rights Reserved. Reproduced from the August issue by special permission.

Source 15.6 Maria Hengeveld, "Nike Boasts of Empowering Women Around the World: While the young women who make its products in Vietnam are intimidated, belittled, and underpaid" (26 August 2016), https://slate.com/business/2016/08/nikes-supply-chain-doesnt-live-up-to-the-ideals-of-its-girl-effect-campaign.html

CHAPTER 16

Source 16.8 Reprinted with permission from Wright's Media.

Source 16.9 CAPITAL IN THE TWENTY-FIRST CENTURY by Thomas Piketty, translated by Arthur Goldhammer, Cambridge, Mass.: The Belknap Press of Harvard University Press, Copyright © 2014 by the President and Fellows of Harvard College. Used by permission. All rights reserved.

CHAPTER 17

Source 17.1 Le Monde, (12–13 May 1968), trans. Mitchell Abidor (2008), https://www.marxists.org/history/france/may-1968/night-barricades.htm Reprinted with permission from Mitchell Abidor.

Source 17.4 "Interview at Tiananmen Square with Chai Ling." Asia for Educators (Columbia University), http://afe.easia.columbia.edu/special/china_1950_chailing.htm

Source 17.6 Peter Rosset and John Vandermeer, eds., Nicaragua: Unfinished Revolution – The New Nicaragua Reader (New York: Grove Press, 1986), 181–89, 181–82, 184, 186, 188.

Source 17.7 Kwame Nkrumah, Neo-Colonialism, The Last Stage of Imperialism (London: Thomas Nelson & Sons, 1965), https://www.marxists.org/subject/africa/nkrumah/neo-colonialism/

Source 17.8 Survivors Fund (SURF)

CHAPTER 18

Source 18.5 Zhora Drif, Instead the Battle of Algiers: Memoir of a Woman Freedom Fighter, trans. Andrew Farrand (Charlottesville, VA: Just World Books, 2017 [2013]), 106, 113–16.

CHAPTER 19

Source 19.3 Rebecca Kanthor, "'I Was on the Front Lines of the COVID-19 Outbreak in Wuhan': A Doctor Shares His Story" (27 March 2020), https://www.jnj.com/personal-stories/meet-doctor-helping-treat-coronavirus-outbreak-in-wuhan

Source 19.4 International Center for Transitional Justice, "'It Was a Way to Destroy Our Lives:' Tunisian Women Speak Out on Religious Discrimination" (14 June 2016), https://www.ictj.org/news/tunisia-women-speak-out-religious-discrimination-TDC (Consulted 8 January 2021).

INDEX

Page numbers followed by *f* and *t* refer to figures and tables, respectively.